THOUGH *the* DARKNESS

Rebecca Martin

THOUGH

the

DARKNESS

Medicine, Missions, and

Meeting God in Nepal

A MEMOIR

To those who serve in unseen ways with enduring fidelity,
And especially to the Tansen Mission Hospital team —

Sabaiko lagi, Dhanyabad

You say I am repeating
Something I have said before. I shall say it again.
Shall I say it again? In order to arrive there,
To arrive where you are, to get from where you are not,
You must go by a way wherein there is no ecstasy.
In order to arrive at what you do not know
You must go by a way which is the way of ignorance.
In order to possess what you do not possess
You must go by the way of dispossession.
In order to arrive at what you are not
You must go through the way in which you are not.
And what you do not know is the only thing you know
And what you own is what you do not own
And where you are is where you are not.

- T. S. Eliot -

Holy, Holy, Holy
though the darkness hide Thee…

- Reginald Heber -

Author's Note

This is a memoir. As such, I have tried to recreate events, places, and conversations based on my best recollection of them over time. I verified these memories against journals kept during this period, and through conversations with those who shared the experiences described. That said, all of the characters in this story are composites, a decision intended to protect the privacy of friends, colleagues and patients integral to its telling. Additionally, some events were compressed, and parts of dialogue recreated, without materially altering the veracity of the experiences portrayed.

Preface

There is a photograph I treasure, taken by a Tansen colleague. The subject is an older man, a village farmer perhaps in his early seventies — although age, I've come to learn, is nearly impossible to gauge in Nepal. He may be in his forties, or over a hundred.

It is taken neither in profile nor in direct portrait, but rather as an angled view from the right. Light from a window behind him backlights this mid-afternoon scene, while also illuminating an X-ray film held aloft in his hands. Weathered fingers grasp the edges of thin, transparent, blue-tinged polyethylene. He is regarding it as patients sometimes did in Tansen — curious, perhaps, to grasp a bit more of the workings and mis-workings of his own mysterious body. I can't help but notice that the X-ray shows quite a lot of fluid gathered around his left lung. Likely from tuberculosis, a resolving pneumonia, or perhaps a brewing cancer.

Although he appears frail, each of the gentleman's forearm bones are clearly visible and edged with the sinewy strength of a lifelong farmer. A worn leather belt cinches his baggy waistband; his trouser cuffs are rolled back at the ankles. He's draped his paper-thin hospital gown over a cheap polyester button-down shirt, sleeves rolled up to his elbows, ever-primed for work.

This manner of wearing a gown over clothing is a curious yet ubiquitous practice at Tansen. In the winter, of course, the wards are far too chilly for a thin cotton gown alone. And it must have been a brisk day, judging from the ribbed beanie-cap and gray scarf he also wears. Yet the gown seems superfluous on someone already fully dressed. I suppose it is part of an unspoken understanding woven into the culture — here, as in the world over — that each member of this medical pantomime plays his or her role, don the proper costume. A bit of lightly soiled medical tape secures an IV to the man's wrist. This small piece of medical technology strikes me as the most out-of-place element in the scene, anchored to a wrist heretofore accustomed to the freedom of wide-open spaces.

But what really captivates me in the photo, the place where I get lost in this time-frozen moment, is the man's eyes. Looking intently at the film, examining grayish-blue tones filtering through the mystery of plastic vellum, I wonder to what extent he quite grasps that these shadows reveal what is inside — *inside* — his own body. There appears to be in his face a mixture of awe, curiosity, and confusion. He is engrossed, lost in wonder, his mouth slightly agape, momentarily oblivious to anything around him.

I find this photograph engaging because of a deeper story it tells — that of crossing worlds. How often I glimpsed the enormous gap between my own experience and that of my Nepali patients. It came to me at times when I noticed, for instance, a patient struggling to operate the doorknob while exiting my exam room. Fixtures even as basic as doorknobs are rarely encountered in rural Nepal.

How much more foreign must be our beeping machines, blinking lights, and mysterious cyan-blue lines charting the course of heartbeats on computer screens? Or bags dripping clear "water" through plastic tubing taped to forearms? Or fuzzy black-and-white images on thin plastic film that somehow — alarmingly, impenetrably — relate to their own innards? The world my patients inhabit is at least as obscure to me, filled with elements I, too, find mystifying.

The very nature of the physician-patient relationship is that of bridging gaps. It is the work of reaching out, of extending a hand to those who suffer, of crossing the chasm that separates the contented from the grieving, and those flourishing from those in pain. Medicine is, most fundamentally, about addressing the gap between illness and health. But that also means attending to the gap illness creates between your sense of being broken, and that of being whole. It is about bridging the gap that opens around the sufferer, being willing first to recognize, and then reach out across, the crevasse that threatens to engulf them. Though just a single moment in time, this photograph brings into focus countless other moments, before and since, that continue to call out from those same chasm depths.

Paradoxically, this gap can provide the very occasion for transgressing a clinician's sacred duty to guard the vulnerable, by neglecting to hold with tenderness the space around them. It can be too easy for the powerful to forget what it means to be weak, too easy to lose sight of their own vulnerability, if indeed they ever had sight of it to begin with. Too many of us start out our professional journeys as robust, healthy twenty-somethings who know far too little of others' frailty, never mind our own.

Confronted with an endless stream of need, and often stretched far too thin ourselves, we clinicians routinely fail to hold this mystery, this intimate sense of wonder. For those who are anything like me, it is possible to become frayed and frustrated by the vulnerability we encounter, our own emotional resources at low ebb, rendering us unable to care from any place of wholeness within ourselves. We are all human, wearied by waves of need we are insufficient to fully meet. Whether or not we dare admit it.

A wise friend once told me that "missions is all about going, not much about doing, and everything about being." It would take a long time to absorb the truth of those words, if indeed I ever have, even now. Yet those two years in Nepal taught me that, just as Jesus came to us to bridge this fundamental chasm, we are called to do likewise — called to stand in the gaps of our fractured world, called to be vehicles for reconciliation, called to build bridges.

This was the impetus that led me to explore medical missions for a year or two — dipping a toe in as it were, uncertain of where the current might take me. I had a sense that, as both a physician and a Christian, I would meet more of Jesus in going to Nepal than if I stayed. And indeed, I did. It's been said that God always calls His servants closer to Himself. What I didn't realize was that this meant meeting Christ in His sufferings and, even more profoundly, in my own desperate need. It would be a meeting on terms of engagement I hadn't negotiated.

These pages that follow tell one story of "going, doing, and being" in that liminal space.

Rebecca Martin
Ossining, New York
September 2023

Prologue

How on earth did I end up under this tarp?

Somewhere between exasperation and exhalation, I trace over the events of the past few days, all that has transpired to bring me to this moment. As I lie motionless on the hard-pebbled ground, trying not to awaken the snoring bodies lined up on my left and right, my mind whirs in the dark. The thick darkness is incensed with earthy smells of woodsmoke from a fire long since gone cold and damp.

I am wedged between Dan, a fellow Tansen doctor, and Urmila, a young woman from the village of Keraunja that has given us refuge. We are lined up in a long row of sleeping family members and other villagers. Dan is a trusted friend, and I am thankful that he put himself between me and the reporter from Kathmandu whose lecherous advances kept me vaguely on edge all evening. I am thankful, too, for the hospitality of the villagers. They had shared their ration of *dal-bhaat* with us that evening as we sat in a smoky circle, our faces lit by flames licking the makeshift hearth.

I am especially grateful to be here at all, glad to have survived the rocky helicopter flight and cliff-top emergency stop, where we waited out a thunderstorm *en route*. A blue plastic tarp hangs from cords anchored to the rubble of surrounding shelters, shielding us from a constant drizzle of rain. I'm even glad to be lying on another tarp, if nothing else.

Uncomfortable though the rocky ground is, that millimeter of plastic is incomparably better than a night in the mud with the leeches. I have already flicked a few from my ankles.

I think back to this afternoon, hastily boarding one of the last helicopters launching from the grassy roadside flat. We waited there most of the day, uncertain when, whether, or even *to* where we would depart. When our assignment came through, Dan and I had no idea where the village of Keraunja even was. Urmila, Dan, the reporter and I squeezed into the commercial-grade helicopter, picking our way over huge sacks of rice packed tightly on the floor. I noticed the *U.S.A.I.D.* logo on several blue industrial-weave plastic sacks, all of them stenciled with official-looking imprints. Rice, maybe. Or temporary shelters.

Awkwardly, I'd taken my seat on the tight bench behind our pilot. He had an *avant-garde* look, this pilot. He was even wearing aviator sunglasses, along with khaki cargo-shirt and jauntily tied cravat. *He looks just like a character-actor in an eighties film*, I thought to myself, which simply added to the surreal feeling of it all. And then we lifted off, flying headlong into a black horizon, ominously thick with thunderclouds.

This is how it happens, I thought. *This is how relief workers die.* That thought would come more than once during those seventy-two hours, when I found myself suddenly and unexpectedly on the inside of a story that I'd only ever glimpsed through the filter of books, films, or a news anchor's lens. I'd always assumed that people in these situations had things under control — a clear plan, an exit strategy. Now I wasn't so sure. Maybe *everyone* feels like they're making it up as they go.

Lying under the tarp, I feel my backpack's uncomfortable bulk, a makeshift pillow beneath my head. When throwing items into it a few days earlier, I'd grabbed my Bible, a small pocket version well-worn with years of use. Between its thin pages was a small scrap of paper I knew well, having sought comfort there many times over the years. It was a verse that spoke of God's companionship and presence. Where was God in all this now?

Could it have only been only two days ago that my interim director asked me to join a team of volunteers with International Nepali Fellowship on a post-earthquake relief mission? We'd be traveling to the Gorkha district, near the epicenter, to provide medical support and obtain a situational assessment. It was, by that point, late in the afternoon, the shadows already long. Our team was to depart at five the following morning.

Then my mind wandered back to three days earlier, when I first understood that nothing on earth was a given. Not even the earth itself, solid beneath my feet. Was this what I thought I was signing up for in coming to Nepal? The reality was quickly becoming more terrifying and unpredictable than I could have imagined.

Part 1 - Going

I am a bow in your hands, Lord.
Draw me, lest I rot.
Do not overdraw me, Lord. I shall break.
Overdraw me, Lord, and let me break.

- Nikos Kazantzakis -

Is not this the fast that I choose:
to loose the bonds of wickedness, to undo the straps of the yoke,
to let the oppressed go free, and to break every yoke?
Is it not to share your bread with the hungry
and bring the homeless poor into your house;
when you see the naked, to cover him,
and not to hide yourself from your own flesh?

- Isaiah 58:6–7 -

CHAPTER ONE
One-Way Ticket

I'd never bought a one-way ticket before. Even after months of mental preparation, it was still harder than expected to actually click the "Confirm" button on the Emirates website. So irreversible! But once I did, and in the weeks that followed, I enjoyed a deep sense of peace, mixed with delicious excitement for what was to come. The trepidation of the preceding months had thankfully dissolved away — at least for a time.

Later that same week, I worked my final hospital shift, moved out of my DC apartment, and became happily nomadic for the next six weeks, couch-surfing with friends and family up and down the East Coast. It would prove an invaluable time in which to say my goodbyes, while soaking up the last bits of the only homeland I'd ever known.

True, it wasn't exactly my first transplant from one terra cotta pot to another. The experience of several moves over the preceding few years — from New York to Virginia and back again, then from New York to Pennsylvania, and Pennsylvania to DC — gave that unique moment in time a strangely familiar feel. I recognized the excitement of an impending transition, and the anticipation of starting somewhere fresh and new.

Yet it was different this time, and not just because of the obvious move to an entirely different continent and culture, huge though that was. This time, I'd also be terminating my cellphone account, cancelling car insurance, and purchasing travel health coverage. I had to forward mail to my parents' home, notify my credit card accounts of "upcoming travel," and set up a new, "travel-friendly" account to avoid piling up international fees.

Those weeks were busy with lists of "essentials" compiled from various online travel-blogs and my *Lonely Planet: Nepal* guide, which warned me not to forget duct tape, iodine tablets, sunscreen, and Q-tips. I opted to forgo the bag of twist-ties and fifteen feet of parachute cord they also recommended. I'd already confirmed that my passport was valid, and registered my imminent move with the U.S. State Department. Required immunizations were almost up to date, including those against typhoid and tetanus; I would just need shots for rabies and Japanese encephalitis, which I could get there. My new Skype account had been set up, and my contact information imprinted on the back of "missionary prayer cards" I'd ordered to share with family, friends, and supporters.

I'm sometimes asked how I ended up in Nepal in the first place. In truth, while the seeds of following Jesus where He led were planted over the course of decades, my desire to pursue medical missions was kindled during residency training. There, I worked alongside patients poorly served by our healthcare systems, and witnessed their difficulty accessing desperately needed medical services. At the same time, I met colleagues who had spent time serving abroad, and reflected alongside a group of friends discerning similar questions of vision, calling, and purpose.

At the end of my medical training, having completed three exhausting, exhilarating years as a Family Medicine resident in Lancaster, Pennsylvania, I emerged a freshly minted attending, afire with aspirations to serve the world. Yet I opted to stay for an additional year at the same hospital where

I'd trained, working as a physician for our local refugee clinic's inpatient service. It seemed a good way to get more experience in a familiar environment before moving abroad. I carried a daily census of around twenty patients, often more. Almost all of them were non-English speaking, hailing from nations across Eastern Europe, Central and South America, the Middle East, Southeast Asia, and sub-Saharan Africa. The schedule was a grueling 120 hours of solo coverage every other week, comprised of back-to-back, 36-hour shifts in which I covered all admissions, discharges, daily rounding, floor calls, ICU calls, Code Blues, and rapid response emergencies for the clinic's admitted patients.

Although it seemed like a daunting role when I signed my contract, I was filled with the overweening energy and confidence of youth. I was sure I could do it. Yet the schedule proved as terrible as it sounds; chronic sleep deprivation left me feeling vaguely nauseated most of the time. That hellish schedule would, after a mere three months on the job, cause me to collapse in a hospital stairwell one afternoon, thirty-two hours into a shift, and cost me a front tooth.

One morning, while finishing up some orders on my last ICU patient of the day, I was surprised by a harsh bleep from my pager. Glancing down, I saw the Emergency Department's extension appear on the pixelated gray screen. It was a number I already knew too well, but this early in the day? We had been through this before — how did they *still* not understand I wouldn't be open for admissions until five PM? The unit clerk and I had gone over this more times that I could count.

Today I was in no mood. Twenty-three patients on the census, nineteen still to go, and most of them requiring use of blue translation phones I'd have to hunt down on each unit. *Haitian Creole, Karenni, Ukrainian, Arabic, Amharic, Spanish,* and yes, *Nepali* — then still as cryptically unintelligible to me as any other tongue. It was going to be a long day.

"Why can't they keep the call schedule straight?" I moaned. Trying to contain the irritation edging my voice, I punched in the extension, barely giving the ED clerk a moment to say "hello" before I launched into my frustration with these errant pages.

"Oh, I know *that*. It's not an admission. Dr. Herr wanted to speak with you about something else." Now she was the one restraining her irritation. "It's a personal connection, I think — a mutual acquaintance of yours."

Pacified for the moment that at least I didn't have another admission piling onto the day's already overwhelming task-list, I immediately began running through my patient census, thinking this might be a personal friend of Dr. Herr's, upset with my care. I mentally scanned potential exam findings or critical lab results I may have missed on goodness-knows-who.

Had I misdiagnosed a spinal epidural abscess as muscular back strain? Sent a patient home with pneumonia or meningitis, thinking it was a viral syndrome? Overlooked an atypical heart attack in a patient without classic risk factors? The wait was unbearable. My license was on the line, no doubt about it. I was already mourning a career cut short too soon.

Suppress the urge to defend yourself, Becca, I quietly counseled myself. *Whatever happened, it's bound to be a valuable learning opportunity.* I felt very much the green attending I knew myself to be, still with much to learn.

Finally, I heard Dr. Herr's voice on the other end of the line. He was, as usual, cool, calm and collected. I braced myself for news of my clinical mistake.

"Hi Jim." This was a new thing, calling my former attending teachers by their first names. They were now technically my colleagues, but it still felt weird. I tried to sound casual. "Everything okay?"

"So, you know the Jansens, huh?"

It took a minute to register. This was way out of left field; I was totally thrown. My befuddled, awkward silence must have betrayed me, so he offered some context.

"Anneke and Willem Jansen? At Tansen Hospital? In

Nepal?"

Suddenly it all came together. I'd been in communication with Anneke Jansen, a physician at Tansen, some weeks before. I was trying to get more information that I hoped would help me make the decision to go abroad, considering whether to serve at a mission hospital in the foothills of the Annapurna Himalayas.

We'd sent a few emails back and forth — she, gauging my interest, and me, trying to ascertain whether this was something of which I was even remotely capable. Yet somewhere in the flood of new attending duties and pressures — not to mention sleep deprivation — I'd placed the whole thing on a back burner. Survival, just getting through each day, had become my only goal.

"Oh, yes!" I exclaimed, finally awakening to this collision of worlds. "How do *you* know about Tansen?"

"I served there for several years, Becca! My wife and I went there with our kids, back when they were little. It was quite a while ago now, but Tansen is still very dear to our hearts. The Jansens have remained close friends over the years. Anneke made the connection that you and I were both here at Lancaster General, and reached out to tell me about your interest. It sounds like you're thinking pretty seriously about heading over there?"

We set a time to meet the following week. I went to their home, where they introduced me to my first Nepali *dal bhaat*, the nation's staple meal of rice and lentils. It was a sumptuous experience — really a *bhoj*, or feast — of all kinds of authentic, aromatic dishes they'd learned to prepare during their years in Tansen.

"It's been a long while since I've had a reason to cook these dishes for company! Sometimes I make them for our family," his wife confessed a bit shyly, but with a twinkle of fond recollection. "You know. . . for old times' sake."

Speaking with Jim that evening, I also got my first glimpse into the harsh realities of this path I was considering. He spoke of weighty decisions and endless diagnostic uncertainty; of long, hard hours; of cases that still haunted him to this day, working at his limits' edges. Jim remembered one patient in particular with advanced lung disease, whom he had tapped in the clinic to remove some fluid, yet who passed away later that night. He was haunted by the thought that something he had done might have caused his demise, acknowledging that he couldn't ever know — was it his intervention, or simply the natural disease process, to blame? Diseases presented at such advanced stages there that doctors were often unable to offer much help. I got the sense that death lurked close at hand on those packed wards.

Yet the evening was encouraging, even as it was sobering. I was glad to know that someone had walked this path before me, emerging intact on the far side. Those challenges were — in theory, at least — survivable. Jim had learned the language and medical skills needed to be effective there, then successfully reintegrated into American medicine upon his return.

Other guidance of his would prove heartening even much later, on the far side of my own time in Tansen, when I was troubled to be abandoning a call to missionary medicine that had once seemed so certain. He likened missions to a relay race. "Some of us are purposed to carry the baton for a short time, and others for longer," he had written in our correspondence. "This is nothing to be ashamed of, but rather to realize that we are doing what we are called to, in God's great, unfathomable purpose."

Most affirming — and ultimately, confirming — were the tears I saw in Jim's eyes that night as he talked about their years in Nepal, revealing his deep yearning to be back in Tansen. Those emotions spoke more eloquently than could words of an experience that had irrevocably shaped his life. It seemed he now marked time in terms of Tansen's "before" and "after." Whatever such a journey might hold for me, it seemed at least to promise the professional and personal growth I desired, and the deeper sense of God's presence for which I longed.

This opportunity to travel to Nepal, to serve for even a few years, seemed a chance to participate freely in the grounded work of justice. Stirred by Jim's courage to serve in Tansen, the fear of regret was also a strangely powerful source of motivation for me. I did not want this idea to become something "I almost did once." I wanted to live into a larger narrative, pouring myself into a story greater than just my own. Here was a chance to join in God's work of restoring shalom and wholeness to broken places of our world. I saw this as a way to plough back into the figurative soil of this earth some of what I had so generously been given through my education, supportive family, and countless other resources. To do any less, in fact, seemed unjust.

And when would it ever again be this easy to go? I was on the verge of professional transition. I had no spouse or children, no mortgage, no school debt or car payments, no aging parents requiring my care. I could think of no particular reason why *not* to go. Once I began to entertain the possibility, it came to occupy my thoughts intensely, pressing upon me with increasing urgency as the months passed, until finally a decision coalesced within me. One morning, on a day off, I called up the missions agency I was thinking of contacting, and asked their team coordinator if they could use a family doctor for a year.

"Can you come for two?" she replied.

CHAPTER TWO
Mussoorie

In order to explore this commitment further, Jim connected me with friends of his living just down the hill from Landour Community Hospital in Mussoorie, India — a town several hours north of Delhi. I made plans to visit them the following summer, and they arranged for me to spend a day with one of the hospital's physicians, Dr. Abrahms. I set out for Landour that morning with great hope, and a small twinge of trepidation.

Running a few minutes late, I grabbed a handful of dry granola from the kitchen as I bolted out the door and up the hill behind the house. Still not accustomed to the high altitude of this northern Indian hill-town, though, I was huffing much harder and earlier than I would have expected, still with another twenty minutes to go. Happily, the last bit was on more level ground, affording a chance to recover, though just barely. I didn't want to arrive appearing as though I might be a patient in need of their emergency room myself.

After presenting to the security guard at the main gate, I was escorted to a second-floor meeting room filled with rows of Franklin style desk-chairs. The staff was trickling in slowly, and appeared to be comprised almost exclusively of Indian nationals. It was gratifying to see so few expatriates, for it signaled that this mission hospital had apparently been able to transition its leadership in such a way that the doctors and nurses mirrored the population they served.

After we all settled into our cramped desks, a young, handsome man in a white coat stood up, introduced himself as Dr. Abrahms, and began leading their routine of morning prayer. There was a simplicity and sweetness in their sung *a cappella* hymn and prayer of vocation spoken over the staff. I welcomed those few minutes' reorientation, before embarking with them on the day's patient care tasks.

Dr. Abrahms was the senior orthopedic surgeon at Landour, and whisked me along to make rounds with his team. We proceeded from bed to bed on an open ward with around fifteen men, their metal-framed gurneys side by side, not even separated by curtains. The scene jarred my American sensibilities around patient privacy. The patients themselves didn't seem bothered, though. Neither did they seem to mind not understanding virtually anything that was happening to or around them, taking it all in as a matter of course. I pictured a couple of my more entitled patients in the States and wondered how they might fare if thrust into this environment.

At the bedside of the fifth patient, ten minutes or so into rounds, we came upon a young man looking extremely uncomfortable, hunched in his bed along one wall. A brief exam revealed a sausage-like index finger on his left hand, hugely swollen and purplish. It was so large and tender that he was completely unable to move it, shielding it gingerly against his chest. Even from a distance, it was clear this was a serious infection, probably a diagnosis of *flexor tenosynovitis*, where the sheath surrounding the finger's tendon is infected and fills tensely with pus. It was something I'd read about but had never actually seen, recalling only that it's considered a surgical emergency.

The attending evidently thought so too, because he immediately ordered a tray for incision and drainage, and had the patient wheeled down to a procedure room at the end of the hall. Minutes later, I was standing opposite the surgeon, next to two fourth-year medical students from Singapore who were halfway through their global health elective at Landour. The surgeon deftly injected lidocaine to numb the finger, and then made a smooth incision along the entire length of his finger's inner surface. Pus came flooding out as the doctor squeezed the inflamed digit. Unfortunately, lidocaine's effects are limited in the setting of a bad infection, and apparently wasn't doing a lot for our patient now. He writhed in near-soundless pain on the table before us. Occasionally agonized groans escaped at intervals, betraying his intense discomfort.

Standing to my left, near the patient's head, were those two fourth-year medical students. As we watched the procedure together, a refrain of helpful adages scrolled through my head.

Pretty tough to see, huh?

Well, you know, it's actually a lot easier to do these sorts of procedures than to watch them.

Believe me, it really does get easier to tolerate the blood and guts, with a little more experience.

I debated breaking the intensely focused silence to share these generous platitudes of wisdom, but frankly, they seemed to be tolerating the scene with remarkable stoicism, pungent odors and all. I kept quiet.

Instead, in a gesture of solidarity with the patient, I laid a hand gently on his knee. It seemed important to reassure him we were not merely voyeuristic onlookers to his pain.

At exactly that moment — almost simultaneously as I outstretched my hand — I began to feel. . . *funny.* Sounds grew further away, as if heard through water. My vision became spotty with large, gray-purple dots, gradually coalescing from the outside of my field of vision. I could barely make out the surgeon though the cool fog that had descended.

I can't believe this. I'm about to pass out.

Squeezing my hands into fists, buttocks and abdominal muscles clenched tightly, I hoped I could force enough blood-flow to my brain to stay upright, a desperate attempt to keep from drawing attention to myself.

Nope, that's not working.

Determined not to go down in a heap, I slowly backed away from the table, moving as inconspicuously as I could, and lowered myself onto an ancient windowsill, conveniently located a few feet behind me. I brought my head down between my knees as low I could get without letting on as to what was happening. Or so I thought. I glanced back up just in time to meet Dr. Abrahms' steady gaze. He was regarding me over half-rim glasses, his eyebrows raised slightly in amusement.

"Feeling a bit woozy, are we?"

"Hmmm. . . uhhmmm. . . *Yeah.* . . Though I really can't imagine *why*. . ."

On reflection, of course, I could think of a few reasons. A scant breakfast and hasty, high-altitude uphill climb just half an hour earlier, then surrounded by the strange landscape of a 1940's-era hospital and unintelligible drone of Hindi all around me. Each of these elements bespoke immense challenges that I knew lay ahead, if I were indeed to pursue this path of medical missions. It was beginning to seem like a foolhardy venture, ludicrously impossible.

Still, I was irritated that a little blood and pus could send me clear over the edge like that. It felt out of character. This was certainly not the first time I'd encountered that.

And yet. . .

How could those two medical students be so placidly unfazed, handling the whole scene better than I? Were they really that much further along as professionals, even with the rest of medical school, residency and early-career practice still ahead of them? Something just wasn't adding up. I was never one to pass out, nor even to cry. In fact, toughness had long been part of my self-identity. I would usually roll my eyes internally at such displays of weakness.

I was flooded with a deep sense of shame. What had happened to me? Maybe I was growing soft, too far removed from the intense rigors of a medical school surgery rotation? It was horrifying to think that I could go weak-in-the-knees at a little bit of blood. And even more importantly, what did this mean for my hopes to work abroad, where medical practice seemed considerably rawer than the sanitized settings to which I'd grown accustomed in America?

CHAPTER THREE

Medicine's Mask

It wasn't until weeks later that it made more sense, and something clicked into place when I recalled my first day of medical school. Our faculty convened an introductory meeting in the lobby outside of the Human Anatomy Lab. Just beyond the aseptic, swinging double doors lay a room we knew would henceforth define our medical school experience, stamped in our memories as it was for countless students before us. We clustered in the stairwell landing, four students to a team, and waited with apprehension. We were about to meet our cadavers.

Entering the cavernous, skylit space — a penthouse atrium filled with sunlight, and specially equipped with a sophisticated ventilation system to mitigate the acerbic formaldehyde fumes — we were greeted by metal gurneys lining the room in long, uniform rows. Their lumpy burdens, unmistakably human in shape, were covered by pristine white sheets. In short order, those sheets were about to lose their crispness, as our fresh scrubs grew pungent. The ease we would eventually come to feel in that space was mirrored in greasy stains of human fat and preservative fluid at our waistlines. Though just weeks away, such a casual attitude was unthinkable to us that first morning.

In those initial, tense moments, none of us wanted to be "the one who couldn't handle it," the one who either reacted with an embarrassing show of emotion or, worse yet, got lightheaded and passed out. Happily, I succumbed to neither. I was a star student in this first lesson of steeling myself to the task at hand, and very quickly grew proficient at shutting down even the smallest hint of emotion. As such, this experience proved an important initiation into the art of clinical detachment. We knew, even then, that such imperturbability was necessary for maintaining level-headed coolness in the heat of crises. It was the *aequanimitas* of which one esteemed father of modern medicine, Dr. Osler, had often spoken. Even the cadaver was given a role in this drama, introduced to us as "our first patient."

What I didn't realize then — what I wouldn't dare articulate even to myself until many years later — was this. Along with my peers, I had diligently practiced the skill of clinical detachment during those countless hours of dissection. We'd all honed it to such a well-practiced habit that, when faced with the suffering of our first real, *living* patients on the wards, we would view them as little more than still-breathing cadavers.

That is how any of us manage to get through the intensity of our first encounters with profound suffering. It is an initiation by fire. I still remember my first patient, a "still-breathing cadaver" on my surgery rotation. As a brand-new student on the wards in July, I had slipped into my crisp, new white coat, pleats still impeccably pressed, and walked into the room of a debilitated, cachectic old man who had already undergone numerous abdominal surgeries. His mucous-caked tracheostomy tube tethered him ever so tenuously to this world. From the bedside, his nurse barked at me to help turn him so she could clean and dress his wounds. Excruciatingly, we rolled him to his right side, exposing his entire, raw sacral bone, easily visible beneath the open skin of his bedsores. I had never seen such a sight, where the "inside" and "outside" of a person were so unnaturally juxtaposed.

Yet I swallowed my revulsion, and didn't allow myself even to blink.

The pain of connecting with such a man — *as* a man, as someone's father and grandfather, or uncle, as perhaps their piano-tuner, or at least their friend — is overwhelming. The student may be forgiven if she goes to a place of numbed quietude, encountering similar pain in similar faces a hundred times more in the span of mere months, compressing and internalizing discomfort as if it were nothing out of the ordinary. No one wants to bear the ridicule of a cynical nurse or resident deriding an emotional display, whether it be fear, or shock, or grief. Nothing is more shameful in the world of medicine than weakness.

And so the mask hardens quickly, and it is worn faithfully. The same tough exterior that got me through that first day in the anatomy lab would prove immensely useful in the years of training that followed. It would protect each of us as the medicine's call drew us in deeper, inviting us to become increasingly involved in the uninvited pain of others.

More often than not, we would find ourselves playing a direct role in their suffering, as we poked needles through skin and bone, or examined broken limbs, or relayed news of a terminal diagnosis, or pronounced death. In the name of healing we would, as often as not, inflict suffering as bear witness to it. To this day I still don't know which is harder.

It turns out that the task of training, then, is also about reintegrating the humanity of the person with the reality of their suffering. This is vital, in order to hold those two elements in tension. The broken body before you has a story. She is a person who has known the sting of betrayal, the gnawing edge of fear, the weight of grief, the mystery of wonder. And you are asked to play a role in her suffering — to bear witness to pain that breaks open her world, or perhaps to bear the grievous thunderclap of news by which she will henceforth mark time. No wonder so many of us find it impossible to hold that tension in balance, choosing to be distant rather than crushed.

Speaking one afternoon with my friend Jane, I told her about the man with the infected purple finger. Jane had been a longtime friend ever since we met as college roommates, and again during our residency years, when we trained together at the same hospital. As I finished telling her about how I almost passed out, just like a novice, Jane listened thoughtfully. After a pause, she noted, "You know, you only felt lightheaded once you reached out your hand to console him."

Was it simply that gesture of care, one human being connecting with another, that overwhelmed me? As my best friend, she certainly knew me well; as an astute physician colleague, she also had first-hand insight into what was happening at that professional-personal nexus.

"But Jane, I've always been able to simply 'shut it down' when I have to. What if I can't, someday? What if I just can't contain the emotion?"

Perhaps, had I maintained the stoic silence of those two medical students looking on impassively, I might have spared myself the embarrassment of, ironically, appearing the novice. I could have avoided the betrayal of emotion. Yet what a cost that mask exacts.

Before heading home from Landour Community Hospital at the end of that day, I met a young American physician serving there with his wife. They were early in their first term at the hospital, and had been there less than a year. I spent an hour shadowing him in the outpatient clinic. "Yeah, it's been tough," he said, when I expressed some of my own concerns. His weary expression said it all. I wish I could say that my ambivalence was assuaged by a peace-beyond-understanding, some profound sense of clarity and calling rooted in unwavering faith. Even a small word from the young doctor might have relieved my misgivings, assuring me that if I truly sensed this missionary call, the rest would work itself out, and everything would fall neatly into place.

Instead, as I trudged out of the hospital and back down the hill that afternoon, I was dizzy with the enormity of the task into which I was rushing, headlong. The day had raised a torrent of questions. Could I really do this? Could I manage such intensity in treating unfamiliar diseases, or performing procedures I'd never even *seen* before, let alone done? And could I do it all in a totally foreign language?

Deflated, I slumped into a plastic chair on the porch, feeling utterly unequal to the mammoth commitment I'd already begun to make.

CHAPTER FOUR
Final Farewells

Having made the decision to move to Nepal, one final, daunting task remained: I had to weed through several years' worth of accumulated *stuff*. It's staggering, really, to note how easily things like books, stationery, household goods, kitchenware, clothing, and furniture so readily fill the corners of your physical and mental space. Nature abhors a vacuum. It was time to sift through the bulk, deciding what items were essential enough to merit packing up and hauling into the basement and attic spaces of my obliging friends. There's a subversive, unexpected thrill that comes with purging your belongings. It brings a sense of delicious lightness deep within the soul. Ironically, this path to freedom is the exact opposite of what our materialistic society promises. We live in a world that unapologetically preaches a gospel of *more* is more.

Over the past few years, perhaps in response to materialism's subtle drag on the soul, there's been some reversal of this trend in favor of minimalism. Sometimes it's couched in eco-green logos, other times advocating a back-to-basics approach, but it generally always channels a relaxed, Zen-like look. Championed by such titles as *The Joy of Less, Simple Living, Minimalism Made Easy,* and the empire of joy sparked by Marie Kondo, books with appealingly clean lines crowd the best-seller tables. It has spawned a movement that's tough to miss, if also tough to attain. We've become a nation tired of excess. Heavily laden. Maybe Jesus was on to something when He advised the young man with lots of stuff to sell it all for the sake of the poor.

The eighteenth-century Methodist revival preacher John Wesley had his own radical approach to materialism. It seems that one particular event dramatically shaped his attitude toward spending. While a young professor at Oxford University, he enjoyed the comfortable income of thirty pounds per year — a sum more than adequate to sustain a single man in his day. As the story goes, Wesley purchased several decorative pictures for his room one cold winter day. On his way home, he came upon a chambermaid shivering in the cold, clothed in only a thin linen gown to shield her from the frigid weather.

Reaching into his pocket for money to buy her a coat, he was dismayed to find that he had nothing left. He was immediately cut to the quick with deep grief, realizing that his lifestyle had left no margin to care for the vulnerable around him. Chastened, he asked himself, "Will thy Master say, 'Well done, good and faithful steward?' Thou hast adorned thy walls with the money which might have screened this poor creature from the cold! O justice! O mercy! Are not these pictures the blood of this poor maid?"

Though aware that the acceptable standard of giving was the "tithe," or ten percent of one's annual income, from that time on John Wesley sought to give away his money with exponentially increasing generosity. He was concerned with the risk of becoming too attached to material goods, and was of the opinion that as a Christian's income increased, their standard of *giving*, not living, should increase. By the end of his life, he was cheerfully expunging up to 98% of his entire income. He once proclaimed, "When I die, if I leave behind me ten pounds. . . you and all mankind can bear witness against me, that I have lived and died a thief and a robber."

It calls to mind the words of another faithful servant of the poor, Saint Vincent de Paul, who was once quoted by activist Shane Claiborne as saying, "when we give food to the hungry, our posture should be to get on our knees and ask forgiveness, for we are only returning what is rightfully theirs." I returned to such difficult words often as a lens for discerning my own vocation, a call to live my life in response to God's love. He is not a God bent on guilt-tripping us into acts of generosity and service. Rather, His heart is for fullness of life. Far from levying a burden of guilt, He looks at us and *loves us*. That's meant to come before all else. His love is our first and best motivation for any acts of care and beauty in the world, because it is an invitation into the very love that He Himself, in the glorious dance of the Trinity, has enjoyed for all eternity.

As I loaded cookbooks into cardboard boxes and sealed bedding in plastic garbage bags, I wondered who I might be on the other side of this adventure, filing these books back onto bookshelves after two years abroad. Even in the mundane process of tying up loose ends of my material world, I couldn't escape the sense that significant transformation loomed large on a near horizon. In the midst of a transition that was as familiar as it was frightening, I found comfort that at least the uncertain road ahead bore well-traveled grooves of others who'd walked it before me.

And so it was that, within the year, these seemingly small decision points led ultimately to the final commitment, the final packing and storing, the final goodbyes. My Subaru hatchback had held up well over some 5,000 miles driving up and down the East Coast, and I'd survived a six-week marathon of sleeping in a different bed (and usually in a different state) every few nights. The exhaustive trek concluded in Boston on a mid-September weekend, where I bid my family goodbye before I was to board a plane at Logan airport and commence my one-way flight to Kathmandu.

One afternoon during that final weekend with my family, we strolled along the Gloucester waterfront, bracing against the autumn air gusting in from Massachusetts Bay. My mother was walking up ahead with my sister Jessica, and I watched as they turned onto a wooden pier reaching out from shore. Gray water lapped against its pilings. I noticed that the pier widened to accommodate a bronze statue set on a generous cube of granite. The nautical theme fit its setting flawlessly — a confident young man in rain gear and Wellingtons, the perfect look for an iconic New England harbor city.

As I grew closer, I could see the sailor leaned against the ship wheel, which seemed to steady his powerful, weary frame. His gaze was locked resolutely on the unknown, uncertain horizon ahead. Standing as a memorial to three centuries of brave seafarers, his future was hinted at only by a simple yet ominous phrase carved into the pedestal beneath him: "They that go down to the sea in ships."

I joined Jessica and my mom, who had paused to regard the inscription. We stood silently for a moment, taking in the courageous, valiant, windswept face of one about whose fate we knew more than did he, himself. Then I glanced back behind me, my father and brother-in-law approaching slowly from several paces behind. I sensed that this moment, frozen in time, would one day be a memory, and each of our lives would look different from that future vantage point. Emotion flooded through me as I regarded the resolute, courageous look on the statue's weathered bronze face, with its themes of journey, commemoration, and grief.

It seemed strange, even self-indulgent, to feel nostalgia for a moment that hadn't yet passed, and sadness for the loss of a moment that was still unfolding. I suspect that on each of our minds was an inevitable thought, that the memories we were making might possibly be our last as a family — moments suspended in time that would be recalled in retrospect for their poignant finality. That is the dark underbelly of adventure — fear in the face of an unknown, barely-conceived-of world.

After our walk, we drove back to Boston and stopped for

lunch at Panera, sitting in a corner-booth surrounded by walls swathed in geometric swirls of burnt orange and basil green. All around us flowed the steady drone of overlapping conversations, mostly in English, as friends caught up over familiar foods, surrounded by familiar restaurant smells, in franchise-manufactured ambiance.

I'd always rolled my eyes at these generic strip-mall storefronts featured from Dorchester to Denver, their prominent logos recognizable on the highways and byways I'd been traversing continually for the past six weeks. These franchises always seemed devoid of character. There was no trace of the struggles borne of local, independent hideaways that they'd replaced in less than a generation. Yet the corporate food industry was virtually all I'd ever known, an American girl raised in American cities with ambitiously American growth trajectories.

What would a world look like without the predictability of McDonald's, Dunkin' Donuts, Subway, or Applebee's? These familiar spots were always easy to take for granted. It was convenient, even, to view them with a measure of cynical suspicion. Now, on the cusp of leaving it all behind, they felt like secure anchors. How many other things had also taken on that glow of "home" recently? I knew that soon, in a far-off time zone, even telephone calls and texts — the *immediacy* of my relationships, as much as their physical proximity — would also lose that predictable security.

My father's health had also been failing in recent years. Signs of age and debility had begun to creep in to his once-strong frame, betrayed in his graying beard and shuffling, hesitant gait. I noticed that his face, once full of enthusiasm and keen intellect, now often bore an expression of vague confusion, as conversation seemed to go over his head. In the pictures we'd taken that morning, he looked like an old man. I wondered if he would even appear in a future snapshot, whenever our family could gather again. Would *I*? We were standing on the brink of what would be the longest and furthest separation our family had ever yet experienced.

That weekend with my family was characterized by a hesitant truce with uncertainty. Predictably, my impending departure infused our time with a hyper-awareness of each moment shared, creating an acute, even artificial, intentionality. None of us wished to acknowledge it aloud, of course, but in a melancholy sort of way, the future was casting its intrusive pall over our present. We tried valiantly to make everything feel normal, careful to savor the moments, creating a space that would, in our memories, sustain us through the separation to come.

Then, hardly before I could believe it, certainly before I was ready, I was saying goodbye to my family in front of the Panera, hugging them in the parking lot of the South Bay Mall. Such a huge moment, and yet strangely anticlimactic. We embraced tightly, they got in their car, and I waved goodbye until they disappeared around a bend.

Suddenly I was again five years old, standing in front of the kindergarten teacher as my father waved farewell down an unfamiliar hallway, imparting to me the courage to step into a new classroom. It was that same wrenching, pit-in-your-stomach sadness of a separation that you fear perhaps might be permanent. A homesick wave of grief washed over me. Overwhelmed, I fought back tears, aware that the next halting steps of independence were mine alone to take.

CHAPTER FIVE

Arrival

Some people live their whole lives on a track, a straight shot from points A to B. As someone who took an unwavering path through grade school, high school, college, medical school, residency training, and fellowship, I get that. When I interview medical student candidates who knew from pre-school that they wanted to be doctors, I recognize that as my story, too. By process of elimination — once "astronaut" had lost its luster, and "violinist" seemed (ironically) too demanding — the allure of "doctor" somehow stuck.

So certain was I of this vocational calling, in fact, that as a high school senior, having just sat for a positively *abysmal* passport photo, I knew exactly where I'd be when the time finally came to renew it in ten years.

"Well, there's the rest of this school year, then four years of college, and four more of med school. Then into residency... I have to wait until my *second year of residency* before I can get a new passport photo?" It seemed unthinkable. With disgust, I regarded the over-exposed square, my pallid face merging with pallid hair against a blindingly white background. The most engaging element in the photograph was a red crew-neck sweatshirt I was wearing, gaudily outcompeting for attention. A regrettable clothing choice.

As poorly planned as that photo was, my life was anything but. It was clear, carefully ordered, and thoroughly mapped out. I was an intensely driven, serious young girl with one, three, five and ten-year plans. I knew exactly how things were supposed to turn out — how and *when*. There would be no messy, meandering paths for me.

Which is not to say that I lacked an intrepid spirit — far from it. I adored the bold spirit of Theodore Roosevelt, and as a teenager, memorized part of his famous 1910 speech. I knew Roosevelt was speaking of me when he described the person "who knows great enthusiasms [and] great devotions; who spends himself in a worthy cause. . ." His courageous escapades filled my imagination with possibility. I longed to "dare greatly" and "strive valiantly," and was tenacious in my pursuit. I never wanted to be counted among "those cold and timid souls who know neither victory nor defeat."

Once, on an international trekking adventure as a young woman, I fell ill, briefly but violently, with feverish diarrhea. At one point during a night of hazy delirium, I lifted my head with great effort and regarded the white-washed cinderblock walls around me. The room was furnished with Astroturf carpeting, one metal table, and a single, bare lightbulb suspended from the ceiling. I flopped backwards onto my pillow with a contented sigh at the perfection of it all. This was truly *living*. When it came to adventure, I was a hopeless romantic.

Yet the idea of risking failure can sound noble and appealing only to one who has never experienced it, at least not really, not in any meaningful or sustained way. In Nepal, I would eventually discover the depths to which my own failings could plunge me, descending in a turbulent undertow that did, eventually, yield its promised growth and depth. Even had I known how those few years would play out, I probably would still have gone. Yet it would have been with considerably tempered enthusiasm.

Thirteen years after that disastrous passport photo, a marginally better one mounted into my passport, I landed on the tarmac of Kathmandu's Tribhuvan International Airport. I had, by this point, completed my medical training, and spent the previous year discerning a call to missions — something of a left-turn in the plan, by most people's reckoning. It was autumn then, but as recently as the preceding summer — living a nomadic existence with the details of an international move still being hashed out — I wasn't sure whether I'd even be on the same *continent* several months hence. I had definitely jumped the well-worn grooves of my track. And it felt wonderful.

As it turned out, when I arrived in Nepal, I had to get yet another passport-style photo for my Nepali Tourist Visa application. I waited in the large, echoing customs hall, which reeked of bureaucracy from a bygone era. Hundreds of people milled about in what was meant to be a queue, waiting for the self-serve photo booth to slowly churn along. An industrial fan hummed in one corner, thick clumps of dust tenuously clinging to its ancient wire slats. A few clumps of that dust — microscopic remnants, really, of tourists from time immemorial — broke off and drifted through the air, landing on this new batch of weary travelers.

Above the fan's whirring rattle were sounds of languages I made out to be Hebrew, German, French, and a few others I could only guess at — a Scandinavian varietal, possibly Norwegian? And something with a more Slavic tone? The line inched forward. I waited, my mind wandering to the question of how, in this crush of people, I would ever locate the Scottish pastoral care couple who were meeting me at the airport that evening.

"What were their names again? Callum and Midge?" I wondered aloud to myself. I pulled out a small stack of folded papers and thumbed through it to an email I'd printed out. Yes, once through customs, I should look for a couple named Callum and Midge. Their smiles were warm and friendly in the photo they'd sent. I breathed a small sigh of relief that someone knew I was here, and could help with the first step of getting to my guesthouse. It was already past ten at night, and I didn't have an internet connection, or even a cell phone. The line slowly nudged forward. Finally, it was my turn, a photo hastily taken and handed to me.

Immediately an official waved me over to a metal-corralled chute. A sign above it, printed in English and Nepali, read "Tourists, Aliens and Non-Residents." I shouldered my hefty, 36-liter Osprey pack and tried to keep my footing amidst the throng of humanity around me, while regarding my new passport photo. I'd thrown a pink scarf casually around my shoulders, the look of youthful confidence in my expression, eyes steady and level to the camera. A faint glint from my nose ring caught the light. On the verge of adventure, I was keen to enter this new world — and perhaps a new life altogether.

CHAPTER SIX

New Horizons

The first weeks in a new country are bound to be an adventure. Nepal, of course, was no exception. I met up with a new Australian friend, Maddy, to explore my neighborhood one afternoon. Trained as an anesthesiologist, she'd spent the last couple of years establishing a surgical obstetrics program and conducting anesthesia training at remote health posts in Nepal's far western region. Maddy was also going to be my flatmate once we got to Tansen, though she would be moving there a few weeks before me. She had been living in Kathmandu for several months, and already knew the area fairly well.

We walked to the end of the alley behind my guesthouse and turned a corner onto the busy road that rimmed our little maze of dirt paths in Kathmandu's *Jhamsikhel* district. The sidewalk was narrow, abutting a torrent of cars, motorcycles and tuk-tuks, which all honked loudly as they careened along, in a way that seemed insanely chaotic. We paused our conversation briefly to walk single file through a section of crumbling sidewalk. The shrill car horns and unmuffled motors made communication nearly impossible anyway.

Ahead of us, power lines sagged from wooden telephone poles, and after several paces, I saw some strands of black-coated electrical wire had fallen to the ground, strewn haphazardly along the sidewalk. I stopped short, assuming them to be live, capable of delivering a nasty, if not fatal, shock. Yet Maddy breezily stepped right through the coils of cable. I took a deep breath and gingerly picked my way across as well. Trying to mirror her casual air as I caught up to her, it occurred to me that this was a good time to accomplish some errands I'd been putting off.

"Maddy, where do you withdraw cash — Nepali rupees, I guess? I need to find an ATM that takes my bank's debit card."

Since few of the streets had names, everyone navigated by landmarks. "Do you know where that three-way branch point is, near *Moksh*?" she asked. "There's a secure ATM just a few shops down from that." I shook my head. I had no idea where — or what — *Moksh* even was.

"We're pretty close to it now," she continued, "and anyway, I have to get some cash out too. I'll show you." She confidently turned left, down another road. I tried to make mental notes of where we were going for the next time I needed an ATM.

"That's a great spot for authentic *chiya* and *momos*," she said, pointing out a hole-in-the-wall tea shop on the corner. I had recently learned that *chiya* was the Nepali word for chai tea, and *momos* were a kind of Nepali dumpling that could be either steamed or fried. I was keen to try both, but knew my command of Nepali was still too meager to attempt ordering in a local restaurant. I thought back to a story someone told me right before I came here, about when she lived for several months in Israel. She'd said a low point came one afternoon when she simply wanted to buy a chocolate bar at a local convenience store, but couldn't tell one kind from another, since all the wrappers were printed in Hebrew. At the time, it struck me as a weird reason to be demoralized. Now I was beginning to understand what she'd meant.

Each day after language class, I took a break to wander the neighborhood surrounding my new home — or at least, the city that would be "home" for the next two months of language training and cultural orientation. Many things were noticeably different from my actual home. It was hard to avoid the extreme air and noise pollution, or the chaos of indiscernible traffic patterns. The sharp pitch of barking dogs frequently interrupted the solitude of my language study.

At the same time, I breathed in premodern smells of wood-fire smoke and rain-drenched mud, immersed in a cacophony of squabbling hens and crowing roosters in my neighbor's garden. These sounds intermingled with cries of village peddlers punctuating the air, as rail-thin men made their way along congested streets and alleys, calling out their wares in long, low, melodic syllables. These were the sounds and smells of an ancient-modern world that lay just beyond my bedroom window, crying out to be explored and experienced.

While in Kathmandu, I also got to know another family right from the start. Dan, Leah and their two children originally hailed from North Carolina, and had arrived in Kathmandu just a day before I did. We would be serving together in Tansen for the next two years. They lived down the road from my guesthouse, and we were going through the same language and orientation program together. As we became introduced to the city's vibrant ex-pat community, we often shared meals with new friends from all over the world — England, Scotland and Ireland; Australia, the Netherlands, Norway and America; Hong Kong, Malaysia, South Korea; and, of course, Nepal. Not infrequently during those first few weeks, we also spent evenings together playing board games like *Settlers of Catan* and *Carcassonne*.

One Saturday afternoon, I joined Maddy, Dan, Leah, and a few other ex-pat friends on a "stroll" over one of the "hills" along the outskirts of the city. The walk, which started out at a comfortable pace through a relatively level wooded path, quickly veered up a steep ridge and eventually unfolded into a six-hour trek to the peak of what seemed to me a *legitimate* mountain — but in reality, at a mere 6,000 feet elevation, barely registered as a foothill. Struggling myself at times, I was impressed at how readily the seven-year-old in our group kept pace the whole way. Occasionally this narrow dirt path led us through yards of traditional Nepali homes. Children sometimes ran over to try out their English on us, shouting, "HELLO! WHAT IS YOUR NAME!" — delivered more as a statement than a question. Older women passed us on the path, their beautiful, furrow-wrinkled faces adorned with ornate nose rings, a fresh *tikka* on their foreheads, and a faded red *sindoor* along the part of their hairlines. They cheerfully returned my "Namaste, Didi!," pressing palms together at their chest in the familiar Nepali gesture, even when carrying impossibly mammoth loads on their backs.

One front yard we passed was filled with faded prayer flags draped back and forth in thick, colorful swaths, shimmering in the breeze. Seeing a woman hanging laundry, Maddy called out a greeting and walked over to strike up a conversation in Nepali, addressing her as *Aama*. Though translated as "mother," the term is used for any older woman as a sign of respect. Even though Maddy had only been in the country for a couple of years, hearing her speak fluent Nepali astonished me. She seemed to be so comfortable. My own command of the language was so weak that I couldn't even distinguish where one word ended, and another began. Maddy appeared to be asking directions, confirming that we were on the right path. They chatted and gestured back and forth, their fluid jumble of sounds forming a verbal counterpoint to the prayer flags flapping aimlessly above our heads. Nodding to the woman, Maddy cheerily said something else, ending with a word I recognized as "Thank you," and then rejoined us on the path. It seemed impossible that anyone could acquire such skill in so brief a span, yet here she was, living proof that it was possible.

Back on my guesthouse balcony the following morning, still exhilarated from the prior day's jaunt, I felt wide awake to the peculiarities of this new life. On the rooftops all around me, saris were draped from neighbors' balconies, their laundry forming beautiful, happenstance banners wherever they'd been left to dry. Two women laughed together as they hung clothes on a line, while down below at street level, another woman swept rhythmically in front of her doorway with a stick-broom. Everywhere, people were moving about their morning routines. A cool breeze picked up, wafting down into the valley from the surrounding hilltops. Everywhere I looked, life was happening, pregnant with a sense of meaning and adventure.

This was a unique world I'd entered, a dizzying eddy of sound, smell and color, churning together in a confluence of cultures. Even among my newfound and fascinatingly varied ex-pat community, I often found myself in unfamiliar territory, a foreigner among foreigners. Yet for all that, it was not difficult to imagine growing fond of this place. Through the eyes of a jet-lagged newcomer, one for whom everything was unusual, fresh and filled with wonder, it was a beautiful sight.

CHAPTER SEVEN
Bideshi Wanderings

My first week of language classes completed, I stepped out of the building, blinking in the sun, and headed home. I would be meeting Dan and Leah in a couple of hours for dinner, and really looked forward to seeing them. My head was spinning with everything involved in learning a new language. I walked through the garden at the heart of our organization's headquarters, where our language tutorials were held, and through the front gate. As I drew closer to the main road, I could feel the air buzzing with nervous energy. Car engines and diesel trucks rattled by on rutted roads, punctuated by the harsh, flat-pitched car horns of European-made hatchbacks.

Sometimes, I also heard the uniquely South Asian sound of men from the *Terai* selling fresh fruit and vegetables. They would ride by, their lean, lungi-clad frames perched atop ancient bicycles, advertising produce for sale. I watched, mesmerized by their long legs peddling in fluid arcs, rubber-sandaled feet angled outward to keep their knees from striking the handlebars. In time, I began to even understand their nasal-toned Hindi calls, accented differently from the Nepali I was studying each day, but with shared words for cauliflower, eggplant, bananas, oranges, mangos, green beans: *Kauli.* . . *Baanta.* . . *Kera.* . . *Suntala.* . . *Aapp.* . . *Hariyo Simi.* . .

The fresh smell of fruit — more vibrant and richly aromatic than all the waxy, hothouse produce piled high on supermarket shelves back home — was tantalizing. Yet it mixed jarringly with more pungent street odors — the acrid smell of trash-choked gutters and smoke from smoldering garbage heaps; earthy smells of goats tied at posts along the roadside, screaming wild-eyed with alarm at the passing stream of cars; the occasional tucked-away corner smelling faintly of stale urine.

I turned down the path into a bustling commercial district of shops and small restaurants. Cauldrons of hot oil sizzled in open-front stalls set a few feet back from the road, deep frying an assortment of sweets that, aside from being different shapes and sizes, looked otherwise identical. Each was the same golden-brown color of deep-fried dough. They all appealed to throngs of black flies swarming in frenetic loops, making only brief concession to a languid hand swatting at them distractedly from time to time.

One afternoon on the way home from class earlier that week, curious to try a piece of this deep-fried dough, I had thought about ordering one. But stepping up to the wooden counter, I realized I didn't know what words to use. I didn't know how to ask the shopkeeper about the cost, nor would I have understood his answer anyway. I couldn't even read the prices on the wall-mounted chalkboard, as the numbers were written in Nepali, rather than the more familiar Arabic numerals. Flushing a deep shade of red, I could only point to what I wanted with an inquiring gesture.

The shopkeeper had seemed to understand anyway, and held up five fingers — five rupees, roughly equal to a nickel. I nodded and handed him the money, but as he fished out one of the sweets, he turned to a woman in the shop and said something that made them both laugh. She looked back at me and said something else, still laughing. I guess they were chuckling over how funny it was to see a *bideshi*, a white foreigner, eating Nepali *kaaja*, street food. There was nothing malicious in it, just plain, good-natured teasing. But I felt uncomfortable just the same. I already felt very much the outsider. This particular afternoon on my walk home, I noticed two elderly women squatting along the curb up ahead. As I drew closer, I could see them tending a small cast-iron basin of coals on which corn cobs were roasting, sending out a deliciously smoky, charred aroma. It smelled amazing, and I felt starved. I'd missed lunch that day, as a loud rumble in my stomach suddenly reminded me. Slowing down over those final twenty feet of sidewalk, I was ready to stop and buy a piece, but then recalled the awkward exchange a few days earlier. As appealing as that roasted corn was, I knew the sight of a *bideshi* ordering one on that crowded sidewalk might draw a small crowd. It didn't seem worth the unwanted attention.

It was all good-natured fun, I knew, but I rarely had the energy for it. On these walks to and from class, which took about forty minutes each way, I rarely saw another *bideshi*. Longing for anonymity, I just wanted to blend in. It was beginning to feel like a fragile space, one in which I was utterly unmoored from anything or anyone familiar. I walked on around the corner, eyes straight ahead, trying to project a self-assured confidence I didn't feel.

Several hundred yards further down on the left, a bridge crossed the Bagmati River, a festering slough that reeked of all manner of waste. Grey-yellow flotsam foamed as it gathered along its stagnant river-edge. A dead dog floated there too, pinned against brush-weed in the rocky shallows, its carcass bloated and limp. It would still be lying there weeks later. The banks of the river were crowded with corrugated tin and cardboard structures, a makeshift shantytown for the city's poorest inhabitants. Those who live there eked out an existence that was unimaginable to me.

Crossing the bridge, I wanted to avert my eyes from the sight. Yet I recalled the first time I crossed this bridge with Maddy, that first morning she showed me how to find our organization's headquarters, where language classes were held. Her words echoed in my head now.

"I want to look away too, Becca," she'd said quietly. "It's tempting to ignore the sight of all that poverty. It's far easier to pretend that they're not there at all, than to be confronted by such desperation."

I had nodded at the time. It was a lot to take in.

"But every day," she continued, "when I walk across this bridge, I make myself look, anyway. I want to offer these neighbors of ours at least the dignity of being seen."

On my right side, traffic streamed across the Bagmati Bridge, cars moving in such close proximity and fluidity that they looked more like people navigating a crowded passageway than vehicles driving on a road. Young men stood casually on the running boards of mini-vans known as *micros*, hawking passengers who knew to embark briskly as the vehicle slowed near the curb. Even if I could have understood their fast-paced slang, I wouldn't have had a clue about the routes or destinations of these *micros*. They didn't seem to be published anywhere, and there was no signage I could see, nor even any apparent stops. Walking was easier, and helped preserve the modicum of privacy and personal space to which I clung.

I glanced up just as another *micro* sped by, its conductor a lanky teenage boy leaning out of the window with lithe grace and the unshakable confidence of youth. One of his arms looped casually through the open front window and hooked on the doorframe. Our eyes met and locked for a second. So brief a snapshot, yet time lingered as I regarded him and he, me. I absorbed his look, but did not comprehend it. Quizzical curiosity? Bewilderment at the unexpected sight of a foreigner in this sea of Nepali faces? Perhaps nothing more than an imagined reaction? He appeared confident, comfortable, bearing the look of one who belonged fully to his world. Clearly I was not, and did not.

Then, as quickly as it appeared, the *micro* was gone, rushing on down the road, and with it, the boy's face, disappearing into a cloud of exhaust that made me blow black boogers later that evening. The exhaust somehow managed to be even hotter than the stifling, sun-scorched air. Sweat gathered in beads on my upper lip, between my breasts, down my back. I turned down a side street, passing rows of storefronts advertising their contents in loopy, *Devanagari* script that I could only hope one day to cipher. Some of the letters, at least, I could now recognize as sounds.

There was a small statue that marked my turn home at the Kandevtasthan Shrine. It was uniquely Hindu — a giant bronze caste of two ears. I took it to be an altar to an Ear God, or perhaps a shrine to Saraswati, the goddess of language, insight and sound, but those were mere guesses. Each pinna was the size of a young child, and they were mounted beneath a pagoda roof to shield them from the elements. In the newness of everything, the strangeness of it didn't occur to me — the fact that enormous bronze ears had become the most familiar marker on my daily commute.

A couple of blocks from my guesthouse was Gyanmandala, a delightful little artistic enclave comprised of a bookstore, coffee shop, cafe, jazz school, and the Moksh music bar Maddy mentioned on our recent walk. I'd also discovered a small yoga studio tucked into one corner of Gyanmandala, which was proving to be an unexpected haven. For years, I thought I had hated yoga. The group setting always felt too exposing. I was fearful of making mistakes, unfamiliar with insider language like "down dog" and "bound angle," unable to distinguish a *chakra* from a *chaturanga*. Yoga always seemed like something for "other" kinds of people. And as a Christian, raised in circles suspicious of anything smacking of "New Age," I also wasn't sure if attending a yoga class was even a good idea. I might be unwittingly duped into heresy.

Yet there was something peaceful about this studio, quiet yet welcoming. The lights were kept dim, which lent a reassuring air of concealment, and I found the juniper and sandalwood-scented candles intoxicating. If anything, exploring this yoga practice had brought me closer to God.

With each deep breath and pose, I imagined resting in His presence with my whole being — body, mind and soul fully His. For me, yoga had become a discipline of embodied prayer, opening myself more deeply to His Spirit with each inspiration. It would be lovely to attend a class that night. Perhaps I could go before meeting up with Dan and Leah.

Finally arriving home, I turned the handle of the metal gate to our alleyway and up the stairs to the front door. It was a big step up over the threshold of Trinity Guest House. The thick wooden door closed heavily behind me, latching with a finality that slightly rattled the house's frame. It was uncommon back home to encounter such sturdiness in the built environment, except perhaps in a few old edifices on college campuses. I stepped across the threshold into a quiet, dimly lit corridor with bare walls and bare halls, where the only sound was the echo of my own footsteps in the stairwell.

CHAPTER EIGHT
Premonition

I stepped out onto the dirt path outside my guesthouse one Saturday afternoon, craning my neck to look for Maddy. We were meeting for a late lunch, and planned to check out a Japanese restaurant nearby that had recently opened.

The culinary variety available in Kathmandu never ceased to amaze me. It made sense, I suppose, since people from all over the world came to live there. Because our neighborhood was concentrated with ex-pats, a glut of international food choices naturally followed.

I saw Maddy walking toward me up ahead, and jogged over.

"Hey! How's it going? Good day so far?" I asked.

"Pretty weird day, actually. I went down a rabbit hole online and learned *way* more than I ever wanted to know about earthquakes," she replied.

"What? Why *earthquakes?* That's such a random thing to be researching!"

"Umm, not really! Think about it, Becca. This part of the world gets a ton of earthquakes. How else do you think the *Himalayas* got here?"

I considered this. Within view were the tallest peaks on earth, which meant they were also the youngest, geologically speaking. And how do mountains form, but by two tectonic plates crunching against each other over millennia, buckling up the space between them?

She went on. "The last large-scale one to hit Nepal was back in 1934, the *Bihar-Nepal* quake. Something like 12,000 people died. And that was *ages* ago, when Kathmandu was basically a little hamlet. There was barely anyone living in the valley, and the city wasn't built up at all, not like it is these days. Kathmandu's population is over a million now!"

We continued to walk along the rutted dirt path, an occasional Vespa buzzing past. "Based on a 70-year geologic cycle in this region," Maddy continued, "seismologists think the next big quake is already overdue by nearly a decade. They say it's not a matter of *if*, but *when*."

She stopped. "Do you want me to share what else I learned today? It's gonna freak you out." She glanced over at me, clearly wanting to process it all aloud, but unsure if the information would be too much to just drop on me, unexpectedly.

"Yeah, I guess so," I ventured. "I mean, it's true whether we hide from it or not, right? Better to know it all, I think."

She took a sharp breath in, then continued. "They're predicting the loss of life to be enormous, whenever it does eventually strike. Experts say that the earthquake will probably be the typical "Pacific-rim" magnitude, like the massive one that struck Japan several years ago. Remember how huge that was? Something like 9.0 on the Richter scale. But Nepal's infrastructure is closer to that of Haiti. The quake that hit there in 2010 was only a 7.0 — just *one-hundredth* of the magnitude! Yet think of the colossal damage it did. They don't even know how many people died in that one, exactly, but maybe more than 300,000, between the disaster and the wake of chaos that followed."

We had just reached the restaurant and settled into our seats. "So it sounds like it could be the worst of both worlds."

"Yeah. Really scary stuff. You can see why it freaked me out." She paused, considering whether to share this next item, then went on. "Apparently, the S- and P-waves will likely reverberate back and forth within the Kathmandu Valley."

I had never heard of S- and P-waves, but I let it go. She was on a roll.

"Experts use terms like *liquefaction*." She shuddered at this last part. We were both trying not to imagine this city experiencing total, liquifying destruction. "They're having us put together Go-Bags in our orientation program, though. There's even a whole day of training on earthquakes, called 'Disaster Preparedness' or something like that."

I was beginning to wonder just how helpful any more information on this would be. What if it only made me more fearful, and didn't actually accomplish anything productive? Funny how "morbid curiosity" is strangely absent when it's your own life. Besides, what could we do about it?

Pausing for a minute as the waiter came to take our orders, I considered my family and friends back home. The thought of their grief if I were killed or injured here was heavy on my heart. The last thing I wanted was to worry them even more. It was stressful enough on my family to have me living halfway around the world, so remote that they were powerless to help. I knew this was a burden to keep to myself, and resolved not to share anything I'd just learned.

"It definitely *is* scary stuff," I said, when the waiter was out of earshot. "I hope I can sleep tonight! But what can we do about it, anyway? We can't control it. We can *maybe* prepare for it. So either we stay in Nepal, or we leave. Aren't those the only two options?" She shrugged, nodding. "And since we're both planning to stay. . . the less we worry about it, the better. . . right?"

CHAPTER NINE
Language Travails

After nearly three weeks of language class, I'd finally pinned down all 46 characters of the Nepali *Devanagari* alphabet. Numbers — whose characters, as well as names, are distinct from the familiar Arabic numerals of the Western world — were slowly coming along too.

Pigeons cooed and clucked on the windowsill of the guest house room where I studied, descending in huge waves and rendering the narrow outer walkway a white-crusted mess of guano. Yet I found their familiar chatter comforting, my first "community" in what could sometimes be a lonely place. With a rush of flapping wings, they were flushed away by a group of American *bideshis* in the alleyway below. These Americans were heading home from a two-week Nepali adventure, their luggage clattering as it rolled along the flagstone path. I felt a touch of envious longing, realizing that they were *en route* to the airport, and home. Their noise faded into the distance, replaced with the close, crisp sound of one neighbor calling to another across our small garden yard. She was shouting something that I was far from understanding, yet spoke in an intimate, amicably teasing tone that transcended words and worlds. It gave a nudge of hope that one day I might understand their meaning.

Still, it was exhausting to strain my ears against this dense, enigmatic language all day and understand virtually nothing. Differences in words like "*dan*" (a donation) and "*dhan*" (a rice paddy) were extremely subtle, hinging on a mere breath of air. I'd say "*dhan*," trying to puff out an aspirated "*dh-*" sound with just enough air to see my breath in the cooling weather of late autumn, and then say it again, "*dan*," without leaving any breath behind. Even with supportive language teachers in my daily one-on-one classes, it was embarrassing to sound constantly like a kindergartener, having to employ linguistic "work-arounds" because of my limited vocabulary.

For instance, I went out one day to buy a cork board, so I could hang some photos on my wall. I went to a small office supply shop nearby, unsure if they even carried these, and waved the shopkeeper over. "I need a thing," I began, hesitating as I realized I had no idea what the word for "*cork board*" was, nor even how to say "*wall*."

Haltingly, while waving my palm in a circular motion over the shop's nearest wall, I continued, "I need a thing to put on this, a thing for this part of the house, where I can keep things. Something where paper can be put. . . Do you have any kind of *paper-putting-thing* here?"

The shopkeeper looked at me blankly, then bobbled his head side to side with a slightly irritated frown. Was he irked because my description wasn't landing, or simply because he didn't carry the item? Either way, I walked home that afternoon without a cork board.

My mounting discomfort culminated one afternoon on a concrete park bench in a residential corner of Kathmandu, where I was sitting with my language teacher, Indira. We were on a rare excursion out of the classroom, employing that painful but necessary tool of "immersion," which would later become a commonplace part of my language-learning. We'd taken a break to rest, after buying "a half kilo of bananas and two mangoes please" from the fruit cart parked around the corner. Even that brief exchange rendered my face a uniform vermillion under the vendor's amused gaze.

Newly burdened with this bounty of fruit, we retreated to a nearby park bench to practice reading. Having familiarized myself with the Nepali alphabet, I was migrating to the next developmental stage — that of putting together those elegant, headline-anchored squiggles into words. I sounded out each letter with an agonizing degree of deliberation not seen since preschool, when I first worked through such seminal texts as *The Cat in The Hat*.

At that juncture, two pre-teen girls dressed in the uniform of a nearby grade school came skipping by, slowing for a moment at this unexpected sight. Here was a tow-headed *bideshi* woman, three times their age, struggling over one- and two-syllable words — a toddler's vocabulary. They took in the scene, eyes alight, and then scurried on, craning their necks behind them for one last look, before collapsing into giggles and whispering conspiratorially behind cupped palms.

Far from home and all things familiar, my defenses were at low ebb — or edgily piqued, depending on how you viewed it. An internal dialogue of defensive thoughts raced through my mind. *Sure, laugh! I have a terminal degree from a high-ranking graduate school in a developed nation. And this is my* third *language.* I am not at all proud of this thought.

Thrown suddenly into that place of shame on a Kathmandu park bench, I was getting my first glimpse into the lamentable reality of arrogance. When wounded and vulnerably exposed, it is not in my nature to absorb that pain magnanimously and respond with gracious, loving concern. No, when my defenses are down, and my defensiveness is up — when life perturbs the smooth surface of my being, and strips bare all that gives me a sense of worth — it is not the generous version of myself that comes out, the version I fancy myself to be at my core. I had somehow managed to live under that delusion for years.

A modicum of comfort came one afternoon soon a few days later, while studying in my room. Thinking myself alone in the empty guest house, I got up to stretch my legs and get a glass of UV-treated water from the kitchen, then returned to my room and wearily began folding some clothes scattered on the shelf, glad for something to distract me from the tedium of language study. At that moment, a single, sweetly melodious note drifted down through the stairwell. It was followed by another, then a third. The sound of it arrested me on the spot, stilled and captivated by this swell of interweaving harmony, its strands drifting just beyond my full grasp of hearing. Harmonies as beautiful as any I'd heard in a long time began to resonate through the spacious guesthouse hall.

To hear better, I stepped out into the hallway, realizing that a group of women were rehearsing two floors up. Their song had a simple, traditional sound, perhaps an old Nepali hymn. As if suspended in time, the moment stretched into what felt like hours. In the music, so heartbreakingly lovely, were echoes of solace transcending human language. Overcome, I leaned against the wooden door frame of my room and wept. I was raw with longing for beauty, and aching for a reminder that such beauty was alive, still, in this impenetrable world that was to be my home.

CHAPTER TEN

Linguistic Nuance

As the weeks progressed and my own comfort with the language deepened, I began to absorb nuances of meaning through a unique perspective granted only to linguistic outsiders. It became fascinating to notice how Nepali vocabulary, like any lexicon, seemed to reflect the most important elements of a culture. Consider, anecdotally, that Italians have many phrases with which to articulate love, while far-northern dwellers, like the Swedes, Inuits and even Scots, reflect a nuanced appreciation of various kinds of snow. I was keen to note what things had a similar *de facto* significance in Nepali culture.

There were words for different kinds of rain — *chhadke paani* for slanting rain, *simsim paani* for a drizzle, *musaldhar paani* when it's a heavy, drenching rain — reflecting the centrality of monsoon patterns. And there were just as many words for rice — the growing kind, the harvested kind; raw rice, beaten rice, cooked rice, puffed rice, toasted rice; rice flour, rice porridge, rice pudding. . . So vital is rice to the Nepali diet that there's even an old proverb, "*Bhaat nakhaandaa, pet nai bhareko jasto laagdaina*" which roughly translates "When you don't eat rice, it's as if your stomach is empty." Whenever we had Nepali friends over and served something other than rice — like pizza or lasagna — I learned that afterward, they would sometimes prepare an entire dinner of rice and lentils when they returned home, even if they were stuffed full. Otherwise, it was as if they'd been snacking all day without taking in any real, substantive food.

Yet what I found most fascinating of all were the specific technical terms for *every single member* of the family, based on painstakingly precise relationships to each other. In some cases, people didn't even *know* the names of their more distant relatives. They instead referred to one another simply by how they were interconnected: *didi* for older sister — in fact *any* female older than you, related or not. The same held true for *bahini* (younger sister), *dai* (older brother), and *bhai* (younger brother). Just by the terms *jetho, mailo, sailo, kailo* and *kanchho*, you knew exactly which of her five sons a woman was referencing, because each one was specifically designated by birth order. Daughters had their own corresponding terms: *are-jethi, maili, saili, kaili* and *kanchhi*.

There was no room for vague generalities like "in-law." Whereas in English, "sister-in-law" could mean your husband's sister, or your brother's wife, or even (stretching it a bit) your *husband's* brother's wife, Nepali culture ensured that each got her own designation. Nor could you confuse your aunts, because your father's sister (*phupu*) was distinct from the wife of your father's eldest brother (*thuli-aamaa*) and that of his youngest brother (*kaaki*). Even the husband of your *oldest* sister got a different name from that of your *youngest* sister.

What astonishing specificity.

Despite all this, I was surprised to learn that there was, incredibly, no term for "cousin." It was just "brother" or "sister." So when I asked my friend Tenzing one day how many siblings he had, it was a while before the answer came, and involved ticking off all ten fingers and a few toes: "Sixteen — no, *seventeen*." He was including the children of his father's four brothers — kids he had grown up with — as his own siblings. All of this pointed to the strength of extended family networks in rural Nepal, a traditional world where multiple generations still lived together and cultivated the same, ancestral land.

There was another aspect to culture, reflected in language, that went even deeper than vocabulary. Early on, I had to learn three different levels of respect — "high, middle, and low" — for verb conjugations in both the second person ("you") and third person ("his/her"). Patients found it strange when I addressed a child in the pediatric clinic with the "*tapaain*" form of "you," when everyone knew it should be the "*timi*" form, for peers or children. And I never even bothered to learn the "low" form, since that was used only to address animals, something I rarely did. It all seemed a bit much. Then my friend Jane reminded me that it could be worse, since proper Korean etiquette observes *seven* levels of deference. Imagine, I once thought the "*tú - usted*" distinction in Spanish took formality too far.

My head was spinning after each day's lessons, but everyone reassured me it would come with time. As challenging as Nepali could be, I was still glad not to be learning *English* as a second language. That seemed to require a small miracle. Those are brave souls who persevere through the mess of English grammar and pronunciation, where exceptions reign more commonly than the rule, atypical word-spellings are rife, and entire swaths of letters lie silent! Nepali rules were, if nothing else, highly consistent and predictable.

Several months later, when I had already arrived in Tansen and my command of Nepali was reasonably functional, I still often struggled to make myself understood. This made for frustrating, and occasionally humorous, interactions. My foreign-accented Nepali was doubtless a challenge for native speakers to understand. It was rendered all the more incomprehensible by preconceived notions that, as a white woman, I surely couldn't speak their language. Patients would respond to my opening question, "*Ke kolagi aaunubhayo?*" (*What brought you in?*) with a frantic, "*Angreji aaudaina!" (I don't speak English!)* To which I would reply, dryly, "*Ho, tahaa chha — tyesko-kaaranlei Nepali boldaichhu."* *(Yes, I know — that's why I'm speaking in Nepali.)* When a woman's grown son or male neighbor accompanied her for the consult, they would simply repeat my own Nepali words back to them verbatim, confirming that my message was indeed getting through to someone.

I wish this didn't bother me as much as it did, but I found it wearing, at least by the eight-hundredth time it happened. Usually after patients settled into our encounter, they could give and receive information with ease. Not always, though. During one particularly cumbersome exchange with a female patient in clinic one afternoon, an image of the Swedish Chef suddenly flashed through my mind — the gleefully oblivious *Muppets* cook, exuberantly gushing Scandinavian-sounding nonsense. His hands would gesticulate wildly above a pot of meatballs he's cooked up as he spoke, all the while blissfully unaware that his well-intentioned communication is understandable to. . . absolutely no one. I was overcome in that moment with the thought of how ridiculous this scene might look to an onlooker, and struggled to suppress a fit of giggles. To this, the woman's perplexed look only deepened.

I came to realize early on that, no matter how comfortable I might grow with the Nepali language, no matter how facile at expressing myself through an improved accent or expanded vocabulary, I would forever remain an outsider to this culture at some level. It was an unsettling thought that I might never be able to connect with patients and friends perfectly through this language. At the same time, it also took some of the pressure off.

CHAPTER ELEVEN
Cuisine's Insights

In Nepal, I soon learned the standard greeting, *"Khana khanubhayo?"* It translates, *"Have you eaten?,"* and is a way of making small talk, like when people in other countries comment on the weather. In Nepal however, it's quite odd if one *does* bring up the weather. Perhaps that's a topic too banal, or too far beyond the reach of control, to merit comment. Instead, Nepalis ask about food. I've also heard people lead conversation with questions like *"Bhaat paakyo?"* *(Has rice been cooked?)* or *"Bhaat khayo?"* *(Have you eaten rice?)*

Early on, I assumed my companions were asking these questions because they really cared about my eating patterns. I tried to answer their greeting literally, recalling and diligently sharing every detail of my lunch break. But after a while, it dawned on me. This was a kind of conversation filler — more like "How are you?" than a true, culinary fact-finding mission. Along the same lines as the cultural insights gained from language study, I wondered if this could lend insight into core Nepali identity and values.

I'm told that the Guugu Yimithirr, a tribe of Indigenous people in Australia, start their conversations by asking, "Where are you going?" Not coincidentally, the Guugu Yimithirr are a people possessed of phenomenal sense of direction. Their whole cultural ethos is centered around the cardinal directions of East, West, North and South — so much so that they actually refer to a table standing in the "north-northwest corner of the room," or a fly that landed on the "eastern side of your northern leg."

I was therefore curious to know why Nepali people seem to be so concerned with food and eating. It was not a feature of general conversation alone. Once in Tansen, virtually every patient asked me, *"Ke ke khanuparcha?" (What foods should I eat?)* — which struck me as rather odd. Most foods are generally fine for most patients. Sometimes certain salts or vitamins need to be limited in a particular chronic disease. Yet the staple Nepali diet, *dal-bhaat-tarkari* — a balanced blend of rice, lentils and curried vegetables — is in fact a meal that safely and nutritiously hits the major food groups.

It turns out there are some interesting reasons for this almost obsessive focus on eating. Some might be inclined to think it stems from the fact that Nepal has long been a subsistence culture, long plagued by high rates of malnutrition, with little margin for food shortage or crop failure. During my two years in Nepal, I saw several children falling well below the third percentile on World Health Organization growth curves. However, the basis for taking this interest in food likely derives from its perceived medicinal properties. A culture deeply rooted in Ayurvedic medicine, the ancient healing tradition of South Asia, Nepal places enormous emphasis on precisely which foods are acceptable, and which are to be discouraged, for given personality types or physical conditions.

As in several other Asian cultures, the traditional understanding of health is intimately linked to concepts of "hot" and "cold," which are innate to different constitutions, illnesses, and foods. You'd be taking your life into your hands if you *dared* eat something cold, like yogurt or orange juice, while suffering from a "cold." Parents sometimes called my medical judgment into question when I made the ludicrous suggestion that they offer warm soup to their child with a fever.

Ayurvedic medicine affirms the principle that certain foods are "warm" or "cold," but this is based on inherent properties of the food itself, rather than their thermal state. A number of foods are understood as possessing unique attributes that can deeply impact the body and its metabolism. Each is associated with certain properties, and foods can be broadly categorized into two groups based on their *Virya*, or potency: *Ushna* (hot) and *Shita* (cold).

"Hot" foods include elements like turmeric, honey, ginger, mustard, cumin, black pepper, saffron, sesame seed, cinnamon, onion, artichoke, garlic, pickles, root vegetables, most sour fruits, and herbs like basil, oregano, and mint. These foods have combustive properties that help aid in circulation and digestion, and impart a feeling of lightness in the body and mind. Medicinally, they are thought to keep the body warm, and are thus useful in managing the common "cold." Taken in excess, however, "hot" foods can lead to vomiting, heartburn, ulcers, and rashes. It was also understood that as a rule, consumption of hot foods is forbidden for pregnant or nursing women.

Cold foods, like banana, yogurt, melons, coconut, asparagus, cucumbers, coconut, cauliflower, and most sweet fruits, as well as fennel seed, tofu, green tea and even rice, provide nourishment and encourage strength and steadiness in the body. They are purported to help manage excess build-up of fluids, but can also impart a sense of heaviness in the body, being harder to digest. Also, because they are believed to negatively impact the immune system — and also, of course, are "cold" — they're forbidden for patients afflicted with colds or respiratory conditions such as asthma.

Consideration of body type is also key, as this is thought to influence a person's response to "hot" and "cold" foods. Echoing the ancient Hippocratic tradition with its four humors, Ayurvedic medicine conceives of three physiologic categories: *Vata* (wind predominance), *Pitta* (bile predominance) and *Kapha* (mucus predominance). When preparing a meal, it's important to balance "hot" and "cold" foods with respect to these body types. I remember a Korean friend sharing with me once that her father, who had a naturally "warm" body type, consumed a certain spicy dish and broke out in hives as a result.

Ayurvedic theories aside, food plays deeply into my own memories of Nepal. If I close my eyes and breathe deeply, I can still imagine the evocative smell of a street vendor's onions frying in cumin and turmeric *masala*, the scent wafting out from storefronts as I walked home each evening. While in Kathmandu, we discovered some amazingly delicious, and criminally cheap, meals of *roti* and *curry* at hole-in-the-wall Indian tandoori kitchens all over the city.

After moving to Tansen, *momos* also became a favorite treat. They're a kind of Indian-Chinese fusion dumpling, which makes sense when you consider that Nepal is sandwiched between these two nations — "a yam between two boulders," as the saying goes. Momos can be steamed or fried, crescent-shaped or circular, and made with meat, veggies, or cheese. Each momo place has its own distinct folding technique and style of seasoning. A cup of hot *chiya* and a plate of steaming momos with friends was therapeutic indeed — whether or not I had a "cold."

CHAPTER TWELVE

Callum & Midge

The *Dashain* festivities began in mid-October, one month into my time in Nepal. *Dashain* (pronounced *"dasai,"* with as much nasal inflection as you can muster) is probably the most important holiday in the Nepali calendar. This festival celebrates the ancient victory of Hindu gods and goddesses over demons, and each day involves elaborate rituals closely observed by my devout Hindu neighbors. In addition to the ritual slaughter of thousands of goats, sheep, chickens, and buffalo across the country, the holidays offered two weeks of school vacation and kite flying for Nepali children, card games and leisurely chatting over *chiya* for the adults, new sets of clothes for those who could afford it, and long bus trips to visit family on rural, ancestral farms.

It was around this time that I first became jarringly disabused of the fantasy that the meat I consumed always came in clean, pre-packaged Styrofoam trays wrapped neatly in cellophane. One afternoon, while walking around town doing errands, I passed two goats tied up in front of a shop, screaming mindlessly, as goats are wont to do. Twenty minutes later, on my way home, I was horrified to see one of the goats lying on the ground, its head severed clean from its body, a pink tongue lolling from its mouth. A garden hose rigged near the gutter flushed red-tinged water from the cobblestones. A man was bowed over the carcass, skinning off hair in handfuls of messy clumps. The other goat was tied in the same place, and understandably, still screaming. It felt like I had jumped back in time.

One morning soon after the *Dashain* holidays had drawn to a close, I was getting ready for language class, and reached for my Bible to do the morning's reading. I was trying to work through a structured Bible-reading plan, hoping this time I could stick with it. Regular "devotions," as I was encouraged to do from childhood, have always been hard for me. At best, I've made sporadic efforts tinged vaguely with guilt at my repeated failure to keep the habit. But on this day, at least I'd remembered, and turned to a passage from Isaiah 2:

He shall judge between the nations,
and shall decide disputes for many peoples;
and they shall beat their swords into plowshares,
and their spears into pruning hooks;
nation shall not lift up sword against nation,
neither shall they learn war anymore.

Pausing there, drinking in this vision for peace that felt so unimaginably far from the raw realities of our world, it occurred to me that never in my life had I seen a pruning hook. In truth, I wasn't quite sure what one even looked like, let alone how you could craft it from a spear. Still, I was moved by the passage's meaning, and thought, *Boy, do we need that kind of peace.* With that, I gathered my things and headed out the door.

Half an hour later, I arrived at our mission headquarters in Kathmandu's Thapathali district. I was uncharacteristically early, and thankful to have some relaxed time before class. Just as I reached the front gates, I saw a gardener pruning the hedge with — I'm not kidding — a tarnished metal, hook-shaped tool. *Aha! A pruning hook*, I thought. It was surreal to be immersed in a world where, all around me, ancient and modern elements were seamlessly intertwined into daily life.

Walking along the compound's sidewalk, I saw Callum and Midge wave me over to a plastic table in the garden, where they were taking their tea break. This couple, serving as the pastoral care team for our organization, had become fast friends since we'd met at the airport on my first evening. Though they had arrived in Nepal only a year before me, they already seemed wonderfully at home in their community and daily routines. I marveled at their grace and ease.

"That man is actually using a pruning hook!" I exclaimed when I reached their table, gesturing behind me. "Can you believe it? I was just reading a passage from Isaiah this morning about beating spears into pruning hooks, wondering what that even was, and there's a gardener using one! What are the *odds* of that?"

Midge laughed, delighted by this unexpected burst of enthusiasm. Callum chuckled too, then asked, "How was your trek, Becca?" They knew I had spent my *Dashain* vacation with a few friends, hiking through the Helambu region northeast of Kathmandu, near the Langtang range.

"It was great to be out and about! I really needed that exercise. It's been tough to find opportunities to get into nature around here."

They nodded, groaning. They knew such opportunities were few and far between, and not always easy to access. Callum and Midge had often lamented the pollution and traffic of Kathmandu, and how difficult it was to find open-air spaces to walk in the area.

"Well, it did rain pretty much the entire time, which was kind of a bummer. And the public bus back home was an adventure in itself! The whole five hours, I was squeezed between two women, my knees wedged up against the metal-framed seat in front of me. There were enough people crammed into the aisle to fill a small banquet hall! Someone even thrust their infant into my arms as soon as I sat down, and I had to hold him almost the whole way. At one point, that infant was crying *and* I had a nauseated seven-year-old girl in my lap, while the two women were leaning out the window, trying not to vomit. And on top of that, a flock of chickens squawked and fluttered in the aisle the whole time. Can you believe it? After this, Greyhound will feel like a luxury!"

I wagged my own head in disbelief, then continued. "The highlight, though, was that we spent our final night with a *Sherpa* family my friends met along the way. They struck up conversation on the path, and then invited us to stay with them. The man's wife cooked our meal on a wood-burning stove as we sat wrapped in blankets around their hearth. I didn't really understand any of the conversation, but it was *such* an intimate experience, being welcomed into their home like that! I even got to drink yak-butter tea, something I've wanted to try for years! Have you ever had it?"

They both shook their heads, laughing again at my enthusiasm. I realized I was talking a mile a minute, happy for this unexpected chance to catch up with friends.

"I also overheard this charming snippet of conversation with an elderly, topi-wearing Nepali gentleman along the path one afternoon. My friend had to translate it for me afterward, but he said that, when that elderly man heard we were Americans, he asked, almost disbelievingly, "They say that it's dark in America now. . . Is that true? Incredible! Could it really be night-time there? Well, that's what people *sometimes* say. . ."

Callum got a kick out of that, and laughed his deep, belly laugh. "Can you come over for dinner tonight, Becca?" he asked. "It would be such fun to catch up more, and we would love to get to know you better."

"That would be great!" I answered with a vigorous nod of my head.

Midge smiled with enthusiasm. "Lovely! Come around half-five, and we'll have a little something ready."

"Oh, wait — what about the new *bandh* that started today?" Callum interjected. "Will that cause any problems for you traveling to our place?"

In anticipation of the country's upcoming elections, a ten-day nationwide strike, or *bandh* (the Nepali word for "closed") had just begun. These strikes were a relatively common means by which various political groups gave voice to their agendas. Vehicles were prohibited on the roads, shops were closed, and usually there was an increased presence of armed military police on the streets. A few times already, I'd seen groups of armed uniformed men in full SWAT gear — gas masks, bulletproof vests, and full-sized plastic shields — patrolling the streets.

We'd heard from others that violating a *bandh* was very risky — vehicles could be harassed, stoned, or even torched. At intersections, groups sometimes burned tires to create dramatic road blockades, as black smoke and flames leapt high into the air. Just the other evening, in fact, I'd heard a loud explosion not far from my guesthouse, only to learn later that a pressure-cooker bomb had been detonated in front of a nearby building. Yet Nepal was a place where, despite such disruptions, life went on as usual. It's amazing what you can get used to.

I shook my head. "No, I'm sure I won't have any trouble on foot. It's what, a fifteen-minute walk to your place? It's only vehicles that are targeted. And besides, they generally ignore *bideshis.* Either way, I'll still be home before the curfew."

Then, looking at my watch, I balked at the time. "Oh no, it's already five minutes past! I've got language class now!" I darted off. "See you this evening!" I called over my shoulder, as I bounded up the steps to our classroom two at a time.

Part 2 - Doing

There remains an experience of incomparable value.
We have for once learned to see the great events
of world history from below,
from the perspective of the outcasts, the suspects, the maltreated —
in short, from the perspective of those who suffer.

- Dietrich Bonhoeffer -

And the Word became flesh and dwelt among us.

- John 1:14a -

CHAPTER THIRTEEN

In Tansen

In early December, ten weeks after I'd landed at Tribhuvan International Airport, it was time to make another move — this time, a day's journey west to Tansen. I again condensed all my belongings into a few large duffle bags and boarded the "Buck," a vehicle so named because, in a former life, the hospital's main means of supply and transport was a "bus-truck" — a half bus, half truck chimera. Over the years, this morphed into a vehicle that was essentially a tourist-style bus when I arrived, though the name "Buck" had affectionately stuck. I made the comfortable overland trip in nine and a half hours. It was a luxurious experience, in that I had my own seat and some decent leg room. As I had learned, that's not something you can expect to find on every bus.

As the Buck pulled past through the hospital's lower gates, I looked up to see a sign emblazoned with Tansen Mission's motto, "We Serve, Jesus Heals." It was written in English and Nepali, and with effort, I pieced its *Devanagari* letters together into the Nepali translation. Still. it was unnerving to realize that in a mere week's time, I'd have to walk through that gate knowing enough Nepali, and tropical medicine, to begin seeing patients. I was comforted to know that everyone else once began where I was. And apparently, no one yet had to give up because the language was too hard.

I stumbled off the Buck and breathed in cool dusk air. Anneke Jansen, a senior physician and Tansen's ex-pat coordinator, was waiting to greet me.

"Welcome to Tansen, Becca! It's great to finally meet you. Remember how Jim Herr made that connection with us a few years ago? You were still in Lancaster then, I think?"

"Oh yes, goodness, that feels like another lifetime! It's great to be here — a dream come true!"

"You must be exhausted," said Anneke kindly. "Your house isn't on the hospital compound, but it's near several other Tansen families. Willem and I live out there too. The cluster of homes is called *Gairi Gau,* located just off the Middle Road. It's sort of a small neighborhood within Tansen. You'll love it there."

Even though it was only a ten-minute walk from the hospital, I was thankful that Anneke had arranged a taxi to haul the two overstuffed duffle bags I'd brought. Our taxi pulled away from the hospital gate and bumped along the unpaved "Middle Road" — not to be confused, I would soon discover, with the aptly named "Upper" and "Lower" Roads that wound through the rolling hills of Tansen's outskirts.

We arrived in *Gairi Gau* and carried my bags down a quaint, overgrown footpath to a small, mud-walled structure, padlocked on the outside. Anneke handed me the key, and after struggling with the lock and deadbolt for a minute, I stepped over the threshold, ducking my head just in time to avoid hitting its low wooden lintel. Off the dimly lit, narrow hallway were steep wooden steps ascending to the second floor. It felt just like the sort of place a Hobbit could live. I fell in love immediately.

After dropping my bags in a little room opposite the small galley kitchen, I stepped back outside. "I'm going to feel right at home here, Anneke, thank you!'

"Yes, well, the house comes fully equipped with electricity, wireless internet, and a flushing Western-style toilet. I'll let you get settled in. If you need anything, you already have my number. And you can also reach out to Dan and Leah — they live right over there." Anneke gestured to the house next door. "Maddy already moved in here a few weeks ago. I think she's working in the Operating Theatre today, but should be home later this evening."

Before leaving, she turned away from the house, and we both looked out onto an enormous valley extending hundreds of miles before us in the distance.

"Isn't that magnificent?" she said with quiet reverence. "We call that the 'White Lake,' because in the mornings it fills with cloud."

I woke up the next morning to loud chirping of birds and a truly ethereal sight — thick, white clouds pooling in the distant valley beyond my window, as the sun crested the Himalayas on the far horizon. I had a hard time believing I was really here. Compared with Kathmandu, the air was cleaner, the stars brighter and more numerous, and the wildlife more abundant. Happily, the weather was also warmer, reaching a comfortable 55 degrees Fahrenheit during the daytime. Yet I discovered how quickly the temperature dropped once the sun set, and noted with some dismay that none of our houses were heated.

Anneke returned mid-morning to go over some logistics, including arrangements with my "Didi." Although technically the term means "elder sister," it also refers to women employed as housekeepers in Nepal.

"Your Didi will come here three days a week to help. She knows this house well, and worked for the woman living here before you. Maddy gets on famously with her."

This surprised me. I hadn't expected to have a housekeeper. "Oh, I don't think I'll need that, Anneke. Surely not." I felt uncomfortable with the idea of a "house helper." It seemed so archaic, like a disturbing holdover from an earlier era and its colonial sensibilities.

"Oh, I think you'll definitely want to work with her, Becca. Keep in mind that everything is done manually around here — *everything*. Almost nothing is automated. That includes washing laundry by hand, purchasing and preparing your food from scratch, and doing all the other usual household chores and gardening."

She paused, still sensing my reluctance. "You're going to be very busy in the hospital, Becca. Take it from me — it's exhausting work, even under the best of circumstances. You won't have time or energy to do all of this yourself. Besides, this has been her job for years. If you refuse her help, that means putting her out of a job."

"Hmmm. I see." It was more complex than I'd initially realized. In my knee-jerk response, I hadn't considered all that. "Okay, I guess we can see how it goes," I hesitantly conceded.

I met Didi later that week. She was only two years older than I, but had been married for years, with two teenage sons. Our worlds were vastly different, yet it was easy to imagine her becoming a trusted friend, and a guide in my journey to understanding this complex culture.

Within days of my arrival, the time came to get acquainted with Tansen Hospital. After touring the hospital complex with Anneke one morning, I spent the rest of the day shadowing Willem, and found it completely overwhelming. Returning home that afternoon, Maddy took one look at me and suggested we sit down in the kitchen for a cup of tea.

"I really don't know if I'm up for this, Maddy! I spent all day with Willem Jansen on the maternity ward and female OPD." Maddy nodded, aware of the demands of our "OPD's," or "Out-Patient Departments."

I continued, "He's not only *really* good at medicine, and unbelievably fast, but also completely fluent in Nepali! He seems as comfortable in it as he is in English. How is that possible? He didn't appear to struggle or search for a word even once! Rounds flew by — I think he saw all thirty women *and their babies* in less than three hours! Then he blew through, like, *ten* patients in Female OPD in under an hour before going back to finish consults on the gyn ward, doing an admission in the ED, and in somewhere in there dipping back to maternity to sew up a cervical laceration! I haven't done OB in three years! What am I even doing here?" I lamented, taking a sip of my tea.

Maddy nodded again, saying nothing.

"I mean, the medicine itself seems do-able, though the volume is insane. But think of doing it all in Nepali! That seems virtually impossible. At this point I'm able to say, *"Hello, are you well?"* To which a patient quizzically looks at me, as if to say, *'Of course I'm not well! That's why I'm here in front of you right now!'* Maddy, what do you say to start your patient encounters?"

Maddy replied, "I usually say something like, *'For what reason did you come here today?'* I know it sounds awkward in translation, but I think that's the most straightforward way to put it in Nepali."

"Thanks, that helps. I mean, I'm not sure I even know how to ask if they're in pain, or what all the body parts are called when they tell me. I'm not comfortable with the past tense either, which is kind of important when you're taking a medical history. I barely even feel like I have the present tense down."

Maddy made a sympathetic clucking sound. "I totally get it. Starting was really hard for me too. But don't worry yet, Becca — you'd be *amazed* at what total immersion can do for your language skills. And the residents are always willing to help. Maybe try sitting with one of them in the clinic, and you can see your patients in parallel? That way you'll help them with any medical questions, and they can get you out of any language binds."

That sounded like a great idea, and reassured me a little. I still had one more week of language classes before joining the medical team, and now had plenty of motivation to jump back into my studies with vigor.

CHAPTER FOURTEEN

Kala Azar

All things considered, my first solo day on the job was going reasonably well. For the past few weeks in Tansen, I'd worked alongside a Nepali-speaking resident to get the hang of things. Now I was finally able to see patients on my own in the male OPD, and slowly worked through my stack of charts. One chart had a chest X-ray paper-clipped to it with huge, white spots riddling both lungs. My initial thought was cancer. But then Willem, who was working in the next room, reminded me tuberculosis can look similar, and was far more prevalent in the region.

"Odds are that's TB, almost definitely," he assured me. "You can check a sputum sample."

Near the end of the afternoon, a thin man in his early forties was wheeled in, too weak even to walk, his hunched, cachectic frame dwarfed by the wheelchair his older brother had borrowed for him at the main entrance. He'd been bumped to the front of the line for urgent evaluation by our clinic's triage staff.

Taking one look at his emaciated body and labored breathing, I reached for an admission packet. He would be spending the night on our ward, no question. His brother reached over the patient to hand me a fresh OPD chart they'd been given an hour earlier, and I noticed that his platelet count, ordered by an astute medical assistant on arrival, was remarkably low at 42,000. In fact, all of his cell lines were down — including a dramatically low hemoglobin of 5.1, a third of what it should have been to carry oxygen where it needed to go. His infection-fighting white cells were also well below the usual level. That same medical assistant, clearly more experienced than I, had scribbled "?KALA-AZAR" in pen across the chart and sent a test I'd never even heard of — the RK-39 assay.

This was all very enigmatic. The term "kala-azar" rang a faint bell, something that I might perhaps have encountered in a microbiology course seven or eight years earlier. Some kind of automatic conditioning kicked in from my subconscious, and the phrase *"visceral leishmaniasis"* surfaced from beneath murky waters, as I recalled that "kala-azar" was the colloquial term for this rare tropical disease. Rare, that is, if you live in suburban New York. As a med student, I'd sipped my mocha in a coffeeshop while perusing the short paragraph about it in my textbook, trying to imagine a context for this pathogen afflicting people in far-flung lands. Visceral leishmaniasis actually wasn't that unusual in Nepal, diagnosed mostly in men returning from work in the Middle East.

Mystified, I knocked on the door of the next exam room to consult Willem. "RK-39?" he asked, looking at the chart. "Oh, that's not a great test. It's only useful if you get lucky and it's positive. But not very sensitive — it's usually negative, even in cases that really *are* kala-azar."

Just as he finished speaking, an assistant strode over with a piece of paper in his outstretched hand. He handed me a dot-matrix lab printout with "RK-39 — POSITIVE" printed in blocky purple font, decisively answering our question. I felt lucky.

Turning to Willem, I asked, "How do we treat kala-azar?"

"Oh, just put him on miltefosine."

I'd never heard of this drug. He needed to repeat the name

two more times before I caught enough look it up in the thick *Physician Desk Reference* volume in my exam room. Scribbling various orders and medication dosages on his admission sheet, I sent him off with his brother to get settled on the medical ward. He was to be admitted to our critical unit, an eight-bed medical ward with two continuous cardiac telemetry monitors — the closest thing we had to an ICU.

I plodded through several more patient visits until my stack of charts finally dwindled down. After wrapping up a few loose ends, I regrouped back on the medical ward with Willem and the residents for our evening check-in. This was when the team would follow up on new test results, correct any medication errors our astute nurses had detected, and generally ensure that the service was "tucked in" for the night. This evening, though, our attention was focused on the emaciated gentleman in the far corner of our critical unit, looking considerably worse even than when he'd presented just hours earlier. In fact, he appeared moribund, what you would call "peri-arrest" — barely conscious, eyes half-closed, his thin chest laboring with an ominous breathing pattern. His blood pressure was undetectable, his pulse rapid and thready.

Tenzing, one of our trusted senior residents, was already at his bedside. Tenzing had grown up in Tansen, and had been doing his general medical training here for a few years by the time I arrived. I'd already come to trust him in the weeks I'd spent learning the ropes. In many ways, he had become my mentor during those early weeks on the medicine service. He frequently supplied me with bizarre-sounding, yet highly accurate, medical diagnoses and demonstrated exam findings that were revolutionary to me — like an interesting maneuver to elicit a particular neurologic reflex. But he always shared his knowledge with good-natured humility and a slightly wry smile that never caused me to feel as painfully "green" as I knew I was. Such is the gift of teachers fully at ease, comfortable in their own skin. They are a safe and secure presence because they, themselves, are safe and secure.

Now though, Tenzing looked over at me with concern in his face, which made me even more nervous for our patient. I felt my American Doctor Brain kicking in, and turned to him with an urgent flood of orders.

"We need a stat ABG, Tenzing, and he's probably going to have to be intubated right away. Let's get him on the vent ASAP — he won't be able to keep up this work of breathing much longer. I think we should definitely broaden his antibiotic coverage too. I started Zosyn when I admitted him, but we'd better add Vanc to that now."

Tenzing responded with an equivocal little head bobble that, in time, I would come to learn meant "No."

"Well, Ma'am. . ." I could see he was making an effort to put this gently. There was a weight of concern in his own eyes, too. "We don't have ABG's here at Tansen. And he's not meeting our vent criteria." *We have vent criteria? I thought.* "And about the Vanc. . . Well. . . The antibiotic vancomycin is very expensive, Ma'am. We generally check with the family before we add something like that."

As if through the looking glass, I'd been sucked down a rabbit hole into a world upside down from the one I had left just months ago. In that other world, broad-spectrum antibiotics and groundbreaking technologies were tossed around without even a passing nod to their cost, let alone their availability. Anything we requested came in minutes, summoned at the swipe of a pen or click of a mouse. A minuscule parasite was replicating and overtaking this young man's body, stretching taut the infection-fighting tissue in his spleen. Yet in theory, it was fully reversible, if we could just give his failing organs enough support to buy some time. That meant keeping his lungs breathing and his heart pumping long enough for the antibiotics to kick in and do their job.

I stood for a while at the foot of his bed, gazing at this man on the very threshold of death. The hardest part was how clear both the problem and solution were — but only in an ideal world. A world in which our hands were not bound by realities of cost and access, privilege and poverty. In this world, no matter how hard we tried, there would always be too many patients we couldn't save.

It turned out that man had less than an hour to live, and I was helpless to do anything about it.

CHAPTER FIFTEEN

Pools of Darkness

A month later, while on call at four AM, I was feeling grateful that my overnight shift had been relatively quiet. With just a few hours to go, the medical ward nurse called, asking if I could assess a woman who wasn't doing well. She was in her early fifties, admitted with a longstanding history of alcohol abuse and resulting end-stage liver disease.

Alcohol abuse was a surprisingly common problem in Nepal, mostly imbibed in the form of hard, home-brewed liquor called *raksi*. Raksi is the backbone of local village economies in some regions, and offers victims everywhere a temporary promise of escape from poverty's harsh realities.

The note from yesterday's rounds indicated that this woman had hepatorenal syndrome, where effects of advanced liver disease eventually destroy the kidneys as well. Her kidneys, in turn, had not been able to keep up with their usual blood-cleaning duties, nor their role in balancing crucial blood salts like potassium and bicarbonate. Her liver, of course, had long since given up its share of cleansing duties as well, and was now actively sabotaging her remaining organs.

By this point, her potassium level had climbed dangerously high, but without a dialysis machine to do the work of her kidneys, there was little we could offer. Medications that help eliminate excess potassium were also not available in Tansen. Even lactulose, the only option we had to remove toxins the liver usually managed, had been out of stock in our pharmacy for a week. The last remaining hope was that her kidneys might have enough life in them for a diuretic to pull some potassium out in her urine — still a temporizing measure at best. In a few hours, those toxins would build up again to critical levels.

Throughout the night, the nurse told me, she had continued to decline. By now, she was totally unresponsive. I wondered why I hadn't heard about the patient earlier, but sadly, such last-minute calls were commonplace. It seemed like more than a month since I'd admitted the man with kala-azar, and learned with breathtaking suddenness about the inexorable grasp death held here.

When I went in to see the woman with liver failure, our overhead fluorescent lights were already on in the ward — never a good sign at four AM. Several of her family members were anxiously surrounding her metal-frame bed, and a few younger ones tossed fitfully on the floor nearby. The woman was breathing in a particularly ominous pattern of heaving gasps. Unnaturally long and fast, these rapid, deep breaths known as Kussmaul respirations were her body's final resort for dealing with acidic toxins building up in her bloodstream. These eerie gasps were made all the more unnatural by her glassy, unseeing stare as she lay on her back, mouth agape, already far removed from the realities of this world.

Her wide-open eyes revealed large, dilated pupils — black pools of darkness staring blankly into middle distance. *She looks just like they do in films,* I thought, taken aback. I'd always scoffed at Hollywood's depiction of the dying, thinking it a lurid dramatization of death. It had never seemed convincing to me, not like it is in real life. Yet how often had I *really* had a chance to witness death in all its rawness? Death unimpeded, not sanitized by the tubes, lights, and lines doctors so eagerly impose? Rarely, to be sure. Perhaps the

Hollywood version was closer to reality than I'd thought. Disturbed, I blinked the thought away.

Back at the nursing station, I pored over her chart and reviewed what labs and imaging I could find, wondering if there was something — *anything* — still to be done. But her chart, down to the progressively destabilizing vital signs inked onto the nursing flowsheet, told the story. Without even a basic medication like lactulose or overnight X-ray services, let alone a hemodialysis unit, I wondered if there was anything we could offer, anything I could think of that might make the difference. Unable to hide behind the security of medical interventions to soothe my conscience, I was left with only the patient before me.

Feeling more helpless than I ever had before, I worried that the only resource I had — my own mind, my medical knowledge — was drastically lacking. Surely I was missing something — some aspect of her diagnosis, some treatment option — that could reverse all of this. Instead, I found myself standing slack-jawed at her bedside, gazing upon a woman in her last minutes on earth, surrounded by a family who would very shortly be plunged into grief as they held vigil in the dead of night.

Then the thought came, unbidden and unwelcome. *This could all be prevented, if only you were a better doctor.*

At a cognitive level, I knew this was untrue. That much was clear, certainly, in light of the myriad limitations with which we were all trying to work. But such limitations have a way of pressing curiously on the mind and heart. In that space, distorted perversely by the trauma of death upon untimely death for months on end, owning the blame for this death seemed somehow an obvious conclusion.

In the narrow bandwidth afforded by that intense period of my life, I found myself bouncing back and forth between two extremes over the ensuing months and beyond. I would lapse, on the one hand, into a pattern of objectifying patients with far too much clinical distance, just as I had been taught in my training years earlier. At the other extreme, haunted by the repeated loss of patients ranging from minutes old to old age, I internalized those tragic outcomes to the point of excess, viewing them as reflections of myself, exposing my deepest flaws.

To be clear, this was not the case of a physician facing medical dead-ends, feeling impotent because there was nothing left to cure. I knew well what to do for this woman from a palliative standpoint. In my experiences with patients at the end of life — dying from terminal illnesses like advanced cancer or end-stage heart failure — I knew that even when there is "nothing left to do" by way of cure, there was still plenty I could do to care, from symptom relief to steady bedside presence. There is a solidarity that bears witness, and refuses for suffering to go unseen.

No, my dilemma was not how to alleviate this woman's suffering, but rather the fact of her death at all. Her family didn't expect her to live. Neither did the Tansen staff. There was an acceptance of death as part of life here, reflecting attitudes virtually unknown in the land that had formed me, with its overweening sense of exceptionalism. And though the grief of these Nepali families was by no means less intense, there was a maturity in their acceptance, a sinewy toughness in their resignation.

Still, I knew this disease process was *curable*. It was a burden of knowledge that weighed me down, try as I might to reason it away.

"You can't compare the medical care available in Nepal to that in America," someone had counseled me before I'd come. "You can't think of what patients could get if only they were elsewhere. Instead, look at the care they'd be receiving if you *weren't* there." Those had seemed like reasonable words at the time.

But they rang hollow now. As with so many of my patients in Tansen, I knew her story could end differently if only she were elsewhere. With short-term dialysis as a bridge to liver transplant, coupled with intensive therapy for her alcohol use disorder in a supportive, accountable environment, she could perhaps live for years. That reality, however, was half a world away, a world that paid too little mind to such inequities. From where I sat, hunched over her chart that night, it might as well have been the moon.

CHAPTER SIXTEEN
Cord Prolapse

Rounding with the medical team in the female surgical ward one morning, we were discussing discharge plans for a forty-two-year-old woman with anemia from chronic vaginal bleeding. Just as we were reviewing how she should take her iron supplement, one of our second-year residents burst through the entrance of the open-bay ward, breathless and looking panicked. "Come quickly, Ma'am. You must come now, to Emergency. There is a cord prolapse."

What? A cord prolapse occurs when the umbilical cord connecting infant to mother emerges first, causing it to be clamped off by the infant's head as it presses against the tight cervical opening. It was an obstetrical emergency, something I'd only ever read about in textbooks. Though I had often prepared for it as a potential risk, I had never actually seen one, let alone managed it in real-world practice. My mind flashed to a page from the study guide "OB Essentials," which I'd used in med school and residency:

> *Q: What is the management of a cord prolapse?*
> *A: Elevate the presenting part and prepare for emergency Caesarean delivery.*

"Do you have any more information, like how far along her pregnancy is?" I peppered the resident with questions as we both rushed down the hallway toward the Emergency Department. "Is this her first, or has she delivered vaginally before? And is someone elevating the presenting part?"

"Yes Ma'am, Maya is trying to lift the head back up," she said in careful, clipped English. Maya was one of our more senior residents and had a particular interest in women's health. From our past work together, I knew her to be reliable and adept at patient care, and I breathed a small sigh of relief.

The resident continued, "They don't know the gestational age of the baby. It is her first delivery, but her second pregnancy; the first was an early miscarriage. She broke her water over an hour ago."

She had apparently ruptured her membranes early, before the head had a chance to come low enough in the pelvis to seal itself against the cervix and prevent the floating cord from slipping out first. Now, without the supportive buoyancy of the amniotic fluid around the baby, this cord was being squeezed between the infant's head and the cervix, or donut-like opening between the womb and birth canal. Now, its blood-flow was being cut off with each contraction of the powerful uterine muscles.

"And Maya couldn't feel any cord pulsations," she added meaningfully. If the cord had stopped pulsating with each life-giving heartbeat from the mother, the damage was already done. Maybe we were too late.

Running down the surgical corridor and across the crowded patient waiting area, where the day's outpatient queues were still forming, I nearly tripped over the outstretched legs of a family member sitting inside the ED's entrance, before breathlessly entering the one private room in our cavernous, open-bay emergency ward. This room is reserved for more delicate patient matters that merit an extra layer of privacy, usually obstetrical and gynecological cases. In my first few months there, I had already attended several precipitous deliveries in that room.

Closing the door to curious stares of patients waiting on a wooden bench along the opposite wall, I turned to look at the woman's face. She appeared to be in her early twenties, lying on the gurney, a small but obviously gravid uterus raising the sheet that covered her. I could see Maya's petite frame bent down between the woman's outspread legs, one hand deep inside the birth canal to press the infant's head upward within her laboring body.

"I think I may feel a pulse, Ma'am," Maya said, in characteristic calmness, even as strands of hair were plastered against her forehead. It had clearly been a long morning in the ED, and seemed about to get even longer. I donned sterile gloves and stepped in to relieve her. She gratefully accepted. The ED was chock full of other patients, some quite ill indeed.

I turned to our senior ED tech to ask, *"Sarjanaharu-lai kawar dinubhayo?" Have you told the surgeons about this case?* He nodded, replying *"Aawa tyahaa janneparcha!" We must go there now!*

My fingers were already beginning to stiffen and cramp under the pressure of that tiny head compressed against her dilating cervix with each forceful contraction. I could feel a thin, slippery cord draped limply against the back of my middle finger — this infant's sole supply of oxygen. There seemed little chance that it was bringing any now. I wondered if the infant was still alive, and whether it was far enough along to survive outside of the womb, especially in Tansen.

The nurse was asking the patient when her last menstrual period was, to calculate a rough estimate of the due date, and how far along she was today. If too early, it might not be wise to even put her through a Caesarean section, with all the complications that would mean for future pregnancies. Women in remote Nepali villages who go into labor are often far away from any medical support services, including trained home birth attendants. Vaginal delivery is a risky undertaking for women the whole world over, and while it's possible to deliver "normally" after one C-section, that history only heightens the risk of potentially catastrophic delivery complications in the future.

I guessed this pregnancy to be preterm, given the thin feel

of the cord and her petite baby bump. Yet there was no way of knowing at this point — she didn't know her last menses, but guessed it to be about *mid-Falgun,* the eleventh Nepali month, which calculated out an age of around thirty-two weeks today. We certainly didn't have the luxury of tracking down a portable ultrasound machine and tech who could help us estimate the infant's true gestational age. This was no time to equivocate.

The patient, at intervals gripped by the agony of contractions, was rushed out on a metal-framed gurney, my right arm wedged between her knees as that hand struggled to continue "elevating the presenting part." Simultaneously, hoping to offer a modicum of privacy, I tried to hold a sheet over her bent legs with my other hand, but it kept slipping off to one side. For a second, it crossed my mind that, were it not for the dire nature of this situation, it could have looked like something out of a zany British farce. Yet very real tragedy lay on the line.

The gurney hurtled down the long, irregular corridor, weaving through a crowd of ED patients waiting to be seen, then under a roofed portico connecting two wings of the hospital and through another dense crush of patients waiting for laboratory and ultrasound services. We finally arrived outside the swinging double doors of the hospital's "Operating Theatre." The tight rim of her cervix was still fighting to expel my fingers, now blanched and numbing.

The resident expertly briefed the nurse, while we flew past surgeons scrubbing their hands in stainless steel basins along the tiled hallway. Rolling into the brightly lit, aseptic room, one of the techs stretched a disposable mask over my face. It struck me as a superfluous gesture, but protocols must be observed. Tansen's head maternity nurse was already waiting, ready to take over the infant's resuscitation once delivered. She brought a fetal doppler over to listen for a heartbeat.

Silence. For what felt like an eternity, the room shared a horrifying but not unfamiliar thought, that perhaps an emergent C-section would not be necessary after all. In that brief pause, it occurred to me to whisper a prayer for this little infant, whose delicate, malleable skull bones I could feel shifting beneath my fingertips. So vulnerable, so small. How desperately this little one needed to be received into the harsh light of our green-tiled world.

And then, breathing a collective sigh of relief, we heard the doppler erupt in a staticky *whoosh-whoosh* of two different heartbeats, mom's and baby's, layered on top of one another. The infant's was sluggish, around 100 beats per minute, but it was there, and that was all that mattered.

The surgeons had just entered, scrubbed and gowned, and took their places opposite one another, poised to begin. Our patient was already deep in her anesthetic slumber, draped with sterile green cotton towels, her abdomen glistening the rich caramel of iodine. Given my unique role in this drama, I had a front-seat view as the surgeon leaned in and made a smooth first incision, moving with deliberate, steady confidence. Layer by layer he descended, separating skin, fat, muscle, and fascia in a hypnotizing rhythm. Then, finally, I felt a slight shifting against my fingers, as the surgeon reached the uterus and prepared to make the last, essential incision.

"Tell me when you're going to cut," I said to the surgeon, snapping back with the realization that I might need to move my fingers out of the way when he did.

"Sure — right now, in fact," he replied politely. The exchange was free of drama or hysterics, and so blandly professional that I might as well have been asking him to pass the salt.

Then they were in, expertly extracting the infant and handing her off to our maternity nurse, who whisked her away to a warmed resuscitation table, just as the infant gave its first wobbly cry of protest. It is truly a relief when babies are healthy enough to sound angry! Her protests were understandable, too, given the insult of being thrust forth into cold air and blinding light, a violent contrast to the warm darkness enveloping her for the last eight months. Indeed, from her perspective it must have seemed cruel.

Yet events were unfolding around her, far beyond her understanding or control, and were more well-intentioned than they seemed. All these efforts were singularly focused on one precious, little life about which there had already been much ado. Risks of infant life in Nepal were indeed great. Even so, she was safer now, outside that comfortable but risky womb, than she would be had she remained within.

CHAPTER SEVENTEEN
Time and Privacy Settings

Ever since I was ten, "old enough" to stay up with the adults watching the ball drop over a televised Times Square, I hadn't missed ringing in the New Year even once. But this year, the newness of my first three months in Nepal had left me feeling drained. Which was why, for the first time in twenty years, I opted to go to bed in one year and wake up in the next. It was glorious.

One of the hardest things about a new year is remembering to change the date whenever you write it out. Oddly enough, that was actually not an issue in Nepal. On hospital rounds, as elsewhere in the country, we followed the Nepali calendar known as *Bikram Sambat*. This traditional, luni-solar calendar is also comprised of twelve months, but *its* New Year falls sometime in mid-April of the Gregorian calendar. Strangely, *Bikram Sambat* also happens to be 56.7 years ahead of the Gregorian calendar, which meant that my first New Year's Day in Nepal was really just another day. . . in 2070.

As you might imagine, this added a layer of confusion to hospital work. For instance, a patient might report they'd had difficulty breathing since *Kartik*. But I don't automatically know where the month of *Kartik* falls in the Nepali year. (It turns out to be the four-week span between mid-October and mid-November.) So I'd have to go hunting through my Nepali-English day-planner to figure out how long the patient had been plagued by their dyspnea.

Similarly, ascertaining due dates for pregnant patients in our antenatal clinic presented an irksome challenge — one that only a manual pregnancy wheel (or complicated long-hand formula) could solve. The calculator app on my iPhone was useless when the Nepali year was 2070, giving an estimated gestational age of "[negative] 2,951 weeks." Even though the Nepali calendar is comprised of twelve months, each with up to 32 days, the number of days in each month changes from year to year. Still, a basic pocket pregnancy wheel came pretty close to calculating an accurate due date, give or take a few days.

To complicate matters even further, our medical assistants were in the habit of recording time fractionally. So a patient may have had "nighttime fevers since 3/12." In this context, the notation is meant to indicate that fevers have been ongoing for three months (of the total twelve in a year) — not, as I initially assumed, since March 12th (or alternatively, the twelfth of *Asadh,* the third month in *Bikram Sambat,* corresponding to June 26). Similarly, "Chest pain since 4/7" designates four days (of the possible seven in a week), and "Return to clinic in 3/52" means come back for another check-up in three weeks' time (there being 52 weeks in a year). This all took some getting used to.

The 365-day calendar year is really just an artificial construct, as arbitrary as the culture that invents it. There is no more rationale for starting the clock anew in January than there is in July. Yet observing the changing calendar offers a chance to pause, to gauge the passing of seasons, to mark time. Each New Year defines the edge of something, a way to mark growth — like pencil-lines notching the kitchen doorframe of my childhood home. At the very least, Nepal gave me an opportunity to see how other cultures observe the passage of time, marking it with various festivals and unique notations.

Working in Nepal also gave a chance to see first-hand how every culture has its own norms and boundaries when it comes to privacy. Like calendar-time, it turns out that the variations laid in where those boundaries fell. For instance, take bathing in public. By necessity, this was a normal feature of Nepali village life. Most of my neighbors didn't enjoy the convenience of running water at the turn of a tap, and instead had to haul their water supply in enormous jugs, twice a day, from a communal well. If a neighbor down the road wished to bathe, she did so in a sort of "bathing sari" on the concrete pad near that same communal well — which, I was told, required remarkable skill. Even with the astonishing ability to do so modestly, it remained a relatively public act.

I noticed the same was true of a man urinating at the side of the road. Bear in mind, of course, that interstate rest-stop pavilions had not yet found their way to Nepal. Neither, for that matter, had interstates. By convention, then, it was considered rude in the extreme for another person to so much as *glance* in his direction at that indiscreet time. The onus was on the passing public to make a separate space for someone who, out of necessity, did this generally "private" act out in the open.

Interestingly, it's the exact opposite in the West. By unspoken agreement, we generally consider it the individual's responsibility to hide him or herself as much as possible. I've occasionally had to venture deep into roadside brush myself, when a rest stop wasn't available. The combination of poisonous snakes and sheer cliffs, however, made that a decidedly unappealing prospect in Nepal.

Yet the converse seemed to hold true for medical results and other matters that, in the West, are considered confidential. I shared that observation with Maya one day during a *chiya* break in the canteen. She was also from Tansen originally, but like many of our residents, had completed her medical degree in China, where education and living costs are more affordable. She'd moved back to Tansen a few years earlier, and I was curious to hear her take on this new observation.

"There's this thing I've noticed in Female OPD that I just don't understand."

Maya looked up from her *chiya* with interest, so I went on. "The other afternoon, I was checking in on the OPD and saw that thyroid test results were back on a patient I'd seen that morning, so I called her over. It was a busy afternoon in clinic, and all the exam rooms were being used."

Maya let out a little snort, knowing how busy OPD can get.

"I didn't want to delay the next steps in her thyroid work-up, since she'd already mentioned she had to catch a bus back home. So I quietly pulled her aside to a private corner of the hallway, where we could talk about the results."

At this, Maya rolled her eyes and smiled. "I bet *that* went well! So much for privacy. You were surrounded by, like, twenty other women, right?"

"Yes, exactly! What's *that* about? It was like the other women had *no trouble* eavesdropping on this conversation between a doctor and patient." We laughed, as I added, "I could even see some of them craning their necks to hear more clearly!" Maya chuckled, nodding her head knowingly.

"Of course," she shrugged. "What do you expect? Is it any different in America?"

"Well, yeah, a bit! That would actually be kind of awkward in the States. We have all these laws in America to regulate the private handling of patient information. I mean, you're really not even supposed to mention any patient-related matters in public areas. We have to watch training videos discouraging people from discussing patient cases near nursing stations, or on elevators, that kind of thing." Maya raised her eyebrows quizzically as I went on.

"Sure, occasionally it happens that you *have* to speak with a patient or family member in the hallway. But we try to be very discreet, and everyone in earshot turns away. Their body language makes it clear that they're helping to protect a private space for the doctor and patient."

"So it sounds like *others* take it upon themselves to give

privacy," Maya summed it up. I thought back to the examples I'd already noted of public bathing or urinating.

"Right, exactly — kind of like an implicit social contract," I added. "It's like what everyone does here when someone makes their own 'rest stop' by the side of the highway, you know?" She nodded. "Well, why don't patients do the same thing for each other in the hospital or clinic, when it comes to medical discussions?"

Maya thought for a minute, then said, "I bet the other women were chiming in with suggestions, right?"

"Yes, definitely. And a few women standing closest to her repeated and clarified my instructions: *'When I got my thyroid checked. . . Oh, I had that kind of ultrasound myself once. . .'*"

"I can totally hear this happening!" Maya said. "Some were probably even relating their own experiences." She added to the imaginary script: *"'Don't worry, it's easy. . . First go to counter #3, then down the hall to room #9. . .'"*

"That's exactly right! And it's like that on the wards too — the family members of *other patients* will join our huddle during rounds to listen in! But no one ever seems bothered by it. Why is that?"

"Well," Maya replied, "maybe in the case of your thyroid patient, she feels she's being guided by other women who have walked this path before her. Perhaps this kind of sharing is a source of comfort for patients going through a confusing process, like being admitted to the hospital."

What Maya said made sense. Being in the hospital certainly was a confusing process, especially for patients unfamiliar with the system. It was as if this clamoring crowd of relative strangers represented the secure presence of community — which was especially important in a society that valued community above almost anything else.

I know a lot of folks back home (myself included) for whom this aspect of culture would drive them mad. For most Americans, especially, it amounts to an extreme — and extremely distressing — breach of privacy. But I was learning that "rudeness" in one culture may well be a socially accepted norm in another. *And* vice versa. One culture's "invasion of privacy" may well be another culture's standard of decency — their expected, requisite, help. Like sorting through dates in the *Bikram Sambat* calendar, this was yet another challenge in navigating my new cultural landscape.

CHAPTER EIGHTEEN
Air Under The Diaphragm

For as long as anyone could recall, the Tansen team had been gathering at the Guest House for an afternoon worship service and meal every other Saturday. The Guest House was an airy building located at the far end of the hospital campus, near the compound's residential apartments, and offered room and board for various visitors and passers-through. These times were deeply refreshing, hungry as I was for community and the sound of familiar hymns sung in English.

Late one night, on my way home after one of these gatherings, still enjoying an expansive mood from our time together, I decided to check in on the medical ward and make sure everything was going smoothly for the overnight team. As Saturday was our one day off in the Nepali workweek, two physicians were assigned to take call each Saturday to round on the ward patients and manage any overnight admissions or patient issues. Since we didn't have pagers or an electronic medical record, it was a habit of the senior doctors to look in on our respective services, even when off-duty, if we happened to be on the compound anyway. It was one of the ways in which lines were often blurred between personal and professional life in Tansen, but that didn't bother me much. It actually felt nice, much like what I imagined it might be to serve as a small-town family doctor.

While the rest of our group exited through the hospital's meandering corridors, out the front gate and up the dirt path to our cluster of homes in *Gairi Gau*, I broke away from the pack and skipped down several fluorescent-lit concrete steps to our medical ward's nursing station. I had rounded that morning, and was curious to learn how a few of the more tenuous patients had fared through the afternoon. Their labs and X-rays should at least be back. As I entered the ward, I could smell rice and lentils that two of the night-shift nurses were cooking in a hot-pot in the corner. Our incredible nurses could prepare an entire *dal-bhaat* on a Bunsen burner if they had to.

I was greeted by Sr. Saritha, the head nurse on for the night. She brightened, looking relieved that someone had come by, and handed me three patient charts, flagging the top one as a priority. An X-ray film was hole-punched and folded lengthwise within it. It was the chart of an elderly farmer from a nearby village. His children had brought him in when his abdominal pain continued to worsen despite the usual home remedies and customary dietary prescriptions.

Admitted a few hours earlier, he had continued to decline through the afternoon and evening even with conservative management — bowel rest, intravenous fluids, and decompression of his air-swollen abdomen through a thin, flexible, plastic tube that coursed from his nose, down his throat, and into to his stomach. This was all part of a classically evolving small bowel obstruction, or intestinal blockage. To further assess, Sr. Saritha explained, the team had ordered an abdominal X-ray earlier that afternoon.

She opened the red binder to the X-ray film and laid it out on the bench in front of me. "Read this, Dr. Becca," with a note of concern in her voice.

She said she'd been asking the resident, Dev, to come to the ward for hours, but he couldn't be reached. She raised her eyebrows slightly, but did not elaborate further. The patient had been getting much worse and was "almost gasping now."

Gasping was code language at Tansen, signifying an actual or impending cardiac arrest. Without any intercom system or overhead paging function in the hospital, it wasn't unusual for nurses to try various phone extensions where a physician might be found — the outpatient departments, inpatient adult or pediatric wards, maternity wing, canteen, or call room — with medical issues that arose. When the voice on the line said *"Gasping huncha,"* it meant come *now.* And come running.

Popping open the three-ring meta binder, I awkwardly lifted out the unwieldy film, at once both floppy and stiff. As I unfurled the film, it emitted a musical "pop," a sound unique to plastic vellum waving in the air.

Holding it up to the fluorescent light overhead, I saw an unmistakable dark line tracing the border of both diaphragms. *Free air.* An ominous, half-inch boundary of black separated the lower edges of the patient's lungs from the large, dilated loops of bowel below. Air in the abdomen — that is, air inside the body, but outside of the usually closed tube of gut.

Our intestines maintain an almost mystical separation between the realms of "outside" and "inside," even as they course in convoluted loops within the "insides" of our skin, on a meters-long path from mouth to anus. The world within the lumen of that tube is one of gas, food, and bacteria — a composition much the same as that of the "outer" world beyond our skin. Yet even as it coexists side by side, the deep inner world of our body is different. The part cushioning and shielding those fleshy tubes of gut is an airless, sterile, bacteria-free realm. Or *should* be. If the gut wall is breached, the results are catastrophic, and that gap must be repaired urgently, restoring the intestinal barrier that separates our intimately proximate worlds.

I went to see the patient, and found him looking uncomfortable as he tried to lie perfectly still on his cot, his abdomen as taut as an overfilled balloon. Piecing the story together, guessing that it might be a perforated ulcer in or near the stomach, I made several calls to track down the resident, knowing we would need all hands on deck to arrange for emergency surgery — everything from obtaining consent from his family and prepping the Operating Theatre, to notifying the anesthesia team and calling in the surgeons.

"The resident's not here in Emergency," said the medical assistant, picking up on the second ring. He wasn't in the pediatrics wing either, nor on the maternity unit. The resident call room phone rang nine times before I hung up; evidently not there either. Finally, my last, incredulous call was to the hospital canteen. A woman answered at the cashier's phone, and then I heard her call out the resident's name amidst what sounded like a busy frenzy at the other end of the line. After a long pause, I heard Dev shuffle over. *"Ahhello?"*

I shared the X-ray findings, the patient's worsening course, the need for surgery. *Now.* I tried to restrain the anger in my voice, reminding myself of how good the Tansen residents' care generally was. I asked him why the X-ray hadn't been seen and reviewed, my voice dripping with the accusatory implication of my question. *Why are you eating dal bhaat, while this emergency is evolving?*

Dev drifted back to the medical ward and called the surgical team to get the ball rolling, as we worked together to stabilize the patient with more fluids, antibiotics, blood pressure support, and pain medications. There's not much more that a medical doctor can do in that scenario, surgery being the only real treatment. Yet due to staffing shortages, it turned out there was no general surgeon available that evening at Tansen.

I looked in again at the patient. He was fairly debilitated even before his admission, and was by this point in such critical condition that, truthfully, he was in no shape to undergo a major open abdominal surgery. I wondered if he could even survive general anesthesia, let alone an involved surgery and long post-op recovery period. Was it wise to put him through such an ordeal at the end of his life, and unnecessarily burden his family with enormous expense? Turning to his son, I invited him into the hallway to speak.

"Your father can be transferred to a nearby district hospital if you'd like. It's twenty minutes down the hill, and surgical services should be available there. You'll just need to arrange for a taxi to bring him there." Hospital transfers to and from Tansen were coordinated almost entirely by the family, the onus on them to navigate all of the details with a private vehicle. There were no ambulances or emergency medical services this far from Kathmandu.

"Of course! Why *wouldn't* we bring him there, if he needs surgery?" His son stared at me with confused irritation. I regarded him for a moment.

"I'm worried that he's very sick," I answered gently. "Even the car trip there might be too much for your father, let alone a major surgery. But if you want to try for that transfer, we will absolutely support your decision."

In the end, they opted for a last-ditch attempt to save him, the family hauling his ailing body into a taxi they'd arranged. I wrote out a brief transfer summary on our carbon-copy template, and handed his son the original.

Remembering the other two charts Sr. Saritha had handed me earlier that evening, I flipped open one of them to a resident's admission from the Emergency Department. It still needed all the orders to be written, including two types of antibiotics for severe pneumonia that hadn't been started yet. The last chart had several illegible medication entries, and one clear mistake. *"Metformin,"* a diabetes medication, was written on the top line, but without any apparent indication. It seemed the resident meant to write *"Metronidazole"* instead, especially given that the admitting diagnosis was an intestinal amoeba infection for which that is the mainstay of treatment. I rolled my eyes and made the changes, frustrated because this wasn't the first time I'd corrected similar mistakes.

It was pitch-black outside when I emerged from the hospital gate and began walking home. Far-off stars glittered, brighter than usual in the darkness, as all lights in the surrounding shops and homes had been extinguished by a community-wide power outage. Thankful for the extra privacy this darkness afforded, I succumbed to tears, grief grappling with frustration in a fury of welling emotion.

The following morning, when I arrived for sign-out, I learned that the man had died en route to the district hospital, in the very vehicle his family had called to take him there.

CHAPTER NINETEEN
Living the Dream

Near the equator, dusk falls so quickly that it's as if earth flips a light switch. The transition would occur with such suddenness that it often caught me off-guard. I was working on my computer one afternoon, absorbed in some tasks I'd been putting off, only to be left bumbling about in darkness for the wall switch several minutes later. I found it, and then headed downstairs to our little galley-kitchen to boil a large saucepan of buffalo milk I'd bought on my way home.

I had let another batch of milk boil over accidentally the other day, watching with dismay as it streamed across the counter, down the fronts of our cabinets, and onto the ground, seeping between layers of linoleum haphazardly covering our kitchen floor. That momentary lapse of attention took well over an hour to clean up, and had been my final straw that day. I walked next door to share the story and some tears with my friend Leah. She and Dan had been my neighbors since we all moved to Tansen after completing orientation together in Kathmandu. Their kids often played with other neighborhood friends in the narrow strip of yard between our homes.

The following afternoon, I'd come home at lunchtime to a note on our kitchen table. Printed in Leah's handwriting were the words, "*They say don't cry over spilled milk. But it's okay to cry when your milk not only spills, but also boils and curdles all over your kitchen floor. Enjoy!!*" She had left a luxurious rarity — a pack of Peanut M&M's — with her note. It could only have come from a care package sent by loved ones back home, so the sacrifice this gift represented meant even more than the candy itself.

Maddy or I generally picked up our milk from the local stand on our way home from the hospital. The milk-stand man would ladle one liter into a clear plastic bag and secure it with a rubber band at the top. It always needed relatively quick "pasteurization" by boiling, since our milk came directly from the cow — or more often, buffalo — that same morning. Now, I lifted the bag of milk I'd bought that afternoon out of the fridge, thick buffalo cream swirling richly at the top. I glanced at the clock on our wall. 6:42 PM. Eighteen minutes until "load-shedding," a phenomenon familiar to most of the developing world, and virtually unknown outside of it.

Load-shedding is the colloquial term for scheduled power cuts owing to inadequate electricity production in the region. Truth be told, the hydroelectric power generated by Nepal's rivers, the most water-rich nation in Asia, is actually sufficient to power the whole country. Yet for years, including the decade that spanned my brief tenure there, hydroelectric power was not a well-tapped resource. Fortunately, our Hobbit House came equipped with a battery back-up "inverter," as did many of the surrounding homes in our neighborhood. During winter's dry season, hydroelectric plants produced even less electricity than when rivers are full. Hence, residents experienced upwards of eighteen hours of load-shedding in the most populous cities of the nation, somewhat less so where demand was lower.

I thought back to the evening before, walking home well after dark from the hospital after our Guest House service and community dinner. A six-hour load-shedding stretch had already begun, and scattered points of light — the glow of burning candles and incandescent lightbulbs in homes across the valley— flickered and dotted the landscape, merging with the glow of stars light-years away. The two swaths of black were divided by an invisible horizon, the black sky above indistinguishable from shadowy foothills and flatlands stretching out in the valley-basin far below.

Returning my attention to the kitchen in the nick of time, I noticed the milk foaming to a boil as it rushed to the saucepan's rim. I turned off the burner's flame and blew on the foam, a trick Maddy once taught me. She was working late that evening, managing post-operative patients on the surgical ward with the rest of her anesthesia team. It was she who also taught me how to make yogurt, something not readily available locally (at least, not the thick, creamy sort), which I proceeded to do with part of this warmed batch.

When I was done, I walked upstairs to decompress with a few minutes of yoga. Before leaving Kathmandu, I had managed to find a yoga mat for sale in a shop catering to expats, and when I moved into the Hobbit House, I was able to angle it in just such a way that it lay flat on the floor of my closet-sized bedroom. Besides yoga, there weren't many options for physical exercise in Tansen, as was the case in traffic-congested Kathmandu. I didn't own a bicycle, and of course, there were no public gyms, pools, or tennis courts anywhere near Tansen. Leah and I had tried out an online "ballet workout" video together once in her attic, but had to cut it short when, jumping around, we suddenly remembered our homes were made of mud. Showers of dirt were raining down onto the floor below us with each *sauté, jeté* and *assemblé*.

Even a workout like running wasn't ideal. It was considered very strange, especially for a woman, to run without any discernible purpose. Still, I tried to run a few times a week, but always before dawn, going by flashlight under the cover of darkness, when I couldn't be as easily noticed. It was generally safe, except for the one time I came upon two rabid-acting, feral dogs far out on a mountain road and had to turn around. Running early in the morning, I would often pass village women trudging up the hilly rabbit trails. They carried huge, twenty-liter plastic oil drums anchored by bands across their foreheads, to fill with water at the well for their daily needs. I could feel their stares on my back, but had little idea what they were thinking as I scampered past.

It always felt good to move and stretch, to challenge myself in some concrete, physical way. I could understand *that* discomfort more easily than the amorphous challenges presented in the hospital each day. I stepped onto my yoga mat and leaned into a stretch. A few minutes later, I heard the sound of my name being called, a cheery greeting emanating without any particular urgency through our uninsulated, wood-slat windows. It was Leah, calling from her kitchen window across the narrow strip of grass separating our homes. I went to my window and pushed it open, the deadbolt sticking a bit as I tried to release the latch.

"Saw your light on!" she smiled, her face beaming from her own window across the yard. "Up for dinner and a game of *Settlers*?"

As a child, one of the few sitcoms my sister and I were allowed to watch featured a handy "tool-man" character named Tim, who had these empathic, wisdom-imparting conversations with his neighbor and confidante, Wilson, across their hedge-lined picket fence. In those scenes, only Wilson's eyes and the rim of his fisherman cap were visible. This portrayal of suburban neighborhood life was far from my own experience. My family had always valued clear boundaries, and frequently endorsed sentiments like "familiarity breeds contempt" and "good fences make good neighbors."

This way of being, this neighborly friendship and familiarity — really, the joy of lived *community* — had always appealed to me with an almost exotic draw. Finally, in Tansen, I was experiencing this beautiful intertwining, through shared lives and spontaneous game nights, for the first time. As hard as the work was, I knew there was a community surrounding me, enveloping all of us, sustaining us. *This* was living the dream.

CHAPTER TWENTY

Meeting Jesus

One of the many gifts of the Tansen community was the chance to encounter different faith traditions. Our international mix represented a wide spectrum of Christian belief and practice, from traditional Presbyterian to charismatic Pentecostal. It was here that I first became acquainted with the ancient Jesuit disciplines of "Ignatian contemplation," a form of imaginative prayer that cultivates conversation with Jesus through Scripture. Trying it out one morning on a day off, I opened my Bible to Mark 10, and immersed myself in the story of the rich young ruler. This bit of Scripture had been formative to my coming to Nepal, and I revisited it that morning with eyes open, imagining what it was like to be there as the story unfolded.

I pictured a young man of privilege, comfortable in his wealth, used to having his voice heard and heeded. This young man set out one afternoon on a quest to seek wisdom, yearning for the "good life" and hearing of One who held the promise of an answer. I took him to be genuine in his interest, imagining that perhaps his life thus far had left him vaguely dissatisfied. His restless search had led him finally to an itinerant, rough-shod rabbi named Jesus, a Man who wandered with a ragtag following as He taught and healed.

This preacher, from His peripheral ministry at the margins of society, in backwater towns beyond Jerusalem's city limits, had created no small stir among the intellectual elite, the *culturati* of His day.

Something in the work of this unlikely rabbi — homely, dark, lanky, and yet somehow impossibly magnetic — compelled this wealthy young man. He had come seeking wisdom — nay, more than this, seeking *eternal life*, life so abundant that it could flow seamlessly from this life into the next.

I imagined this "rich young ruler" striding up to Jesus, buoyantly debonair, in a manner of one accustomed to getting what he's after. There, toe-to-toe with Jesus, he spread his upturned palms wide in the gesture of a supplicant and moved in to pose his question. Yet so close to the living, breathing Jesus, he must have been startled by the gravity of this Man before him. I imagined his confident momentum momentarily shaken. This Man was not starstruck by his charisma, like others were. This man had a solidity that seemed somehow to exert its own gravitational pull. It was as if He knew him.

Our young man, perhaps in his early thirties himself, felt his own being de-centered in this Presence. The crowd rippled to stillness, sensing a confrontation building. Regathering his composure, our brave young hero steadied himself and returned Jesus's gaze. He expected the hard-set jaw and arched eyebrows of a smug victor, the alpha-male in a power struggle typical of his daily life. He was surprised, then, to meet instead this Man's relentlessly tender gaze, filled with love. The young man may have blinked, his ironic edge and impressive swagger melting away. He recollected his thoughts and tried to recall the question he'd traveled these many miles to ask.

Good Teacher, what must I do to inherit eternal life?

Even the crowd sensed the genuineness of its source. This was not one of those traps so often laid by fine-garbed Pharisees, with elegant tones and hard edges. They were always posing impossible questions, questions without *safe* answers.

Many in the crowd, detecting this young man's earnestness, grew bored. No blood to smell in these waters. But none of that mattered to him. Like a moment suspended in time, these two young men faced one another, his question hanging between them. *What must I do?*

Jesus responded simply. *You know the commandments: Don't lie, don't steal, don't murder, don't commit adultery...*

Our young man released a small breath, not daring even to show his relief. For he was in compliance so far; he had checked all those boxes.

All these I have kept from my youth.

Here he was, face to face with Jesus. And, the gospel writer tells us, "Jesus looked at him and *loved him.*" Jesus is so often provocative. Yet His provocations are rooted in love, even as they run counter to the grain of our natural inclinations, our broken way of being in a world that is, itself, deeply broken. It's *love* that motivates Jesus to say what He says next.

Then go, sell all you have and give to the poor. And come, follow Me.

I must admit that, until this point in the story, I was tracking along with this young man. He had my number. I, too, had been checking off all the right boxes. I had a "testimony" of being led to Jesus at age nine by my Sunday School teacher, Ms. Baron, followed by a straight line of spiritual growth at youth group, summer Bible-camp, winter weekend trips, seminars, retreats, and campus clubs.

Yet hearing of this encounter, of a rich young ruler coming face to face with God, I realized that Jesus loved him not for all the good that he had done, but rather in spite of it. It struck me with breathtaking force. I had it all backwards. This way of Jesus is entirely upside-down. It's all about love, *His* love. It is this Love that motivates the goodness. It empowers all action, because it flows from a place of full acceptance in Him. His fierce love, as purifying as fire and as cleansing as water, is alone able to push away all the silt and dross that get in our way. Jesus's sole interest was to remove whatever self-righteous mess was keeping this young man from receiving His Love.

It felt like the proverbial no-brainer. Who could refuse such a love? What on earth — literally, *what* in this realm — could compare to joining that dance of eternal love begun before time? A flooding-through-your-being sort of love, more real, more true, more heart-achingly beautiful than anything else imaginable? It was a tasting of the unique, boundless joy — fleeting joy, as J. R. R. Tolkien described it, "joy beyond the walls of the world, poignant as grief."

Who could turn that down? What could even hold a candle to it?

Seen in this light, the young man's response is shocking. He turns away from Jesus because the cost is too great, his wealth too compelling. When I re-read this story in the context of Ignatian contemplation, this reaction hit me like a gut punch. I'd always imagined a "holier-than-thou" look on Jesus's face as the young man turned aside. Yet this closer, imaginative look shed an entirely different light on the scene's tenor. There is deep grief there. Nothing in Jesus's face bespeaks smug self-satisfaction. His heart is breaking.

I'm thankful that we don't know what ultimately became of our rich young ruler. For even in the ambiguity of this unresolved ending, there is a promise of hope. In fact, church tradition holds that, far from having made a permanent decision, this young man *did* eventually repent — he made an about-face, turning around to walk towards Jesus, not away. Tradition goes on to tell us that in the space of a few decades, this same man would meet Peter, hear his first-hand account of Jesus's life, and pen the gospel account that's borne his name down through the centuries: Mark.

I know, too, what became of *this* would-be author that day — or perhaps more accurately, what *began to become,* in a journey that even now is still only beginning. The commands to act justly, to love mercy, and to walk humbly began to make sense as parts fitting into a beautiful whole, framed within a context that offered all the power, motivation, and hope needed to live them out.

Even more than that, the call to follow Christ down a path of obscurity held an unexpected appeal, alluring and tantalizing in its simplicity. *Come, follow Me.* It was a call simply to be in the place where He was, and there to find more of Him in obscure and forgotten places. I longed to know Him more deeply as I loosened my grip on whatever hunger for glory was keeping me from walking closely at His side.

CHAPTER TWENTY-ONE
Tamponade

On one sunny, frigid afternoon in late January, female OPD was crammed, and I was finalizing an admission for a complicated emphysema patient. It was striking how many cases of advanced emphysema we saw here. In the developed world, cigarettes are the leading cause of this debilitating lung disease. Not so in Nepal.

Here, as in many resource-limited settings, emphysema happened disproportionately because — as Willem once put it — "women are just trying to feed their families." A lifetime of exposure to wood fire smoke caused damage that often presented early and aggressively, turning every breath into a labored, conscious effort. I'd seen the smoke-blackened mud walls of village kitchens from time to time, where a residual smell of burnt air lingered thick. A time or two, I had even endured the eye-watering experience of village cooking up close, and wondered at my host's capacity to tolerate hours of billowing smoke at such close range.

The patient before me, a frail waif in her mid-forties, had the characteristic "barrel-chest" from years of trying to maximize what little lung capacity she had left. She was seated on a bench outside my small OPD room, waiting for the result of her echocardiogram, or heart ultrasound, to come back so we could finish the admission and get her settled onto the ward. I expected to see a reading of right heart failure or *cor pulmonale,* a chronic side effect of advanced lung disease that, while relatively unusual in the West, was astonishingly common in Nepal. Instead, I was horrified to see the words *"Cardiac Tamponade"* scrawled across the handwritten report.

Tamponade is an emergency, occurring when a large amount of fluid builds up around the heart and has to be removed. In the context of features like falling blood pressure, bulging neck veins, and muffled heart sounds, the tight space in the center of the chest must be decompressed, to make space for the heart to beat. Otherwise, the patient risks dangerously low blood pressure and even death. In Nepal, tuberculosis was the most common cause, and large cardiac effusions were not that unusual. It was probably the cause here, too. The only way to drain that fluid is by thrusting a long needle under the rib cage and into the sac around the heart, a procedure known as a pericardiocentesis.

Happily, my colleague Willem was also in clinic that afternoon, working one room over, and I ran it by him. He agreed that we needed to get her settled in quickly and perform the pericardiocentesis. Having treated many tuberculosis patients over the years, he had done it a number of times before, and was comfortable with procedures even more aggressive than this one, which required steering a razor-sharp needle right next to rapidly pumping heart muscle.

Quickly tracking down the necessary materials — a portable ultrasound device, tubing, three-way stop-cock valve, fluid collecting basin, sterile gloves and drape, a bottle of iodine for cleansing, and the longest spinal needle that our sterile-supply department could find — I waited for Willem to join me at the bedside, running through the steps and anatomical landmarks in my mind. I tried to picture the large, fluid-filled sac thumping beneath her sternum, straining to imagine where I would put the needle.

There's a saying in medical school training: "See one, Do

one, Teach one." It's often said with an ironic tone, implying a "cowboy" approach to learning that, in truth, was virtually non-existent in my own training, structured and supervised as it was. Yet it does capture the reality of the ambitiously steep learning curve of medical education, especially when learning a new procedure. At some point, you just have to *do* it. Medical training demands a willingness to jump in and, with supervision, try things that you may have seen done only a handful of times before.

Thus I found myself at the bedside of a patient in need of this urgently lifesaving yet risky procedure. A centimeter in the wrong direction and I could easily lacerate the wall of her heart muscle, which would cause her to bleed out in seconds. A med student from New Zealand was working with me that afternoon, halfway through his global health elective. He joined me to watch this "great learning opportunity." It seemed this would be a "See one, Do one, Teach one" moment all rolled into one. Dev, the senior resident I'd had some tension with before, came to the bedside too, perhaps hoping to do the procedure himself. He saw me standing there, holding the ultrasound and equipment, and I thought I saw a small scowl cross his face as he walked away.

Willem appeared through the bedside curtain, and we gloved up. There is something incredibly reassuring about the presence of mentors, the security that comes with those possessing far more experience than yourself. Tansen was chock full of such doctors, bringing with them the confidence that even unexpected crises could be managed. I was thankful for Willem's extraordinary clinical competence and decades-long experience in Nepal. It gave me hope that I wouldn't get in too far over my head.

The five-inch-long spinal needle fit snugly into the turncock adaptor and syringe, attached to a length of tubing draped down to a metal basin where the fluid would collect. Using a bedside ultrasound, it was easy to locate the fluid-filled sac, since the pocket of fluid took up the entire screen. Only a small tip of her heart was visible, fluttering madly in one corner. I stalled for a minute, reluctant to push the needle in.

Drawing in a deep breath, I advanced the barbaric rod under her sternum, requiring more force than I expected. I went slowly, keen to stay well clear of the ventricle that swung dangerously close to the needle's tip with each heartbeat. My focus locked onto that tip the whole time, sucking out fluid with the giant syringe and emptying it into the basin. I marveled at her trust as I hovered over her frail, thin frame, a needle penetrating her chest.

One plungerful of dark red fluid after another kept coming with each pull on the syringe handle. It had the look of old fluid from a blood-tinged effusion, probably from tuberculosis affecting the heart and complicating her already severe lung disease. But there was so much blood. Sweating bullets, I began to wonder if somehow I had pierced the heart's muscle itself and was draining circulating, *arterial* blood. To the relief of everyone present, though, she remained stable throughout the procedure, and the blood didn't clot in the basin, which we took as a good sign.

In the end, we drained 1800 milliliters of that dark red fluid, nearly enough to fill a two-liter Pepsi bottle. Now that her heart again had enough space to pump, her heart rate slowed to normal. And so did mine, due in no small part thanks to Willem's steady presence there, helping me through the white-knuckled ride that was my first pericardiocentesis.

CHAPTER TWENTY-TWO
Triage in Emergency

I was keenly anticipating the start of my vacation the following morning. It would be my first break — and the first time even leaving the town limits of Tansen — since arriving on the Buck two months earlier. I had just one more overnight hospital call to get through. As they often do, admissions kept us busy in the ED until just after two AM, but they were all fairly straightforward, and finally tapered off enough that I could leave what few loose ends remained in the hands of our capable senior resident, Tenzing.

I trudged back to my call room across the compound to get a few hours' sleep, aching for the start of this long-awaited trip. Maddy and I were heading to Pokhara, a tourist town several hours northeast of Tansen.

Maddy's stories of life in the remote Western regions of Nepal — far from town centers, food shops, and even drivable roads — always left me wide-eyed. To one who perceived virtually everywhere in Nepal to be rustic, her simple, matter-of-fact tales of "roughing it" gave me insight into how grim life could be elsewhere in the country. She never told these stories as if bragging. In fact, they were all the more compelling because they were shared as if they were "no big deal," simply just the way things were.

Through our chats, I'd begun to realize that Tansen accommodations were, in fact, relatively luxurious. Still, Pokhara promised a desperately needed break with good restaurants, guest houses, tourist bookshops, and plenty of time for relaxation. Only six more hours to go.

The call room phone jarred me awake in the darkness. I shook the grogginess from my voice and answered it, reaching for my phone to check the time. 4:40 AM. On the other end of the line, Tenzing was speaking rapidly.

". . .must come to Emergency, Ma'am. There was an RTA in Aryabhanjyang. We are notifying of Mass Casualty to the staff."

A Road Traffic Accident. I was suddenly wide awake, my mind whirring at those dreaded words. I'd somehow managed to miss any mass casualties in my first two months of Tansen overnight call. But it was one of several bleak scenarios that my more seasoned colleagues occasionally mentioned in passing. Every time, I dreaded having to face something so extreme. As a family physician, I'd had little exposure to major trauma management.

Well, the time had finally come. Forcing myself to breathe slowly, aware of the violent pounding in my chest, I leapt out of bed and hurried along the maze of hospital corridors that connected rear segments of the compound with the main entrance and emergency room. These passages, now familiar enough to navigate in pre-dawn darkness, had been so confusing when I first arrived.

I finally got to the ED, pausing outside the double doors to catch my breath and gather myself for a moment, imagining the chaos of heaped bodies and tangled limbs on the other side. Yet the scene that met me was, surprisingly, one of total calm. There was a single, stable patient sleeping on one stretcher in the far corner. A medical assistant named Khirel stood next to Tenzing, both of them illuminated by patchy rays from an overhead fluorescent light suspended above the nursing station.

I gave Tenzing a puzzled glance. He looked

uncharacteristically tense, a barely perceptible strain flickering beneath his usually unflappable exterior. He'd always emitted an air of jolly confidence and the ease of natural competence.

"They're twenty minutes away, Ma'am." Then, seeing my confusion at the eerie stillness, explained, "The police gave us notice from the scene of the accident."

I had no idea where Aryabhanjyang was. Khirel made a subtle grimace at the name — as if this was not the first time vehicular tragedy emerged from that fraught area, wherever it was. Having traveled through Nepal and India before, it was not difficult to imagine the hairpin turns, sheer cliffs, and crushed metal frames from previous accidents I'd seen lying in the canyons. Aryabhanjyang, it turned out, was barely more than a cluster of mud homes and shops dotting the narrow highway that wound through the mountains, linking Tansen to the rest of the world.

"A bus overturned," Tenzing went on. "Probably too much *raksi*." He made the universal sign for imbibing alcohol, wiggling his fist in front of his mouth with thumb and pinky extended. I'd heard of drunk driving being especially problematic in the winter months. Bus drivers were apt to take surreptitious sips from flasks of the rice-based distilled liquor. Ostensibly, this was their way of staying warm on long, overnight trips, in public buses that were rarely heated and never insulated. The effect, though, was exactly what you'd expect when you mix nighttime driving with high-proof alcohol. Almost invariably, it resulted in accidents of epic proportions, as drivers fell asleep at the wheel and careened over the edge of a hundred-meter cliff, or into another vehicle head-on. The mountains of Nepal afforded slim margin even for sober drivers during daylight hours.

"How many are coming?" I asked Tenzing, willing my voice to sound calm and self-assured. I recalled Willem mentioning mass casualties with upwards of forty victims at a time, the steady onslaught rolling in on rows of stretchers, then being carried in by volunteers when all available gurneys were taken up. It was the role of the on-call doctor to manage the initial triage. Tenzing had already summoned the surgeons, who were on their way in from home, along with other members of our team.

"They said something like twelve people survived, though most are being taken to the District Hospital." Twelve seemed like a lot, but better than forty. Tenzing reached for a cardboard box under the nursing station desk and produced several color-coded tags — Red, Green, Yellow, Black — with matching colored badges on lanyards. I felt my heart race faster. He picked out a White badge labeled "TRIAGE OFFICER" in big block print, and slipped it over his head.

I recalled a Wilderness and Survival Medicine conference I'd attended the previous year. It was held in the Grand Marquis Ballroom of a fancy Washington hotel, back when I was still living in DC, which now felt like another universe. During the conference, they covered the basics of disaster management, including a victim-sorting process intended to optimize survival for the maximum number of people. Red for critical, Yellow for tenuous, Green for stable, the "walking wounded." And Black, for dead. Dead, *or* critical but unsalvageable — the living, sorted among the dead. It was a macabre thought even then, but still a hypothetical one. Now, though? Apprehensively, I suppressed a wave of nausea.

There wasn't time to think any more about it, though. Tenzing passed me the "RED OFFICER" badge just as the first stretcher rolled through our swinging ED doors and emerged from the shadowy vestibule. I pulled on a pair of latex gloves and took my position in the "Red" trauma bay.

On the medical wards, even with our sickest patients, I usually have some sense of how to proceed. That was my comfort zone, and I was able to settle into a rhythm, anchoring in the basic patterns of my training. But in the surgical realm, including that of trauma management, I felt lost. I had too little experience with it to have developed a framework. Medical training conditions you to approach even the most complex pathologies as a series of related yet discrete problems to manage. Surgery was certainly no different. It's just that I had little idea what their approach looked like.

CHAPTER TWENTY-THREE

Mass Casualty

I stood in the "Red" trauma bay as Tenzing directed the incoming gurney toward me. On it was a fit-looking young man, early thirties, dressed in the blue camouflage fatigues of a Nepali Police Officer. He was lying there motionless, bloodied and unconscious. A gurgling sound was emitting from deep within his throat, his airway blocked by what appeared to be multiple facial and jaw fractures. I noticed he had a crushed right eye socket, large scalp wound, blown right pupil, and clear fluid pooling in the ridges of his right ear. These were all signs of massive head trauma, and of too much blood gathering inside the fixed space of his skull. It seemed he had a brain bleed that was causing it to swell and press perilously against his brainstem, the part of the brain that regulates basic functions like breathing. Simultaneously, the brain's cushioning fluid itself was leaking out through cracks that should not have been there.

His condition was imminently life-threatening, and with no neurosurgeons around for hundreds of miles, I knew we were not prepared to address it at Tansen. I placed a bag-valve mask over his bloodied face, the only option available, though his extensive facial fractures made it a struggle. As I did so, I wondered if anyone on the team had experience with drilling a Burr hole, a procedure designed to temporarily relieve pressure in the brain. I'd read about it years earlier in an Advanced Trauma Life Support course, but had never seen one done. It was certainly not something I was going to be trying on my own, no matter how dangerous the bleed.

"What do you think about drilling a Burr hole, Tenzing? Have you ever done that before? Is that even something we do here?"

Tenzing looked thoughtful for a moment. "We have the tools for drilling a Burr hole, but. . ." He paused, noting the hesitation in my face, then said that it would be ill-advised. "No, Ma'am. I don't think that would help him, not with the kind of care we have here."

He lifted up the red tag pinned to the officer's clothing. I had just been thinking that, in truth, this man probably shouldn't have been given a red tag after all, given his dismal chances of survival. Tenzing, as if reading my thoughts, seemed to be reassuring himself as much, when he said, "No. . . perhaps not. But. . . he's a *police officer.*"

Just then, two more stretchers arrived. I left the medical assistant, Khirel, in charge of resuscitation efforts on the officer, though we both knew there wasn't much we could do. If we lost his airway because of the facial fractures, I didn't feel comfortable doing a cricothyrotomy, where an opening is made in the neck to ventilate him directly through the trachea. That was beyond my skill set, and with only two ventilators in the hospital, criteria for their use were strict. Severe traumatic brain injury was not one of them.

I felt my mind freezing up with fatigue, and the newness of a realm for which I had no mental template to impose structure on the chaos before me. Meanwhile, a heavy-set woman had been wheeled in, moaning in a repetitive, semi-conscious pattern, along with a man who was crying and moaning somewhat more coherently. They each got a yellow tag. The man's blood pressure was low, but he had no obvious source of internal or external bleeding. One of our assistants started running IV fluids while I examined the woman. She had a stiff cervical collar on, placed by the medics in the field, that looked too tall for her, like a medieval torture device stretching up around her chin. Over and over, she cried out for water, *"Pani. . . pani. . ."* Her repetitive litany was all the more distressing against the eerie backdrop of the silent police officer beside her.

The metallic smell of blood hung thick in the air around her, wafting up as I leaned down to examine her head. To my horror, I discovered that her scalp had been split wide open, and I was able to shift it back and forth easily across her smooth, glistening skull, now partly visible beneath lumpy flesh and blood-matted hair. I wasn't sure what to do about that, other than to bandage her head like an injured Civil War soldier in a movie. It was the best we could offer. Microvascular re-implantation surgery was not an option here.

I turned to the next case, noting that the other patients being wheeled in were in similar distress, moaning and semi-conscious, covered in blood and dirt. There was so much blood, in fact, that I could see it dripping and spattering off the plastic gurney mats on the stretchers, pooling beneath a few of them, soaking through torn clothing. After attempting initial evaluations on each, like checking for evidence of spinal trauma or long-bone fractures, I still wasn't sure I'd identified all the issues, but tried to write out what I could on their trauma charts, listing each injury I could think of in the order that seemed most pressing. The section for "Plan" looked more anemic. "Await X-rays. Pain control. IV fluids. Consult surgery." I prayed the surgical team would show up soon.

With relief, just then I looked up as Anneke walked through the doors. The surgeons arrived shortly afterward, and over the next three hours, we tended to the patients, getting them each as stabilized, cleaned up, and pain-free as we could. Finally, it was time to sign out to the day team, handing over responsibility to a fresh set of eyes.

Exhausted, I trudged with my backpack to the lower gate,

where Maddy and I were to meet our vehicle and begin our trip to Pokhara. Normally I'd be ecstatic at the prospect of a scenic car ride and several days' vacation. Now though, I was dazed, barely able to feel even the relief of having survived my shift. The smell of blood lingered thickly in my nostrils. With my last remaining shreds of energy, I threw my pack in the trunk and slumped into the back seat of our cab, staring numbly out the window.

Later that morning, not more than an hour after leaving the hospital, our driver pulled over to the side of the road. Slowing to a stop in the gravel scree, he casually mentioned something about there having been a huge bus accident here overnight, some drunk driver who'd gone off the side of the cliff. We all got out of the car, joining a few Nepali onlookers already gawking. One spectator was clucking her tongue with pity. They had no idea I'd just spent hours intensely proximate to this tragedy.

Standing there with that group of roadside onlookers, I was overcome with a desire to say something, wanting to highlight the bizarre coincidence of this intersection. I also wanted to run as far from the scene as I could. Nauseated, I peered down into the ravine below. Maybe an eight-hundred-foot drop? A thousand? You could just make out the crumpled wreckage far below, sun glinting off the bus's bent metal frame. It was so far down, and suspended among dense vegetation, that I could see little else of the wreckage, not even the colorful hand-painted good-luck symbols that adorned Nepali buses.

Looking down at the wreckage, I began to imagine the crash itself. In spite of myself, unable to put it out of my mind, I pictured the terror of the passengers as their bus rolled in the darkness, tumbling and sliding down the mountain face, crunching over rocks, tearing through trees. My mind drifted to the patients being wheeled in on gurneys. I imagined them laughing with friends at home before saying their goodbyes, then boarding the bus and settling into their respective seats, maybe exchanging a jovial tease with the driver before ambling down the aisle. I pictured them in their clean, dry clothes, their faces intact, sitting comfortably in their seats. I didn't even know how many of the passengers had died.

By five PM, a mere twelve hours after those first stretchers rolled in, I found myself in a setting that could not have been further removed from that emergency room scene. We were sitting at a wood-hewn balcony restaurant in Pokhara's Lakeside district. Maddy and I had dropped our bags at a guesthouse and were relaxing with glasses of red wine in the candlelit mezzanine of this rustic, Tuscan-style restaurant. It was dizzying, this instant shuttling between worlds, as I enjoyed easy access to luxury that most of my Nepali patients would never see in a lifetime.

I was thankful for the privilege to simply walk away from tragedy. It was a relief to be in that restaurant, reveling in the rest and reflective space it afforded. Yet the smell of blood lingered in my nostrils for days. I couldn't shake the deeply disjointed feeling within, echoes of that morning's suffering. It seemed incredible that it could all be contained within a single day.

CHAPTER TWENTY-FOUR
A Day in the Life

Workdays in the hospital generally followed a predictable pattern. After rounding on patients, we would take a mid-morning tea break, then return to the ward to finish all orders, discharge instructions, and remaining loose ends before heading to clinic. There, we met patients who had traveled near and far to see a doctor. The assignments had been worked out over the years to ensure a fair workload, and followed a logical order: male OPD if we'd spent that morning on the adult medical ward, female OPD if on the maternity ward, pediatric OPD if on the peds service, and surgical OPD if on the surgical or ortho services (except for those scheduled to be in the Operating Theatre).

I spent a lot of my time on maternity, so it was usually female OPD for me. To get to the exam rooms at the far end of the narrow hallway, we squeezed past crowds of patients and medical assistants waiting in the vestibule, then slowly picked our way over the outstretched feet of more patients crammed onto wooden benches lining both sides of the hallway.

This experience of navigating through crowds that leave no margin for "personal space," which was apparently not a concept embraced in Nepal, tended to get me off on the wrong foot. Eventually I made it past all the stares, giggles, and muttered comments from our long-suffering queue of patients, who sometimes wondered aloud why we would only be arriving at 11:30 AM (little did they know). By the time I claimed an empty exam room in which to settle down, I could already feel my blood pressure rising. On this particular morning, I drew in a couple of deep breaths before calling the first name on the stack, which elicited another flurry of giggles and chatter over my bizarre pronunciation.

"Reena Paudel?"

I heard a ripple of chatter move through the crowded hallway. "[POWdel]!!? [POdel]?? Ha! It's supposed to be *[PohDEL]!*"

A medical assistant hadn't had a chance to catch me at the clinic's entrance, so he followed the patient into our exam room with a stack of orders to sign, ECGs to interpret, and X-rays to read. He laid the bulky films on my desk, which was already scattered with prescription papers, admission forms, patient charts sorted into various piles, a few medical reference books, and a scrap of paper with notes in a familiar handwriting — probably some reminder I'd scrawled the day before and forgotten to throw away.

As the assistant walked out, he forgot to close the door. I stood up, walked around Ms. Pohdel and closed the door, only to have two patients push it back open, wandering in to ask when their turn was coming. I told them to wait outside, closed the door again, and sat back down.

"What brings you in today?" I asked in my most natural-sounding Nepali.

Just as she began to say "stomach pain," the phone rang. It was a nurse from maternity, with a signature that was missed during rounds by someone on the team.

"Could you come up to sign that right away, because the billing office is waiting on it to complete the patient's account discharge process, and the patient has to catch a bus home."

I asked Ms. Pohdel to wait a moment and walked back up the hallway, against a backdrop of more muttered comments.

One vexed woman said loudly in Nepali, "She just got here, now she's leaving?" I speed-walked through the passageways and up the last ramp at the far end of the hospital, where our maternity department was located.

While I was there, several nurses had additional issues that needed addressing — an order for IV fluids to be signed off, an abnormally low hemoglobin that might require consent for a transfusion, and a patient who needed to be counseled on potential risks and benefits of oxytocin before her labor induction could begin.

Fifteen minutes later, again braving the humanity-filled hallway, I was seated back in front of the patient, and asked my first follow-up question about her stomach pain. "Where does it hurt?"

"Right here," she replied, gesturing to her upper abdomen. Two fingers landed right below the notch where her ribs met. "It's a burning pain after I eat." She was in her late sixties, a smoker, and began to say that sometimes her left shoulder and jaw also hurt, especially when she walked uphill in the morning to collect her household's water.

Just then, the phone rang again. It was the ultrasound department this time, asking me to do a tap on a patient with a huge right pleural effusion — fluid around her lung. It was ordered by the medical team, but "they're in the middle of rounds and can't come up. The patient is waiting on the table, so are you coming right now?" I heaved a sigh of resignation, knowing I'd better go quickly or risk another call from my harried Nepali colleague who was, herself, wading through an ocean of patients queued for their ultrasounds.

Ten minutes later, tap done and documented, I was back in the room asking the usual questions — how long Ms. Pohdel's epigastric pain had been going on (several months), what made it worse or better (nothing to get better, but sometimes worse when walking uphill, or after eating spicy food), what other things were associated (Nausea? Yes; Palpitations? Yes; Chest pain? No; Tightness? Sometimes; Dizziness? Often; Reflux? Most days; Sweating? Yes, when it's hot outside).

The phone rang again, from maternity. The patient we started on oxytocin was having "decelerations," meaning the baby's heart rate was periodically going too low, which can be a sign of distress. It didn't improve with the usual measures, like stopping the medication that stimulates contractions, turning the woman on her side, giving oxygen, and starting IV fluids. The baby's heart rate had been hanging out consistently in the 70s, dangerously low for an unborn infant, and they asked me to come right away.

I again excused myself and went running down the hallway, where I bumped into an older man standing in the middle of the tight pathway. I apologized but still managed to appear an untenably rude young woman to this crowd of bystanders, and sprinted up the ramp to maternity. By the time I got there, the fetal heart rate was back up to 130, which was reassuring, but I reviewed the chart to see if any red flags jumped out that might mean we should get a C-section, especially if a big deceleration happened again.

I returned to the OPD and resumed my visit with the woman who had maybe-serious-heart-disease-or-maybe-just-heartburn. As I walked past the exam room beside mine, I saw that Anneke was already admitting a patient from her stack of charts, and caught a look in her eye that said she was having a similar sort of day.

A resident came in with a question about a patient she was seeing in the next room, followed by the medical assistant asking if I'd read those X-rays and ECGs yet, followed by three more women crowding in behind *him* who didn't want to miss the opportunity of an open door (so to speak) to find out when their turn was coming and *Why it's taking so long!* After dealing with each of these in turn, I shoved the three extra women out and told them, too harshly, that they must wait their turn. My patience was paper-thin by this point, and I forcefully slammed shut the deadbolt on our exam door to keep out any more interruptions, scraping two of my knuckles on a sharp edge of the bolt. They began to slowly ooze blood, which I staunched between lips pursed with frustration.

Then there was one more telephone call about a patient threatening to leave "AMA" (against medical advice) from the female surgical ward, to which I replied, "Hold on to her for another few minutes, I'll be there shortly." I asked Ms. Pohdel several more questions, and was reassured that if cardiac in nature, this woman's pain was most likely due to stable angina, something not warranting admission, and probably had a component of reflux. I offered a medicine for her symptoms, checked an ECG, and encouraged her to quit smoking. Any kind of advanced cardiac work-up like cardiac catheterization or stress testing wasn't available at Tansen Hospital anyway, and she couldn't afford the bus fare to Kathmandu — let alone the cost of those tests. So that's where we left it.

The phone rang again, female surgical ward. "Aren't you coming to see that patient? Her family is very upset!" I hung up the phone and tersely negotiated a follow-up plan with Ms. Pohdel. She agreed to come back in six months — no, she couldn't come any sooner, despite my best cajoling — and we exchanged Namastes as she exited the room. I followed her out on my way to the female surgical ward, hoping we could get their patient to stay another night, or at least provide whatever discharge medications she might need before leaving AMA.

First patient down. Once back in the OPD, I plowed through my pile of paper charts, more or less in the same manner, for the rest of the afternoon. At one PM we all took a quick respite for lunch, and I went for a walk up through the peaceful Srinagar forest. These woodlands were located on a gorgeous hill behind the hospital. From the top, on a clear day, you could enjoy a panoramic view of the southern valley plains on one side, and the entire snow-capped Annapurna Himalayan range on the other. Taking a vegetable samosa and hard-boiled egg in hand, I pressed up the steep hill and 509 concrete steps to gather my thoughts.

CHAPTER TWENTY-FIVE

Providence

In the clinical chaos of each day at the hospital, it was easy to lose sight of the motivation that brought me to Nepal in the first place. One memory that cropped up from time to time helped anchor me in that sense of calling. It was from the year I'd spent completing a fellowship in academic medicine and medical humanities in Washington, DC, just before moving to Nepal. That year offered a rare chance to learn under the guidance and mentorship of one of my heroes in the field, while also working at a hospital near where I lived, to keep up my clinical skills and pay the rent.

And so I found myself covering night shifts for a year at an underserved community hospital in northeast DC, then cycling downtown to Georgetown's medical school campus during the day a few times per week to teach. In many ways it was as far from rural Nepal, both in setting and content, as could be. Yet it was also a year joyfully rich in relationships, and filled with experiences that would prove vital preparation for this next chapter.

At that point, having already made the commitment to move to Tansen for a couple of years, I still felt apprehensive about the decision, sometimes wondering if it was really the right thing to do. Reassurance would come, slowly and gradually, over that year. It crystallized for me one day in particular, while performing the most mundane of hospital tasks: handwashing.

It was the middle of the night, 4:30 AM, and I was in a vile mood. The Emergency Department was humming. Far enough into my twelve-hour shift to be feeling the pain, I still knew seven AM was a long way off, with plenty of time left for more. The ED attending called out from behind the unit clerk's desk.

"I have three more for you — two of them are pretty straightforward."

I was trying to shake off the groggy feeling of being awoken 25 minutes into my first nap of the evening. One of these new admissions was shaping up to be a real challenge. He was a medically complex patient with a laundry list of diseases, unable to give any sort of history at all, and no family at his bedside to supplement much-needed information.

I knew I'd just barely be able to get through those three sets of admission dictations, orders and billing paperwork in time for a seven AM handover to the day team. And *that* was assuming there were no emergencies on any patients in the rest of the hospital, no "Code Blues" or "Rapid Responses" crackling on the overhead paging system. I knew I had to catch a few hours' sleep before heading off to Georgetown again for a small-group session I was leading that afternoon on "Concepts in Evidence-Based Medicine." I placed three blank admission packets on top of the metal chart rack that doubled as my desk. We were in the process of transitioning to an electronic medical record, which meant having to use two systems for a while, a paper chart and an electronic one, to address various aspects of patient care.

On the way to my first patient, I stopped to wash my hands. As I leaned over the deep, industrial-metal sink basin in the middle of the ED and lathered my hands with antibacterial soap, my eyes drifted wearily to nowhere in particular, eventually resting on a cheaply framed sheet of computer paper with words printed in a heavy serif font. It struck me as rather out of place, this attempt at decor pinned to the corner of the dented, sheet-metal backsplash.

I read the first line: "Lord of life, I pray You. . ."

Surprised by its overtly Christian reference, I thought back to a crucifix I had seen hanging outside the entrance to the hospital cafeteria. It was further evidence, as were other items tucked unapologetically here and there, that this was indeed a Catholic hospital. At eight o'clock each evening, the staticky voice of a Daughter of Charity offered the daily *"collect,"* or prayer. It offered a brief pause for patients, visitors, and staff to pray for those who sought healing — and for those who sought to bring it.

I read on:

"Lord of Life, I pray You —
Light my mind to know the remedies for my patients' ills,
and touch my heart to feel compassion for their suffering. . ."

This called to mind a statue standing just outside the hospital's ambulance entrance, a marble of Vincent de Paul, the patron saint of charitable service. An icon of compassion, he also had some pretty provocative things to say about service to the poor. "You will discover that Charity is a heavy burden to carry," he once wrote, "heavier than the kettle of soup and the full basket. But you will keep your gentleness and your smile. . . You are the servant of the poor, always smiling and good-humored. . ." The last line of that quote stunned me the first time I read it: "It is only for your love alone that the poor will forgive you the bread you give to them." Sobering words. And I certainly did not always feel "smiling and good humored," least of all during tough overnight shifts like this one.

The prayer continued,

"When I stretch out my hand to heal the sick,
Let me heal them with a portion
of Your wisdom and Your strength. . ."

There was a small chapel in one wing of Providence Hospital where, in the occasional quiet lull, I would go to reflect and pray. How unusual it was to serve in a place that went out of its way to make space for reverence, a hospital whose very mission speaks of being "rooted in the loving ministry of Jesus as healer." It advocated a special preference for patients who are "poor and vulnerable," endeavoring to serve the surrounding community "with compassion and justice." Somehow, this articulation of mission-in-vocation helped not only to give words and flesh to a growing sense of calling within me, but actually helped shape and form that very calling.

Finally, the prayer concluded:

"And when I cannot heal them,
let me help them on at least to a deeper faith
and resignation in Your love. Amen."

As I read each new stanza, line by line, I sensed my heart opening, softening, stretching past the irritated, peevish place it had been just moments before. Just minutes earlier, I had been irked that these new admissions were interfering with my sleep. Yet with this brief reset, I could now recognize the gravity of the moment, the privilege of entering someone's story at a point of crisis.

I sensed a rootedness in my first and primary calling, that of my own "deeper faith and resignation in God's love." From that place came the calling to participate in the subtle, loving work He does in those around me. And it was a privilege that He uses my hands to do so — hands, I suddenly realized, that were dripping all over the floor and basin edge. I caught an awkward sideways glance from the unit clerk at her desk a few feet away.

Quickly, I dried my hands and made my way through the curtain to meet my next patient.

CHAPTER TWENTY-SIX

Team Dynamics

Criticism of staff should always be carried out...
    (b) in private, to avoid loss of face.
A person's status is determined by...
    (d) family background, caste, age and job title.
Nepali society is best described as...
    (a) hierarchical.

I had nailed every question on the quiz. The concepts of cultural competency were clear, when laid out during our orientation program in obvious wording on a worksheet. The "right" answers seemed almost painfully obvious. How, then, was I so blind to those truths — and their profound import in my daily interactions — when more subtly disguised in "real life?"

As a white, Western-trained female physician in my early thirties, I could not have been more of an outsider. I spoke a heavily accented version of "Nepali as a second language" that marked me as a foreigner, if my blond hair hadn't already made that abundantly clear. It felt like a constant struggle, this crossing of cultural divides to simply *interact* day after day. There were myriad differences, not just in language, clothing, skin, and hair color — the usual, obvious things —

but also more subtle ones, like sense of humor, intonation of voice, even posture and manner of walking. I knew I was coming from a specific context, the quintessentially East-Coast American ethos of life and practice, with an unmistakable flavor of ivory-tower privilege thrown in at no extra charge.

It was with this background that I found myself on a team of medical trainees who were all Nepali, overwhelmingly male, and generally at least a few years older than me. It was an awkward situation, particularly as someone who, technically speaking, held senior status in the hospital's physician hierarchy.

When gathered around patients' beds in our didactic semicircle for morning rounds, I often looked around only to realize I was the lone female surrounded by a group of four or five male physicians. The teenaged nursing students and their supervising ward nurses were typically the only other women on the unit. I doubt any of my male colleagues even noticed. It was something I couldn't help *but* notice.

Even during our break times, I would sometimes sit awkwardly in silence over mid-morning tea breaks in the cafeteria as they argued national politics, regional news, and local gossip, all in rapid-fire Nepali that I could catch in small fragments at best. It was so uncomfortable that I often fantasized about ways to avoid these times. In fact, I dreaded them, much as I'd dreaded the unstructured social interactions of high school field trips all those years earlier. Yet begging out of those tea breaks would have amounted to an unacceptable social affront, an abandonment of supposed team cohesion. And so I went.

These times were also strangely reminiscent of an experience harkening back to medical school, causing me to feel almost as if I'd been thrust back into the role of my third-year surgery rotation in New York. I could almost hear, even, that same voice plaguing me so many years ago.

Loser.

It was implied in his tone of voice, the sneering curve of his upper lip. As he berated me, my med student friends cautiously cast pitying glances my way. That was about as much solidarity as I could have hoped for that afternoon, during a spontaneous "teaching" session that my senior surgical resident, Adam, had decided to offer. Derisive sarcasm oozed from his voice as he grilled me in front of my teammates.

"*Cholelithiasis?* Surely you mean *Chole-DOCHO-lithiasis,* student-doctor?"

I was on my first clinical rotation of third year, the infamous Surgery clerkship, and my head was already swimming with acronyms, abbreviations, and algorithms. Which is to say nothing of the subtle distinctions we were asked to draw between various biliary tree pathologies. Well, as it turned out, I was about to be schooled extensively in the various locations you might find a gallstone, and the deleterious effects resulting from each. It had been a tense week with Adam in particular, for reasons that remain shrouded in mystery even today, and it was about to get worse.

For the previous six weeks, I had been rising well before dawn and jetting about at the beck and call of every attending, fellow, resident, nurse, intern, unit-clerk, and fourth-year medical student on the ward. The surgical unit can be a grim place of post-op patients and chronically debilitated nursing home transfers, all trying their best to recover from the latest laparotomy or bedsore skin graft. They were doing so on a ward that didn't appear to have enjoyed an upgrade since 1980.

Yet I'd managed to keep my head down, mouth shut, and eyes open long enough to have survived to this point. It seemed I'd been well-served by a "nose-to-the-grindstone, get 'er done" approach, earning praise from my resident supervisors and eventually, honors on the rotation. But on the receiving end of Adam's ire, none of that seemed to matter. He went on.

"How did you get this far with such crap work? Did you

even read up on this stuff?"

Days and nights blurred together as I subsisted on the cheapest thing available in the cafeteria — a toasted Kaiser roll for a dollar, with (free) butter — and discovered that sleep truly was an expendable luxury. Showering was optional, connections with family and friends non-existent. Between cases in the OR and at home in the evenings, my reading consisted exclusively of the medical student primer *Surgical Essentials.* But soon this eight-week voyage to the outer rings of hell would be over. Just two more weeks.

On this particular afternoon, with rounds and follow-ups completed, Adam looked particularly keyed up, grunting and pawing the ground, primed for abuse. He seemed keen to demonstrate the age-old medical education ritual known as "pimping," a poor mimic of the Socratic method, based on publicly querying junior learners with challenging clinical questions. It's a form of teaching that, for good or ill, has shaped many a doctor over the decades.

"Why on earth would you say *Cholelithiasis*, student-doctor?"

So went a forty-five-minute pimping session on gall-bladder pathologies. In his crosshairs the whole time, as a small crowd of nurses, med student peers, and one bemused unit clerk looked on, the experience left me breathless with shame and anger. Stripped raw, my insecurities fully exposed, I retreated down a hallway that blurred with hot tears before I could even reach the safety of my car. An impromptu humiliation, courtesy of Adam.

I look back on that twenty-something medical student with a great deal of compassion. Jaw clenched, red-faced with shame, eyes stinging with tears I refused to shed — *no,* not *in front of him* — I felt a gritty determination in the moment. Yet afterward, weeping desolate tears alone in my car on the edge of the hospital's parking lot, there was nothing but resentment and shame. It was months before I could even put words to the experience that afternoon, lending it some semblance of meaning. Defeated, I knew I'd have to return to that same lot ten hours later, when the early-morning fog rose off of an adjacent reservoir in the quiet pre-dawn hours. When I did, I hoped that my puffy eyes and tear-blotched face had somehow rinsed fresh enough for anyone to suspect I'd spent the evening on my couch, sobbing.

CHAPTER TWENTY-SEVEN
Flawed Perfectionism

Morning tea breaks at Tansen Hospital were, happily, nowhere near as dramatic or painful as those med school memories. Yet they exhumed that old, childhood specter of awkward insecurity, of not quite fitting in. And like that day as a student on the surgical ward, it collided with the security I sought in my professional role, as a place to find reassurance through excellent performance.

Therein lay the paradox. This perceived need for perfection — the very thing that had fueled whatever success I'd enjoyed to date — had become my main obstacle. As a physician, perfectionism was commendable, even necessary, for safe patient care. As a teacher, however, it made me unapproachable, forming a barrier to relationships with my trainees. It did not allow for space in which they felt safe to fail.

I tried everything I could think of to connect with them. I arranged extra teaching sessions, and compiled review materials for the medical content they were sure to encounter on their national exams. They generally weren't interested. Realizing that the residents might have felt intimidated, I initially tried a kind, friendly, even bubbly approach, feigning ignorance at times, in the hope this might play better in my overwhelmingly male-dominated world. The residents only gave a funny look, as if to say, *What kind of a self-respecting senior doctor are you, to be so friendly and egalitarian?* When that strategy failed, I grew detached, going about the workday with an airy, aloof sense, as if I could float along without worrying about relationships. Yet that felt like cowardice, and it wasn't an effective strategy if the goal was to help them learn medicine.

I also tried out the role of strict authoritarian, holding them accountable to impeccable standards of care in order to earn their respect through excellence. Predictably, that proved worst of all. Rounding with the residents became a pained affair, replete with uncomfortable shuffling of feet and awkward stares at the tiled floor. As they entered the ward each morning, it seemed like the residents greeted each other warmly, joking and slapping one another on the back, only to physically turn away from me, returning my greeting with a forced "Morning Ma'am" as they brushed past.

Rounds themselves could also be uncomfortable. Most days, I would glance around the circle of six or eight physicians — a mix of ex-pat and Nepali doctors — and look at the faces discussing a given patient. I was generally the only woman standing there in the group. Aside from our nurses, there were rarely any other female clinicians on the ward. Never before in my professional life had I felt so isolated as a woman in medicine. Female role models had abounded during my training — especially in a field like Family Medicine, where women frequently outnumber men. But that was in America. If there were any sexist overtones here, they were more felt than observed — slights inconspicuous enough that I sometimes wondered if it was all "in my head." Yet we humans are fine-tuned social beings, capable of detecting the subtlest of cues.

Adding to the complexity of connecting across these gender and cultural divides, I was in the position of senior attending physician, and was therefore responsible for supervising the residents in their patient care, while also delivering care myself alongside them. Eventually, issues came up in patient care — as they invariably would — and I had to call one of the residents to task.

Opening up a chart one day to review a patient on whom the nurses had noted dangerously low blood pressures, I saw a lab result scrawled in the margin. Looking closely, I recognized Dev's handwriting, noting that he'd written *"Hemoglobin: 5.7"* This patient's oxygen-carrying red blood cells were perilously low.

Yet nothing had been done. There was no type and crossmatch of blood products, no transfusion orders placed, no mention even of a plan in the chart. I thought back to that other evening, when Dev was nowhere to be found during a medical emergency, and wondered if this was part of a more troubling pattern. Just then, he strolled confidently into the nursing station, where a scattering of residents and nurses were standing around. I waved him over for a chat.

"Dev, it looks like you saw this patient's low hemoglobin level." I paused for his response, making space for what I hoped would be an insightful moment of self-correction.

"Yes, that's right. 5.7, I wrote it right there." He seemed pleased with his effort at having done so.

"But it's very low, Dev. She's quite sick. Her heart rate is in the 120s, and her blood pressure has been gradually trending down." I spoke slowly, trying to suppress the hot anger rising within me. "What was your plan, Dev? Why didn't you order a blood transfusion? Did you just write the value down and do *nothing* about it?" Two residents glanced over at us, sensing tension rising in the room.

"Yes, well. . . I wrote for IV fluids!" He suddenly seemed defensive, angry that we were having this conversation at all, but especially in the presence of his peers.

He turned his back to me and walked away, making it clear we were done. Dev eventually ordered the blood transfusion, but the whole interaction felt like a colossal failure. He and the other residents gave me the cold shoulder for days, our rounds an even more uncomfortable ritual. I wondered if I had only acted to confirm their suspicions of me — the *real* Dr. Becca — as someone just waiting to pounce when they screwed up.

The next morning, after handover, I walked down from the upper conference room to the medical ward alone. I was surrounded by a herd of doctors, chatting and laughing excitedly with one another, which only accentuated my sense of disconnection. Small clusters of our team peeled off to their respective wards to start their day as we drifted down a series of ramps connecting each unit.

My eye caught Dev's as he sauntered ahead, before ducking down to whisper something to one of the new interns. This young intern had recently joined our program after completing medical school abroad, in the hopes of continuing his residency training at Tansen after this preliminary year of medical internship. I couldn't help but notice both of them snickering and looking back at me once or twice as we walked along. Reaching the ward's nursing station together, I greeted Dev as he walked past. He halfway turned his head toward me, mumbled an obligatory response, and bent down over a chart that suddenly consumed his attention. I thought I saw him shake his head slightly, as if to say, *Can you* believe *this one?*

"Shall we get started on rounds, team?" I asked, willing my voice to whip up some enthusiasm. I directed the question generally to the room, where the atmosphere now felt thick with mounting tension. One by one, the residents peeled themselves from the counters, Dev last of all. His body language indicated that my senior rank was all that compelled him to join. *It is going to be like this all day?* I lamented to myself. I wished desperately that Willem, Anneke, or *any* like-minded colleague were here now — a mentor, perhaps? Or at least an ally, in this evolving ordeal?

We filed into the critical ward and coalesced around the first bed, beginning rounds on a man with a severe lung infection. One of our interns, the same one who'd walked down from handover with Dev that morning, picked up the patient's chart and began to present.

"This is a thirty-eight-year-old male with typhoid and a large TB pleural effusion, day seven of antibiotics — he's on a combination of chloramphenicol for the typhoid, and R-I-P-E therapy for TB — now four days post-op from a chest tube placement, with persistent air leak. I think he needs a doxycycline pleurodesis today." Dev nodded in agreement, tracking along as the team's supervising senior resident.

I knew by now what a "doxycycline pleurodesis" was, and had even performed it a few times myself. We offered this treatment when a suctioning chest tube, initially inserted to drain fluid from the space around the lung (the pleural space) had failed to self-seal the opening around it. Sometimes, when this normal course of healing didn't happen for certain patients, it was necessary to introduce an irritant into the pleural space, paradoxically causing inflammation in order to reawaken the body's own healing process and create scarring.

In this procedure, we'd empty several capsules of the antibiotic "doxycycline" into a small volume of sterile water, manually tapping the powder out of the plastic pill caps into the basin, then stir it into suspension before sucking it up into a large syringe. We'd then instill it through the tube into the chest cavity, clamp the tube, and instruct the patient to roll back and forth, sloshing the liquid around to coat the inner walls evenly. From there, it was a matter of waiting for inflammation to stimulate healing and slowly scar down the tissues lining the pleural cavity, hoping it would seal together and eliminate the space causing the air leakage.

The intern went on, "Exam normal. Plan to continue antibiotics and do a pleurodesis —"

"Wait," I interrupted. "I didn't hear anything about his vital signs." I frowned my displeasure. "And it's hard to imagine that his lung exam was stone-cold *normal*, with everything he's got going on in there."

Glancing sideways at Dev to see if he had any insights to add to his intern's presentation, I said to both of them, half under my breath, "*C'mon* — I know you can do better than this."

Inhaling sharply, I turned to face the intern and walked him through the basics. "Let's start with his vital signs. It's important to make that a standard part of your presentation, right? So you always remember to check them?"

The intern stared down at the patient's blue bedspread and said nothing.

"Well, did this gentleman have any fevers overnight?" I pressed him.

"No," the intern answered reflexively. "Vitals are stable. No fever currently."

"But what about in the last twenty-four hours? You know that fevers come and go. Did you check?"

I picked up the chart laying at the foot of the bed and flipped to the sheet where our nurses recorded the vitals. "Look here! He spiked to 103.8 last night. Had you noticed that?"

He offered me a withering glare, then fixed his gaze stonily back down at the blanket, still saying nothing. With a twinge of paranoia, I could imagine his thought process. Surely whatever opinion Dev had shared about me that morning while walking down from handover was obviously ringing true to this intern. At any rate, he clearly wanted our little "teaching session" to be over.

Yet I could also feel frustration boiling up within me at the fact that this intern, who had already completed his entire medical school coursework, had failed to check something so basic, something an entry-level *student* should have known to do automatically. I wanted to press him to acknowledge his mistake, to own up to it. After all, of course I could help this one patient get his necessary treatment. I knew precisely what the next steps were. But that wasn't the point, was it? I was there to be a teacher, at least as much as a physician. I had come to Nepal to help trainees *learn*.

"Do you see why it's important to check the vitals" I asked him, softening my voice a little. "And to present your cases in a systematic way, so you don't risk missing important things?"

To give him a breather, I turned my attention to the group. "So, team — this patient has been on antibiotics for seven days, with an indwelling chest tube for four. Now he's got a new temperature. What are you thinking about in this case? Why the new fevers?"

By now, none of the residents were feeling much like participating, but a few gamely mumbled some thoughts about how his antibiotics might not be effective due to resistant bacteria, or perhaps a new abscess had formed that the antibiotics couldn't reach. I examined the patient, briefly reviewed potential reasons for this new fever, and we reluctantly settled on a plan.

Then we drifted to the foot of the second patient's bed, to continue our rounds.

CHAPTER TWENTY-EIGHT

Chinta Na Gara

I'd been living in Tansen for eleven months by this point, coming to the end of another long day at the hospital filled with difficult diagnoses, sick patients, grieving families, and bewildering team dynamics. I had a med student from Northern Ireland shadowing me on her four-week global health elective, and she was critical of how short I was with a woman in clinic who didn't understand her diagnosis. Or maybe I just thought I detected an air of criticality. Either way, it only amplified the already overbearing voice of self-reproach droning on within.

Female OPD was more of the usual fare — crowds of patients lining the hallways, puzzled by this tall, foreign woman-doctor with too-short *surawal* pants and a laughable accent. A patient had died that morning during ward rounds, somewhat unexpectedly, after nearly an hour of resuscitation efforts. That seemed like a week ago. My resilience was shot.

I bought a bag of fresh-looking apples at a fruit stand outside the hospital's gate, and decided to take the long way home. Attacking the steep hill behind the hospital, I tried to release whatever it was that felt so pent-up inside — *Anger? Grief? Frustration?* I never used to have this much difficulty discerning my own emotions. By now though, inner turmoil had become a familiar, if uneasy, companion.

Breathing heavily, I turned left and made my way along Tansen's dusty Upper Road. Happy for some time to think, I put my earbuds in and pressed play on a soothing Gregorian chant soundtrack I'd recently discovered. Ten minutes later, I came to a narrow, steep footpath branching leftward off the Upper Road that marked my turn home. The path down the hill was rocky and uneven, strewn with boulders and the uneven edges of crumbling concrete slabs. Occasionally, rods of iron rebar poked out at odd angles. In Nepal, these little footpaths are called "rabbit trails" — narrow, nearly-vertical shortcuts bypassing the broader vehicle roads that wind through mountainous regions.

Picking my way down carefully, I reached the point where the rabbit trail joined the Middle Road below, when my Birkenstock-shod left foot suddenly slipped on a patch of loose gravel. I flew through the air, arms flailing, before landing in a graceless heap at the trail's outlet. Wondering for a moment if I'd broken anything, I was relieved to test my elbows, knees, and hips, finding them all intact. Just a scraped palm, sore flank, and severely bruised ego. At least there was no one on the path to witness the embarrassing incident.

I was at that moment greeted by the sound of raucous laughter breaking out on the Upper Road — a group of rowdy teenage boys, clad in the uniform tan sweaters and slacks from the local private high school, peered down at me. So much for anonymity. They looked pleased — what good fortune to happen upon such fine entertainment! Their guffaws echoed as they sauntered away.

Hauling myself up, I gathered my scattered belongings — handbag, earbuds, an empty coffee mug, the kilo of apples I'd just bought. At least I hadn't picked up eggs. Deflated, I repacked my bag, blinking back tears. I resented the rocky, uneven roads and ridiculous footpaths. I resented the dust that invaded every crack and crevice of life in the dry season, only to be replaced by the stink of mildew during monsoon. I resented having to carry all this stuff, by foot, all over town.

Most of all, I resented the mocking jeers of those teenage boys. I seethed over their glee at my humiliation. How could it be that so few people in this world had any imagination for the experience of a foreigner? I felt I'd given up so much to be here. My only thanks seemed to be the mockery that made a bleak day even heavier.

At least it was a sunny day, which gave me an excuse to wear my sunglasses — even though I suspected they didn't conceal my now blotchy, red face. Awkward, sideways glances of a passing schoolboy confirmed this. He politely averted his eyes at the strange sight of a grown woman stealthily crying on the dusty road. I finally reached home, barely containing my sobs as I climbed down the ridge of packed earth.

For once, I longed to be alone. Yet there, on the stoop, was Didi's tell-tale pair of pink rubber sandals. At this particular moment, I didn't care to see anyone at all. Yet when I ducked through the low-hung doorframe, I ran into her as she emerged from the kitchen. She took one look at my face, and with a look of deep, tender concern, dried her hands on a towel and gathered me into her arms. It was an instinctively maternal gesture. Collapsing into the safety of her embrace, I could contain myself no longer, and began to weep.

"*Chinta na gara, Becca — chinta na gara. . .*" she cooed, using the informal, familiar form of address among friends. "*Don't worry, Becca — do not fear. . .*"

She'd made lunch for us, and guided me into the kitchen, rich with the aroma of her amazing *dal bhaat*. Didi said a blessing, and we began to eat. Slowly, I began to open up about everything — my sadness about the patient who had died that morning, and the ward of patients that might still die; the way the family wailed with grief when we told them; the loneliness of our medical team, who couldn't seem to support one another through these sad events; the criticism I thought I was getting from my medical student; my embarrassment at falling on the path; and the desperate sense of my own inadequacy, woven through it all. I faltered at times for the right Nepali words, but she seemed to understand anyway, nodding quietly, saying little. Her eyes were full of compassion, as if she could see straight through to my heart, past all my striving efforts and sense of crippling failure, right down to the desire at my core — to do *well*, and to do *good*.

"*Chinta na gara*," I heard Didi repeat again, like a soothing mantra. I thought about how much she had been through in her life. She had shared some difficult stories over our months of growing friendship, yet it was *she* who offered *me* comfort, speaking these words of peace. After a few minutes, Didi stood up, walked over to the stove, and began ladling out two cups of *chiya*. When we had finished, mostly in quiet silence, she gave me one last encouraging hug, and sent me forth with a reminder. "*Chinta na gara, Becca.*"

CHAPTER TWENTY-NINE

Alabaster Sacrifice

"Time for a quick chat?"

I popped my head over the swinging gate, with its trellis covered in climbing passionfruit vines, and peeked into the small yard. Anneke was sitting in their garden on a rare afternoon off. She'd been away from Tansen visiting family for six months, but had just returned that week and was settling back into life here. While she was gone, I'd also returned home for a brief visit to see family and friends, my first time back to the States since arriving in Nepal. Boarding the return flight here was one of the hardest things I'd ever done.

On this particular mid-summer afternoon, I looked forward to talking with Anneke about everything that had been going on with the medical team lately. Seeing me at her gate, she welcomed me over, then ducked inside to fetch a new mosquito coil from her kitchen. As I settled into one of the plastic patio chairs, I thought about the reason I wanted to speak with her, wondering how to bring it up, how even to articulate it to myself. With nearly a year still left in Nepal, I wondered whether I could make it. Feeling like a frayed, burnt-out shell of my former self, I needed some help getting there. Which is how I found myself swatting at mosquitos in

Anneke's garden that afternoon.

"Of course, of course, come and have a chat!" She welcomed me over with a good-humored smile. Anneke was one of those people — and Tansen could boast of many — whose welcome was *welcoming* indeed. It felt wrong, somehow, to bring the dark cloud of my frustration there.

"I'm having such a hard time, Anneke. How do you do it?"

I began to vent about all the sloppy work that kept me on the medical wards until late in the evening most days, correcting charts and revising medication lists awash with errors. I shared the pain of perceived slights at being one of the rare women on a mostly male physician team on the medical wards. Or the frustration with patients who asked the same questions over and over, seeming not to pause long enough in their anxious questioning even to hear the answers. Or my own inner frustrations, feeling alone, unseen, unknown.

Tears welled up, and I struggled to hold them back, feeling miserable the whole time.

"You know, while I was home a few weeks ago, I went to this global medical missions conference. It was huge, with thousands of young people on fire to join God's mission to the world. I kept hearing the kinds of messages that used to get *me* fired up for missions — the very things that, at least I *thought*, meant I should come here in the first place. This seemed like such a clear calling then. But now? I was so cynical there, Anneke! I felt disillusioned, sitting in those sessions thinking, '*It's not really like that, friends. It's a hard slog, from start to finish.*' How have I changed so much?"

I hesitated to tell Anneke that I didn't even want to come back to Tansen, but then plowed ahead. "While I was home, Dan emailed me to say that things on the medical ward were getting really toxic. With Dev, especially. I didn't even want to come back, honestly. It was all I could do to get on the flight to come here again. It feels like everything is spiraling out of control, and I worry it's all because of me!"

When I finished, my voice catching on the lump growing

in the back of my throat, Anneke leaned back thoughtfully for a minute, regarding me with a look of genuine concern, yet with a certain spark in her eyes. She was possessed of an indefatigable humor that grew, I suspected, from the soil of experiences even more challenging than those I was describing.

"Yes, Becca. Nepal has that effect. It brings you to the end of yourself. It does for everyone. It did for me. But. . . Indeed. . . something *has* changed, yes. . . I noticed it when I first got back. You are not the same Becca who was here when I left."

Her words were unexpected. It was sad to hear I was noticeably different. But I also took some small comfort in being seen. It felt good to know that I wasn't alone.

"I think it must be very difficult for you here, Becca," she went on. "You have such high standards, and such good medical training. How hard it must be to work here, in this setting, where things are so different from how they are back home."

She paused again, as if just remembering something. "You know, Becca, you came to mind this morning as I was reading today's Scripture, and I really didn't know why. But now I think I know."

She got up and ducked back into the house to get her Bible, then emerged, setting a swarm of mosquitos buzzing as she casually flipped through the tissue-thin pages. She said she had been reading a passage about one of Jesus's followers and close friends, a woman who anoints His feet during a dinner party with an expensive jar of perfume, and then wipes them with her hair. It is an extravagant gift, over the top, really, and would have been wildly inappropriate — then, as now.

Anneke described that, at a time when a jar of perfume would have served as a woman's entire inheritance, her gift was so costly as to be quite embarrassing to those present. It's clear she gave all she had to Jesus. She offered Him her possession of greatest value, her entire net worth, and held back nothing. She was not even worried about her own reputation, which surely would have suffered as a result of this demonstration. She was giving Him her whole self.

"It was such a costly thing to do, Becca. And at such risk."

My curiosity was piqued now. I leaned in. I had no idea where she was going with this.

"You know, I can't help but think how very difficult this all must be for you. You come here with great accomplishments, your standards of care, your way of doing things. I think of everything you left back in America." She did not say this with a hint of reprisal or accusation, holding instead that same generous gaze. I heard compassion in her voice, even a note of pity.

"But I wonder, Becca, if perhaps that's why you came to mind, then?"

I looked at her, still confused. She explained, "It's as if you came here to give all you have, to sacrifice everything that's precious to you — even your accomplishments, talents, gifts — so that you could offer them to Him. I wonder if that's maybe what you are doing here, Becca."

Sitting there, I considered what she was saying. Did I feel like my talents and gifts were being wasted, that I could serve elsewhere for far greater "profit," higher "impact," more "effect?" It was true that I harbored a deep, unspoken suspicion that my efforts *were* being wasted. After all this time, what had really been accomplished, anyway? But Anneke said that's what Judas thought of this woman's devotion, too. And yet Jesus praised her sacrifice. He declared she had done a beautiful thing by anointing His body, preparing Him for the heart-wrenching sacrifice *He* was about to make. She had poured out her love on Him.

This conversation with Anneke left me wondering if this was, in fact, where God wanted me. Just to *be* with Him. Her words reminded me of something I heard Willem say once, that "missions is all about going, not much about doing, and everything about being." If my being in Tansen was simply an opportunity to offer my gifts, experiences and whole being to Jesus, then I could do that, for His sake.

J. R. R. Tolkien once said that the praise of the praiseworthy is above all reward. I had just been given immense affirmation from someone I deeply respected, and it felt like an undeserved gift. I knew that in beautiful humility, Anneke had just extended far more credit than I was due. Struck with a biting pang of conscience, I wanted to tell her the whole truth, sharing again how far I really was from giving my whole self. Being an impossible-to-please perfectionist with unattainable standards, and approaching my work with a bitter attitude, is not exactly giving my "all" joyfully from a heart of love and gratitude.

Yet in that moment, even amidst inner protest, something shifted and loosened. A shaft of light crept in, its beam hopeful and luminous and airy. Within that thin ray of light I felt seen, appreciated, and validated. I was called to this particular moment in time, for this particular role, bearing compassionate witness and presence in suffering. It was as though, in speaking those words of Mary's sacrifice for Jesus, Anneke had made them a reality in my own story, too.

CHAPTER THIRTY
Buccha Karaabi Chha

We take for granted the expectation that each child born into the world will survive and thrive. But in Tansen, a child's life is far more precarious. As I was checking in on each ward at the start of overnight duty one evening, the pediatrics team notified me of an infant who had been delivered the day prior. She was born prematurely at thirty-five weeks, around a month early, and was not doing well.

"Buccha karaabi chha," the nurse had said, shaking her head mournfully with a cluck of her tongue. *That baby is serious.*

She was in the newborn nursery, stashed away from her mother in a "protective" incubator. Yet I'd learned that a simple skin-to-skin approach known as "Kangaroo Care" is known to give better outcomes for these premature babies. Especially in resource-limited settings like ours, and for very sick babies like these, it has been shown time and again to save infant lives the world over.

A mother's body is finely tuned to provide exactly what her infant needs — even to the point of adjusting her own body's surface temperature, ever so slightly, to ensure that the baby is kept comfortably warm. So in tune are the two bodies that their breathing patterns begin to match. Their hearts even start beating in sync, coordinating their rhythms through a mechanism no more (or less) sophisticated than the galvanic skin response. Infants cared for in this way tend to feed and grow better, with improved cognitive and social development, and show benefits lasting well into childhood. This infant was too weak to breastfeed, instead receiving breastmilk through a syringe. Still, there seemed to be no reason why she couldn't be brought out of the incubator, and wrapped close against her mother's chest in a skin-to-skin position. I pointed this out to the nurse on duty, who looked at me skeptically. How could simply holding an infant to your chest be better than a high-tech, Western incubator?

Our nurses and new mothers alike seemed to favor the impressive blue plastic box, with its portholes on the sides and radiant warming-lights, perceiving it to be the more advanced (read: "better") way to keep infants warm, safe, and monitored. I thought it made the infant look like a tiny astronaut, about to be unwittingly launched to the moon in her own miniature space capsule.

When I spoke with the mom about holding her baby, she also recoiled. There was no hint of hesitancy in her body language. It was an unequivocal gesture of refusal. Thinking perhaps I had miscommunicated the message in Nepali, I asked the nurse to clarify my suggestion, and she reluctantly joined me at the bedside. The mother, however, would have no part of it. I was confused. It made no sense — neither her refusal, nor my own nursing staff's reluctance to support this clearly beneficial advice. And the stakes were huge. Her child's survival hung in the balance.

Then a sobering thought occurred to me. If I insisted on this alternate approach and the infant died anyway, was it possible the hospital could be blamed for it? I began to imagine an angry mob gathering at the front gate, clamoring for justice in the face of perceived sub-standard care. It seemed unlikely, but maybe an awareness of that possibility had colored the nurse's response, too. Whatever was at the root of this mother's resistance, it seemed part of something deeper, more culturally ingrained. This wasn't the first time a woman on our newborn ward seemed reluctant to bond with her sick infant. Maybe it was rooted in an understandable — and realistic — fear of losing them. This might explain why the Nepali naming ceremony isn't held until the newborn is at least a week old, as if the infant must prove he can make it past life's first major milestone in order to be given the communal welcome a name confers. Too many are lost before then.

I went to look through the chart again and noticed, scrawled on one of the handwritten outpatient forms, the phrase "NND x 1" — shorthand for one prior neonatal death in the mother's history. She had already lost her first child. As I read further, I saw that the death had come mere days after birth, just as this one threatened to. In an American maternity chart, that history would be front and center, as something so fortunately rare in the developed world. Not so here.

Suddenly, this woman's reluctance made more sense. Cringing, I went out into the hallway where the infant's father and uncle were waiting for news of the child.

"She's very sick," I told them. "Very, very, sick. She may not make it."

The father looked stricken, sharing that this exact scenario had played out less than two years earlier. It had been a healthy term infant, born vaginally in an uncomplicated delivery, after an unremarkable pregnancy. Yet that baby, too, had died within his first few days of life.

"Pakeko tyo," he'd said. *The baby was infected.* The father used a term that literally translates as "over-ripe" or "rotten," the same word you'd use for an eggplant that was no longer salvageable, even for curry.

That infant had also received antibiotics in his first few days of life, but to no avail. The history's fragmented pieces suddenly came together. This sounded like a case of "recurrent GBS sepsis," an illness occurring in infants exposed to certain bacteria (specifically, Group B Strep) in the mother's birth canal during delivery. This bacterium can cause severe infection and sometimes death, even when the mother has no symptoms at all.

In high-resource countries, it is standard practice to screen for this bacterium with a simple culture swab around the time of delivery. It's one of the core measures of routine prenatal care. If that testing indicates the bacteria is present, women receive two doses of penicillin at delivery — amazingly, still effective nearly a century after its discovery. This simple approach virtually eliminates the risk of passing along the bacteria to the infant during the birthing process. It's automatic, part of the "routine checklist" of considerations. So much so, in fact, that I asked about it when I first arrived in Tansen, noticing it wasn't done here.

Our head of obstetrics, an extremely competent Nepali surgeon with decades of experience, waved her hand dismissively at my question. "That is a luxury reserved for countries who have already gotten their perinatal morbidity down to single digits from the other causes. That's what you do when you want to tackle the *last* one percent."

The most-cited causes of perinatal mortality in developing nations like Nepal include preterm birth and complications during delivery (such as asphyxia, or lack of oxygen). Yet even in this woman's case — unknown Group B Strep status, in the setting of a prior neonatal death from *any* cause — penicillin could have been given automatically, as a preventive measure. In this case, it might have had lifesaving effect. She lost her little girl a few hours later.

I recalled another baby brought to the ED by her parents a day after delivering at a local health post. The tiny infant hadn't cried since birth, and was lying floppily on the gurney with a very strange look about her. Then it occurred to me that her corneas were opaque; she wasn't even blinking her bone-dry eyes. The soft space of her scalp, called the *fontanelle*, was bulging and pulsating, an ominous sign of a severe brain infection. This was also likely a case of Group B Strep. And those parents had lost another infant in exactly same way one year earlier.

It's a challenging conundrum — giving antibiotics to all

laboring mothers would dramatically increase the risk of adverse reactions and bacterial resistance. Yet with few labs anywhere in the country that can perform bacterial culture testing, screening every pregnant woman isn't feasible either. And so, in a world where "routine screening" for this common bacterium is still not routine, the health system is forced to play the odds that most babies will do alright. And even if 99 percent do, tragedy still strikes once in a hundred times — more often, of course, for mothers already colonized with the bacteria. Mothers, that is, who are more likely to endure this more than once. America doesn't tolerate such odds for itself. Yet globally — and even in segments of America — the situation for mothers and infants is *at least* this bad, well into the twenty-first century. Most of the world considers it acceptable if the risks are *only* one percent.

Look back about two hundred years, and you can find a time when the Western world was not so far from where Nepal is now. For context, this was when Europe found itself embroiled in a series of Napoleonic wars, Beethoven was unleashing masterpieces into the world, Dickens was preparing to introduce the characters of his incomparable fiction, and an Industrial Revolution was dawning on the horizon. Infant mortality was extremely high at that time. Worldwide, it's generally agreed that roughly one in five children died during their first year of life throughout the nineteenth century; half did not live past puberty.

Since then, child mortality rates have declined more than tenfold in the West — remarkable progress in the span of less than two centuries. Such progress has arguably brought benefit to every corner of the globe. Yet disparities between high- and low-income countries remain extreme, and the gap is growing larger. Meanwhile, every day, families around the world lose infants to these preventable infections.

I had come from a world in which these tragedies are vanishingly rare, a world where I had attended many normal deliveries of healthy infants and happy moms, where a "bad outcome" was so thankfully unimaginable that it was seared it into my memory if it did happen. In Nepal, I lost count, in my first six months alone, of the number of lifeless infants I'd held. During one series of calls, we lost an infant each night — three babies in one week — despite prolonged resuscitation efforts after each delivery. As I sat with one of these mothers in the silence, after sharing the unthinkable, I saw her phone buzzing over and over with congratulatory messages. Sickened, I realized her family and friends would hear soon enough.

CHAPTER THIRTY-ONE
Insights from the Burn Ward

Rounding on the children's burn unit was another part of our daily routine for those working on the pediatric inpatient team, a service on which we all took periodic rotations. These kids were mainly cared for by surgeons — from their initial surgeries, to wound dressings and daily burn washes, to eventual skin grafting.

Yet medical management plays a role as well, treating infections, correcting blood chemistry problems, and ensuring that the children received high-calorie nutrition. Myriad issues crop up when our largest organ — the protective outer covering of skin, which forms a vital barrier shielding our squishy insides from the world outside — is breached. We had to stay vigilant every day for even the most subtle signs of infection brewing in their little bodies.

And, just as you would expect, pain control plays a huge part, too. The need for adequate pain management is as crucial as good nutrition or infection management. It's all interconnected — a loss of the protective skin barrier sets the stage for an immune system at risk, while the body works overtime to keep its temperature and fluid balance stable. The skin, of course, with its sweat glands, sophisticated blood supply control, and insulating layer of fat, plays a critical role in all that. Patients with severe burns often have to take in more than double their usual number of calories just to keep up with these extra energy demands. Pain adds even more stress to an already taxed system, further interfering with the body's hard work of healing.

Kids are usually not thrilled to see *any* doctor enter the room. Yet on most medical wards, our young patients might be in and out after a couple days of treatment for gastroenteritis or pneumonia, so they were generally more bewildered by us than frightened. I suppose they didn't yet know enough to be scared.

Not so with our burn patients. After many days, weeks, and even months — for the truly lucky ones who lived that long — they knew our presence meant pain. The pain of being examined, at a bare minimum, as we asked them to lift a scalded arm, or turn a raw and blistered torso. Just as often, our appearance portended pain that came with daily burn washes, or from poking an IV needle into one of the few remaining veins on their bruised little hands, ankles, or scalps. For them, our appearance on the ward meant that they would not be left alone quite yet. Their faces twisted with agony unique to experiences of prolonged suffering, as they watched our crew filing in, helpless in the face of our best-intentioned plans for their recovery.

Even more heart-rending, though, were the children of that six-crib burn unit who did *not* cry. There were some children whose long-suffering faces told a story of more physical pain endured in their young lives than anyone should have to bear, *ever*. It was certainly more pain than I could imagine, even at five times their age. I came to the bedside of one child, squatting down to eye level, and introduced myself. She whimpered softly in response, terror visible in her eyes. I tried, ever so gingerly, to reposition her seared right arm and trunk so I could sneak my stethoscope up to her heart.

Before any big movements or treatments, I liked to give a small dose of morphine, something that I strongly felt should be given at regularly scheduled intervals, to avoid the peaks and troughs of breakthrough pain when their "as needed" doses wore off. We even had a weight-based morphine protocol that Anneke had written out. Yet I noticed that these orders would frequently go unfulfilled by our reluctant nursing staff, who readily gave other pain medicines but were inexplicably wary of morphine.

I felt caught between a moral imperative to relieve suffering, on the one hand, and a cultural attitude against the very means of doing so, on the other. It was distressing to inflict pain unnecessarily — pain that interferes with healing and impairs trust — especially when a remedy was so clearly at hand. It seemed a problem at once disturbing and easily fixed.

Initially I met this resistance with exasperation. "How could they *not* want to relieve the pain of these kids?" I knew it wasn't heartless indifference, for these nurses were the furthest thing from it. I was always moved by their unflagging dedication and gentle, compassionate way with each child. It certainly wasn't oversight or negligence either, for they were, without exception, as conscientious and diligent as they were kind. Our hospital's nurses were professionals of the highest order. Their strict standards, like their starched white uniforms, harkened back to another medical era entirely. What, then, could explain their hesitancy?

It seemed as though there were some general misunderstandings around morphine, for starters, not unlike those I heard back in the States. "Isn't morphine a bit extreme?" patients used to ask me. "I mean, they gave that to dying soldiers on the battlefield in *Saving Private Ryan!*" It seemed that attitudes were no different in Nepal, half a world away.

I tried to explore other reasons by casually chatting with my nursing colleagues, but even there I ran into trouble. These were strong, competent staff, most of them with decades' more experience in medicine than I had. I walked over to one of the senior nurses one morning and waited until she was done talking with a colleague.

"I was just wondering about this patient, Didi," I began, as I unfolded a chart. "There's this order for *'morphine with dressing changes and repositioning.'* It doesn't look like it's been given in a few days, though. . ."

She let out a nervous laugh and bobbled her head, but I could see that her eyes were not laughing. I didn't know what to make of her response.

Pressing a little further, I added in an off-handed sort of way, "I noticed we don't really use morphine very much on the children's burn ward."

I paused, hoping she would offer some insight as to why that was. Instead, she suddenly stood up a little straighter, with a serious, slightly affronted expression, as if I had questioned her team's standards of care. I let it go.

It wasn't until later on, talking it over with Willem, that the rationale became clearer. These nurses had seen their fair share of children die year after year, their little bodies overwhelmed by the stress of extensive burns. During one stretch the year before I arrived, they'd seen a particularly bad string of deaths, one right after the other, all in a matter of weeks. These were children for whom the nurses had lovingly cared hour upon hour, day after day. They had tended to their wounds, and changed their dressings, and fed them by hand. And then, after weeks of care, each of those children had, in the end, succumbed to death.

Furthermore, it sounded like some of those children had died shortly after receiving even a small dose of morphine — appropriately dosed for weight, far too little to suppress the respiratory system and cause death. It may well have been that this modicum of pain relief allowed them to relax sufficiently to die. Yet in the minds of the nursing staff, the morphine itself was to blame — not the underlying process of death, which was by then inevitable. This seemingly causative link, once made, was tough to uncouple.

It was an important lesson that those who, on the surface, appear to be acting irrationally may have their reasons, and quite good ones at that. The nurses' reasoning was certainly better-founded than I had appreciated at first glance. I also realized why change can be hard, especially in a medical hierarchy that limits open communication within the team. Here, an uncompromising ethic of respect limited the nurses' open criticism of, or even true dialogue with, physicians seeking change.

CHAPTER THIRTY-TWO
The Not-Horse Chipper

While boiling a pot of tea one morning in the kitchen, I could barely contain my excitement to see Callum and Midge, who were visiting Tansen that week. As our organization's pastoral care team, they were based in Kathmandu, but came out to Tansen on the Buck for one week every other month. It gave them a chance to connect with each member of the Tansen ex-pat team, and their visits always provided much-needed support.

A few minutes later they appeared on the path out front and called through our kitchen window. I stepped outside holding a tray of steaming teacups and foil-packaged ginger cookies from the local shop. We settled into wicker benches on the porch, the White Lake valley stretching out below us. That sight still took my breath away.

Midge sipped her tea and exclaimed, "It's so good to see you, Becca! How have you been, since we saw you last?"

"Well. . . it's been a lot." I took in a deep breath. "To be honest, I've felt pretty overwhelmed most of the time. I mean, I love living here, and really enjoy our team dinners, Bible studies, Saturday worship services — it's all so beautiful, living in community like this. And I am definitely learning a *ton* of skills in tropical medicine. Still, it feels like I have to learn it the hard way, sometimes."

"What do you mean, 'the hard way'?" Callum asked.

"Well. . . There's just so much *death*, Callum. I'm not used to this — it's different from working in America. I mean, I knew it would be, of course. This was a massive move — not just geographically, but also culturally, relationally, professionally. I feel like I hear all these discouraging messages ringing in my head constantly. *'You dress funny. You walk funny. We can't understand your strange, foreign-accented Nepali. You're the wrong gender to lead, or even to teach. You don't fit in here.'* And on top of it all, *'You must not be a very good doctor either, since your patients keep dying.'*"

Callum and Midge looked at me with alarm. I had just shared a lot. "Wow, Becca. It sounds like you're in a very different place from where you were a few months ago, when we saw you in Kathmandu."

"Maybe so. . ." I looked out again at the White Lake, then back at my friends. "I mean, it's a struggle to buy even the most basic goods — like milk, ladled by the liter into plastic bags and tied with a rubber band, which we have to run home and boil right away, before it goes bad." Midge nodded her head with understanding.

"And the other day, a resident actually asked me if I was working in Nepal because I couldn't get a job in my own country! It's like he thought the reason I was here was because I wasn't good enough to qualify for a job in America!"

Callum laughed, "Well, obviously *that's* ludicrous, Becca. But I can imagine it's difficult to hear that sort of assumption, just the same."

"Right. Even though most of these 'messages' aren't spoken aloud, it's still hard to feel like I'm doing anything good, or that I even have my footing yet."

"You're right, Becca. This kind of international move is really challenging," Midge agreed. "People who have only known their own, familiar culture may have a hard time appreciating what you're going through right now, and just how profoundly disruptive this cross-cultural experience can be to one's core sense of self."

"Especially when those messages are bombarding you for months at a time, with little to counter it! I just wish someone would tell me I'm doing a good job from time to time. But when I mentioned that to someone on the team recently, they just told me I'm such an *American*, always in need of reassurance. That really stung. Seriously, I think we *all* need that kind of reassurance, every now and then. Isn't that right?"

I felt tears coming on, and took a deep breath. "It feels like this move to Nepal uprooted me overnight. Suddenly, I woke up and found I didn't have anyone around me who's known me for any real length of time. Everything is unfamiliar, from language, to food and cultural customs, to the medicine I'm practicing. Even *within* our ex-pat community, where we all speak English, there are still so many different countries represented, each with their own, funny little particularities."

"Yes, Becca, that's so true," Callum agreed. "We feel the same thing even in Kathmandu, being British."

Midge nodded too. "Australians, Americans, even other Europeans like the Dutch — they all have different ways of communicating. It's subtle, but you're right, it can feel like totally different worlds sometimes."

"And take the other night. . . I was walking home with Willem and Anneke from a really beautiful Saturday service at the Guest House. Maybe I was feeling especially vulnerable — I often do, after a beautiful worship service — but I was really overwhelmed, and thought I was going to start crying. As we went along in the dark, I tried to fight back tears. It was embarrassing to be so emotional, especially when both of them seem so strong all of the time. I don't even think they noticed I was that upset. Or maybe they did. Either way, nobody said *anything*. I felt so alone!"

Midge looked surprised at this. "That doesn't sound like them. I'm sure they had no idea how you were feeling, Becca. Maybe because it was dark, they couldn't tell you were so upset. If they knew, they definitely would have said something to comfort you, I'm sure of that."

"Yeah, you're right, Midge. It still felt awful though. I sometimes wish I could just go home, but I'm not a quitter. I gave a commitment of two years. But now, with sixteen months left? That feels like forever. We had a 'going-away party' at the Guest House last week for one of the families, and I just kept thinking, *'I wish it were me.'* Then I felt guilty for even thinking that."

"It's clear you're trying hard to give your patients the best possible care," Midge comforted. "You're doing your best, every day. And even if it doesn't seem like it, the other missionaries are struggling with that too — all the death here, all the poverty. We know it's hard for everyone, even the more experienced ones."

"We've also noticed," Callum added, "that it can be difficult for all of you on the team to debrief with one another about these things. For whatever reason, maybe because the Tansen team is quite small, you each tend to hold it within yourselves, and save it up for when someone comes in from the outside. It's a lot to hold, while waiting for our visits every two months."

I nodded in agreement. "That makes a lot of sense. I think we're all so worried about bringing each other down, when the work is already so hard. It's true, we just don't talk about these things very much."

"You know, Becca, I've begun asking a simple question in my prayers: *'Jesus, when have You felt this way?'* I find it helpful when I'm feeling alone, or disappointed in friendships, or even tempted to despair."

"That's good, Callum, I like that. *'Jesus, Companion for the journey.'* I'll try praying that myself. I've actually tried to be better about prayer. It's been hard to connect with God lately. For the past month or so, I've doubled down on my spiritual disciplines. I'm fasting and praying during the usual lunch hour, and meditating on Scripture — the Beatitudes, actually! You know, where Jesus speaks of those who are 'blessed' — the merciful and the peacemakers, those who are pure in heart, and poor in spirit? I really need to be more of all those things."

At this, an astonished laugh escaped Midge. "Oh my goodness, Becca! I don't know that the *Beatitudes* are exactly the place to go with all this angst. You're setting quite a high standard for yourself, wouldn't you say?"

Then she looked at me thoughtfully for a minute, and said, "I wonder if you take a lot upon yourself, Becca. You have such a keen sense of responsibility, in both your teaching and your patient care."

"Absolutely, Midge. Actually, about that. . ." I began telling them about the incident with Dev that happened a few weeks earlier, when he'd noted a patient's critically low hemoglobin level in the chart, but did nothing to address the problem of her anemia. That spilled over into an account of when he missed a fatal intestinal perforation, because he'd failed to follow up on the X-ray result showing free air under the diaphragm.

"I want to make sure our patients get the care they need, and I always try to model high-quality care in our rounds. But I can tell I'm becoming increasingly impatient, and also maybe a little arrogant about my own high standards. Being on my game, honing my skills to perfection, had always been my safe zone, you know? It's where I go when I'm feeling uncertain of myself. Like, in this new world of tropical diseases and traumatic deaths, at least I know how to manage *anemia*, or recognize a surgical emergency. And of course, that could mean saving a life."

Continuing on, I reflected, "Still, I worry that this perfectionist tendency, my *need* to be right, is forcing a deeper wedge between me and the residents. It makes them feel defensive, nitpicked for errors. Even criticisms that I thought were fairly mild, like the way I handled that anemia case, cut the residents to the quick. It was clear in the hurt and anger I saw in Dev's eyes. It's made him and the others afraid to work with me, for fear that I'll shame them by exposing more mistakes."

"That sounds like a tough situation, Becca. It must be frustrating," Midge said kindly.

The irony, I knew, was that my most natural response, to protect my pride, was establishing a vicious cycle of fear and shame that inflicted even *more* wounds to pride. I didn't know how to start over with the residents. Thinking I needed to project strength, I was too fearful to show the vulnerability I constantly felt about my own uncertainties. I felt utterly helpless to disrupt that cycle. Even as I could see it happening, I had no idea how to do it any differently.

It was also becoming clear that a fear of failure renders impossible the risk-taking necessary in learning. Over time, I knew, fear hardens into a crust of invulnerability, the refusal to accept correction or acknowledge mistakes, because the vulnerability needed for growth is just too painful, too scary. The life of a medical learner is characterized by profound insecurity, the threat of a potentially fatal mistake lurking around each corner of the ward, with senior supervising physicians like me always there at the ready to point out mistakes.

Still, I knew even *that* wasn't the whole story. "The truth is, when I think about Maya and Tenzing, and all the other Nepali residents here, I know I'm not being fair when I talk about 'the residents' all lumped into one big category. Most of them are fabulous — intelligent, kind, always ready to help, and eager to learn. Dev is probably in a tough spot himself, but I wouldn't know, because I never take the time to ask. I just wish I had some guidance on how to teach and connect with these residents!" How desperately I felt the need to be mentored in this space of uncertainty. I wondered what difference such coaching from more seasoned physician-leaders in the hospital might make.

"But we're all tired, I know that. Most of the other ex-pat physicians have been here a lot longer than I, and they already work so hard themselves." I yearned to scream into the void, pouring out my fears and processing my failures with colleagues. Yet in our context, where chronic staffing shortages stretched everyone too thin, complaining felt so. . . *gauche.*

Pausing to take another sip of tea, I tried to change the subject. "Anyway, do you want to hear something wild? The most absurd thing happened the other day! These two twenty-something white girls walked into the Tansen Emergency Department, of all places. They were American tourists, and one of them was sick with a stomach bug. When I walked over to introduce myself, I couldn't for the life of me remember how to start a medical encounter in English! Maybe it was being in Tansen's ED, where all I ever use is Nepali, but I was totally flummoxed for a minute. It was weird!" I laughed sheepishly.

Callum and Midge chuckled along, grinning. Then Callum gently brought the conversation back. Looking thoughtful, he asked, "Have you ever heard that story about Michelangelo, Becca? The one where he was commissioned to carve a life-sized horse statue?"

I shook my head.

"Well, a bystander passed by and asked him how he planned to bring forth such noble equine glory from a block of marble. And the great artist replied, 'I just chip away all the parts that aren't horse.'"

I looked at him quizzically, hoping he would explain this cryptic parable. "It's like that with God, sometimes," he continued. "However painful that chipping process may be, however much still remains to be done, that's what He's doing, too. Knocking off all our rough edges, a little bit at a time, to slowly smooth and shape us into something really beautiful. Remember — as He remakes us in His image, we're just works in progress. But I know it's not easy."

"And God meets us wherever we are, Becca," Midge added gently.

Grateful for their kindness, especially after I'd revealed so much of my own flawed weakness, I felt tears again gather at the corners of my eyes. I nodded, thankful for the profound meaning-making they had each offered me, in their own way.

Too overcome to speak, I turned out toward the valley again, as we sat for a while in silence.

CHAPTER THIRTY-THREE
Dealing with It

One day, I arrived at the pediatric OPD after lunch and tried to settle into a rhythm for the afternoon. The evening before, one of our residents had left to attend a wedding in Kathmandu, and wouldn't be in for the rest of the week. He also hadn't arranged for a replacement, so my stack of charts and X-rays was thicker than usual. I tried not to resent his absence. This sort of thing didn't happen every day, but it was still more regular than I was used to back home. It also seemed unnecessarily last-minute. Surely he'd had *some* advance notice for a wedding?

Glancing at the top chart in the stack, I called in my first patient, a little girl whose weight mapped out below the second percentile for her age and height. Given how tiny she was, she definitely qualified for services. In fact, our community health coordinator had already seen her, recommending a referral to Tansen's "Inpatient Re-feeding Center" at the bottom of the chart. Malnutrition was unfortunately a common diagnosis in pediatric clinics across Nepal, though rates were definitely improving. I reached into a bin of papers mounted on the wall and grabbed an admission packet.

The charts used at Tansen were simple and functional. On

arrival, patients were handed a sheet of stiff, blue-lined cardstock stamped with the Tansen Hospital logo. The header was printed with the patient's name, date of birth, town of residence, and a unique medical record number. Dates of birth were often estimates. More than once, when I asked patients how old they were (to confirm I had the correct chart), they would look back at me with a quizzical expression and say, "Well, you've got the chart right there — how old *am* I?"

After handing the admission packet to the child's mother and explaining next steps in her care, I reached for the next chart in the stack. Glancing at the pile of X-ray films, I thought, *I should really get to those.* Noticing that the next patient had been held over from the morning session, I vowed to look at the X-rays right after seeing him.

Leaning into the hallway, I called out the next child's name. "Prakash Bahadur?" A mother stood up, leading her twelve-year-old son down the hall and into my small exam room. When we were all settled onto wooden stools, she began to share that her son had been having persistent headaches over the past several weeks.

I started to take his medical history, asking details about the timing of his headaches, their quality, associated symptoms, and how he was doing overall, both in school and at home. I had barely gotten three questions in when his mother interrupted to ask, pleadingly, *"Yo kina ho, Daktara, kina?" Why is this, Doctor, why?* I could hear the urgency in her voice, full of fear as she pressed me for an answer. Her anxiety struck me as out of proportion to the problem.

Replying in Nepali, I explained, "I'm not sure yet why he's having these headaches. Let me ask some more questions. And then I have to examine him." She frowned and reluctantly bobbled her head side to side, looking acutely dissatisfied that I couldn't wave my hands and magically elicit a diagnosis and cure with one sweeping gesture.

At first, I assumed his problem would be something benign, like stress headaches, the most common explanation for this sort of complaint in children. She was clearly worried, an anxious mother concerned about her only son. The more I heard, however, the more worried I became. His headaches were indistinct, rather of vague and "all over." He wasn't an anxious child himself, with good friendships at school and no reports of bullying. He didn't have any nausea or vision problems, but hadn't been eating well, and looked pretty thin. What troubled me most was that his headaches were worse in the morning, right after he woke up. With headaches, a positional component can be a dangerous sign, potentially indicating pressure from a tumor or fluid that increases when lying flat.

A complete neurological exam revealed nothing, fortunately. All the same, something was telling me to order imaging of his brain, since they lived far away, and this might be a rare encounter with *any* health system. They could easily get a CT scan just twenty minutes from our hospital, but it would be expensive: a thousand Nepali rupees for taxi fare there and back, five or six thousand more for the CT scan, plus any lost wages for mom if she had to miss additional work to take him there. All told, it could easily cost the exorbitant sum of USD $65 to $70, over a month's income for people living on two dollars a day, not to mention the risk of radiation exposure to his young brain.

It was always hard to make these decisions. A patient needed to be sick enough to justify the costs of such imaging, yet also stable enough to make the trip there and back. I tried to weigh the options, but kept imagining a large brain cancer growing, eventually compressing his brain's breathing center, perhaps killing him instantly one night while he slept. I shuddered to think of this mother walking into that nightmare scenario.

At times like these, I generally worked out my ideas on paper in the chart, organizing and gathering my thoughts while buying some time before making a final recommendation. As I was deliberating, I looked up just in time to see the young boy swaying back and forth, eyes rolled up in his head. He looked like he was about to pass out. Then, a fraction of a second later, I watched in horror as he tilted his chin up and sent a stream of semi-particulate, orange-brown vomitus hurling forward in one graceful, slow-motion arc through the air.

The stream landed with direct impact on my desk, narrowly missing me as I jumped to one side. It drenched his chart, soaking through my carefully crafted note. It also bathed a stack of other patients' charts, arrayed neatly in a line along the edge of my desk. It even managed to work its way between the stack of X-ray films piled in the desk's corner, leaving a nasty residue that made them virtually unreadable. I regretted having put off that task ten minutes earlier.

"Just wait in the hall," I snapped, as I hastily ushered mother and child out of the room. It was almost more than I could bear. This unwelcome incident sealed my decision to proceed with a CT scan. Sudden, unexpected vomiting was another potential danger signal, indicating that there could already be pressure on the brainstem. I stepped outside to complete the triplicate order form at the nursing station and handed it to the mother, who looked relieved that her concern had been heard, and something was being done about it.

Returning to the exam room, I stood there for a few seconds in stunned silence, struggling to balance empathy for the child with my own disgust. It took a minute to absorb the full impact of the clean-up ahead, the thought of it paralyzing. With the help of our clinic's medical assistants and tireless housekeeping staff, we managed to get everything sopped up and rinsed off as best we could, setting some of it out to dry on a sunny windowsill. I tried not to think of how these other charts would be handed back to patients at the end of the day, once dried out, to be brought home until their next OPD visit. This vomiting incident was the sort of thing I couldn't have imagined handling a year earlier, yet here I was dealing with it, like it or not. Much of life in Nepal, I was discovering, consisted simply of "dealing with it" and moving on.

In the end, I never found out what happened to that child. Like many stories at Tansen — whether because we had no centralized medical record in which to track outcomes, or because they were seen by another physician or simply didn't follow up — this one would have to go without a resolution. In the case of young Prakash, as with many patients from Nepal, I still wonder what happened to him, questioning whether I should have done anything differently.

CHAPTER THIRTY-FOUR

Jesus the Homeless

One chilly afternoon in January, having worked in Tansen for just over a year, I was relaxing at home after a busy night in the hospital and catching up on podcasts. A story from the BBC World News came on, documenting the plight of Syrian refugees fleeing violence in the city of Aleppo. Temperatures there were near freezing, even colder than in Nepal.

The news anchor spoke of insufficient clothing, blankets, and shoes. Among the millions of displaced refugees, the reporter said, many women and young children were suffering, as snow had begun covering the ground. Without even the most basic tarp shelters available, many were already dying of exposure.

Sitting there at my desk in our unheated home, a warm blanket cozied around my shoulders, I began to shake with tears. I wept over the images this radio newsfeed so readily conjured in my mind's eye. It all seemed so close, so readily imaginable. This was a story of the suffering of people who could be my next-door neighbors. Given a different set of circumstances, it could easily have been me. Before moving to Nepal, this humanitarian crisis would have been the sad plight of others, the suffering of masses "out there" in the world, far beyond my own lived experience. Yet in the year

I'd spent in Tansen, these stories had gradually morphed into the plight of my own neighbors and friends. The suffering of faces I could imagine. Pain I could grieve.

In downtown Buffalo, New York, at the corner of Church and Pearl Streets, there stands a bronze statue. Or more accurately, there *lies* a statue, taking up most of one park bench. It is the rumpled form of a man stretched out on one side, a blanket pulled up over his head and obscuring his face. One hand hangs limply to the side, slightly outstretched. And then, only after looking closely, do you see it — the scar of a deep, penetrating gash on the palm of that outstretched hand.

I came upon a photograph of that statue, *Jesus the Homeless,* one afternoon in Tansen, and it was on my mind during hospital rounds later that week, when a nurse called for Tenzing and me to come quickly to a patient in Bed #27 who was "gasping." Hurrying to his bedside, we arrived to find a small, disheveled man lying stiffly in bed. He appeared to be choking, the whites of his eyes wide with fear as his jaw made rhythmic, rolling mastications, the only movement in his otherwise rigid frame. He said nothing when I asked him how he was, though his eyes glanced briefly to meet mine before returning to stare into the middle distance. I slipped on a rubber glove and gently pried his lower jaw open, discovering that his mouth was filled with chunks of boiled egg. Odd, strangling noises suddenly began to emit from the back of his throat.

I'd been working there for over a year and never faced anything quite like this. Normally, when someone is choking, you would encourage coughing, and attempt the Heimlich maneuver if they're awake, as he was. Or you would sweep the mouth clear and do chest thrusts if they were unresponsive. . . as he also seemed to be. A suction machine wasn't available, and it was such thick, particulate matter that it would be hard to suction out anyway.

This was confusing. I was reminded of a time years earlier, while I was on duty as a brand-new lifeguard and a young man with a seizure disorder fell face forward into the pool.

Then, as now, the victim was neither fully awake nor fully unconscious, but in a sort of semi-frozen state of catatonia. The man in the pool was having a partial seizure, still aware but unable to interact with me. Then, as now, I did not know which maneuver to employ. The man before me clearly needed his mouth cleaned out, but that rolling, chewing jaw precluded any such attempt. And forcibly pushing on his upper gut seemed likely to make things worse.

We opted to roll him on his left side, or tried to. He remained stiff, flailing his limbs slightly in a spastic gesture that seemed to resist our movements, then succumbed in a moldable sort of waxy flexibility. It was all so disorienting, not at all the usual picture of a critically ill adult, and the way forward was in no way clear. In the end, we were able to turn him to one side, but his stiff body required me to support him in place, my face so close to his that I could smell boiled egg spilling out of the corners of his mouth. He was breathing more comfortably now, and no longer making that distressing, choking sound. Tenzing leaned over and confided that this man had arrived earlier that morning, confused and speaking incoherently, with handfuls of dead leaves packed into both coat pockets.

The extent of the pathos we were witnessing overwhelmed me. If other patients are desperately poor, how much more so was this man? The others at least had shelter, clothing, food, family. Their basic needs were met, if only barely. And their decision-making ability, their general faculties, were usually preserved. They were not utterly alone.

Once, on my way back from Pokhara after a weekend away, I stared out the window as our car threaded its way through several small villages. "Villages" may be too grand a word for clusters of mud-walled homes and a couple of open-storefront shops — the kind whose side lintels are smothered by garlands of potato-chip bags linked together in their air-puff packaging. These little communities dotted the narrow, paved road connecting Tansen with Pokhara.

At the outskirts of one such community, I'd happened to

notice a figure up ahead. He was weaving back and forth along the rim of dirt at the edge of the asphalt road, dipping dangerously for a moment onto the pavement itself. Just beyond him, the road turned a blind corner. Our driver hugged the double yellow line to avoid hitting him. As we passed the man, I could see more closely his disheveled clothing and matted, filthy beard. He staggered under the weight of a ragged cotton cloth sack slung over one shoulder, presumably filled with his belongings. I could see his mouth moving as we sped by, muttering something aloud to himself, or perhaps to no one in particular.

I had wondered what becomes of such a person in rural Nepal. Could he scrounge enough food and shelter to survive in a place like this? I knew there were no government-sponsored safety net programs to speak of here. Now, my attention returning to the patient before me, I realized that he could have well been the same man, or someone very much like him. I cleaned some more flecks of boiled egg spilling from the corner of his mouth, then rubbed his shoulder for a minute, until a nurse came to take over his care. Standing there beside this figure lying catatonically on his mattress, a phrase flashed through my mind. *As you did it to one of the least of these My brothers, you did it to Me.*

To Me. To Jesus, who spoke those words in the urgency of His last hours on earth. His words in Matthew 25 had become for me a focus of devotion over the preceding few years. With them, He was sharing with His disciples a vision of what will matter most in the final accounting — namely, that our love for Jesus will be revealed most truly in how we cared for the poor and marginalized in our midst. Jesus seemed to be making clear that in following Him, we are called to live out with our hands what we say we believe with our hearts. So closely does Christ identify with the vulnerable, in fact, that in caring for the man before me, I was caring for Christ Himself.

In this light, the immediacy of Christ's shame left me stricken. I was horrified at His humiliation, only to realize the humbling reality — that it was all for me, all motivated by love, all necessary. How far He was willing to go, and still goes, to identify with the weakest in our midst. How far He will go to assume, in Mother Teresa's words, "the distressing disguise of the poor."

The call was clear, the gauntlet thrown down — to serve Christ in the poorest of the poor. Clear, too, was my repeated inability to do so. My daily prayer eventually became, *Lord, let me recognize You today in my patients, and let them recognize You in me.* It was an impossible prayer.

Not long afterward, I was on a brief trip through Kathmandu for one reason or another, and signed into Skype for a conversation with my friend Jane. It was early morning in Kathmandu, just after six AM, and I could see the sun rising over the city's eastern horizon. In New York, Jane was almost ten hours behind me, so it was still evening for her, which tended to be the most convenient time to catch family and friends. I was sitting on the rooftop deck of the Trinity Guesthouse in Kathmandu's *Jhamsikhel* district that had been my home during orientation more than a year earlier. So much had happened in that time. Jane asked how I was doing, and a deluge of frustrations poured forth like waters through a burst dam.

This was, I feared, becoming something of a pattern with friends and family on the other end of my calls, yet I couldn't hold it back. Fortunately, I was surrounded by friends gracious enough to hold that space. As Jane listened, my stream of words morphed into a worry that had been evolving for me.

"Jane, what if *I'm* the only glimpse my patients ever get of Jesus?"

"What do you mean?" she asked.

"Well, patients come to Tansen Mission Hospital from all over, and even if they know nothing else about us, at a minimum they know that the ex-pat doctors are all Christian. I ought to be showing the kindness of the God I'm supposed to be representing. But instead, my patients have to deal with a condescending, short-fused white doctor who clearly needs an attitude check! I mean, recently my prayers each morning as I enter the front gates of the hospital are simply that God will grant me the grace to see Jesus in my patients, and that they would see some of Jesus in me. Yet I am failing on both fronts. *Constantly.* What am I even *doing* here, Jane, if not that?"

Now, the thing you must know about Jane is that she is nothing if not direct. Loyal, loving, faithful, brilliant, hilarious — and always direct. We both think and speak fast, which has made for a stimulating, fast-paced friendship over the years. Her words are also full of good humor, yet delivered with a bracing clarity that often begins matter-of-factly with, "Well of COURSE, Becca. . ." That phrase has preceded countless reality checks she's given over years of longstanding friendship. So, upon seeing this weighty burden of guilt I'd lobbed forth, she energetically returned the volley.

"But c'mon, you don't have to be *GOD!* I mean, think about it Becca — you *can't* be Jesus to them! Because you're not Him!"

She paused for a minute, considering something, and then said, "You *need* Him, in fact. I mean, duh, I know you know this. But do you hear yourself? Why are you carrying all that?"

I hadn't thought of it that way, and didn't really know what to say. She was right, of course, but how could it be that easy? She finished up with an emphatic flourish, as only Jane could. "*Of course*, Becca. . . *You* don't have to be God, because *He's* God!"

And then, her voice softening, she affirmed what I so needed to hear: "And Jesus is *Jesus* for you too, Becca."

Her words were straightforward and bracing, yet full of kindness. It would take me years to absorb their full impact. This was a mammoth truth, one that I needed to learn and re-learn many times over. Mere striving would not suffice. This "learning" required a sea change within the heart, a turning from my usual bent-in self to a humble posture of self-forgetfulness. Brennan Manning captured it poignantly when he wrote, "'Lord, when did we see you hungry and feed you?' Those declared blessed at the Last Judgment will have no memory of meeting Jesus in those whom they fed, sheltered, and comforted. They won't remember because in those moments when urgent need surfaced, they forgot themselves. In unselfconscious freedom, they responded to human need without seeking to be noticed, unconcerned about impressing anyone, and unworried about getting gold stars for their behavior."

This is not a truth easily received by self-sufficient perfectionists. Even recovering ones, those of us who recognize that perfection is not actually achievable, however tantalizingly within reach it may seem. Despite my most vigorous resistance, I was coming to see that my need of Him was the whole point. Perfection — even, and perhaps especially, perfection in ministry — is a weight Christ alone is fit to bear.

CHAPTER THIRTY-FIVE

The Long Lens of History

On a warm afternoon in early spring, I was walking along the row of brick apartment homes at the far end of our hospital compound. Warm sun filtered down through jacaranda blossoms that grew along the brick wall. Flowers blossomed, joyfully overstepping their rock-edged beds. Turning the corner, I saw our hospital's gardener bent down in one section, clearing out weeds with a hand-rake. For years, she had cultivated beauty throughout the hospital grounds, and possessed an amazing gift of care for growing, living things. She rose stiffly from her squatting position in the garden, adjusting her cotton sari, and flashed a friendly grin as I pressed my hands together in greeting.

I turned up a flag-stoned path and through the swinging porch door of *Annapurna II*. All the compound houses were named for Himalayan peaks, many of them visible along the northern horizon on a clear day. I entered the galley-style kitchen and knocked on the doorframe of the living room just beyond, alerting Willem to my entrance.

"Yes!" he cried out in a firm Dutch accent, leaping up from the bench on which he had been reading. His hyperkinetic energy always amazed me. You would expect it in a man thirty years his junior. "Come in, come in!"

"Have a minute?" I asked, thankful that he was home and not hiking or cycling in the area, as he usually was on an afternoon off. I'd joined him on hikes before, a small group of us exploring crests and valleys surrounding the hospital. The effort was always rewarded by gorgeous views — even on rainy monsoon days, whose gloomy skies held their own beautiful mystique.

Today, though, I was feeling pretty low, and glad for an afternoon to rest. I'd just finished up in pediatric OPD — thankfully, an unusually light morning. It was a breather in the season between winter's onslaught of pneumonias and summer's monsoon bloom of tropical diseases.

I flopped on the couch. "I'm just so frustrated, Willem. I'm really struggling." Even as I said it, I realized how good it felt to finally admit that aloud. "What difference am I making here, anyway? I mean, I've been working here for over a year, and nothing's any different!

"When I came, I thought my biggest contribution would be teaching the residents, even more so than clinical care. That has a more lasting effect, right? The whole, 'teach a man to fish' concept? What does it matter if I see as many patients as I can in two years? Well, sure — that's obviously of *some* value for those patients individually. But shouldn't I instead be focused on training a handful of young Nepali physicians to give good care? In the grand calculus, it's a no-brainer in terms of how best to allocate our limited time and effort, right? They'll be here long after I leave. And I can at least teach them *diligence*. But I see so many mistakes — most of them just careless errors — in important things like medications, antibiotic dosing, and overlooked critical lab results."

A question began to surface deep in my mind, one that I didn't want to consider. Why was I again lumping all the residents into this one category, when really it was just a small few, like Dev, that I had in mind? I pushed the thought aside, carried along by the energy of this newly vented irritation.

"Or how about their failure to consider an alternate

diagnosis, because they anchor in on a single, obvious seeming one that ends up being wrong. I mean, Dev wrote a *three-line* admission note the other day! All it said was: 'Headache + fever. Abdomen soft. Dx: Enteric Fever.' The patient had florid neck stiffness and was totally delirious when the nurses called me over to evaluate him. I'm sure he was on the verge of convulsing. He had *meningitis*, Willem!"

Willem furrowed his brow into a small frown, but said nothing. Another thought threatened to surface, rooted in the memory of mistakes I had made as a medical student and junior doctor. Some of my own "teachers" — like that obnoxious resident, Adam — had raked me over the coals for them, even though I knew I was trying my best at the time. It disturbed me to think that maybe I was doing the same thing. I swallowed, pushed the thought away, and continued enumerating frustrations.

"What am I supposed to do with that? I can correct those mistakes while I'm here, just like we all do. I mean, I'm glad I got there in time for that patient, but sometimes it's too late, like that man I told you about who died of a bowel perforation because no one bothered to check his X-ray in time. What about after we're gone? It seems like such a broad issue, this attitude of just getting by with the bare minimum. And it seems to get worse as the residents rise through the ranks, almost like it's a sign of seniority to get *less* involved!"

I paused in my diatribe, sensing I was getting myself really ramped up. At that point, there were a great many things Willem *could* have said. He could have easily pointed out, for instance, that I, too, was once a trainee. Or that I, even as a senior attending, sometimes got tired and lost my focus, still entirely capable of making careless mistakes myself. He could also have identified the overwhelming arrogance in my voice, or the fact that I was making sweeping, wildly unfair generalizations in judging all the residents as one, when I just had a few in mind. Almost all of them were doing just fine, and many were excellent.

A few of the Nepali trainees, led by our senior residents,

had even initiated a voluntary Journal Club to meet early in the mornings a few times per week before work, in order to review particularly challenging or confusing cases as a team, and share what the literature could teach us about evidence-based ways to manage them in the future. I was impressed that they had taken the initiative to do that. On the whole, Tansen delivered vastly superior care compared with anything else in the region, despite being embedded in an educational system that hadn't exactly prepared these residents the way my own medical school had.

Willem could have even pointed out, devastatingly, how little I had really done to build relationships with residents like Dev. Why should he take correction from me, or strive to emulate someone so distant and disconnected from his own experience?

Yet in his wisdom, he said none of these things. Instead, he looked at me with a humbling depth of compassion in his eyes, lovingly filled with fatherly concern. In those eyes I could also see the impish glint of humor that animated his elf-like features. His face remained somehow youthful, even as it bore the imprint of years that had imparted to him the very wisdom I lacked.

After a pause, he responded in his inimitably straightforward manner, characteristic of so many Dutch friends I'd come to know, honest and direct without being rude. "No offense, you know, but really, you're just a small cog in a big machine here. A small cog in the work God has been doing in this place for a very, very long time, in fact. You know, Becca, there were missionaries who came to the border of India in the 1930s and '40s, praying just to *enter* Nepal. Missionaries who spent their whole lives in those dusty towns, never knowing if this kingdom would even open to outsiders. It ended up taking decades. Can you imagine?"

At his words, I had a sense of time telescoping back, visualizing my own tiny place in that timeline. I was just one single point on a far grander trajectory. I suddenly felt gloriously small, just a grain of sand on God's vast plain of time. Could those faithful missionaries have ever imagined the fruit that would come from their prayers, as the borders eventually opened, and hospitals (including ours) were built? I wondered what they would say if they could see basic needs being met, as infrastructure was slowly built to provide electricity, running water, and sanitation services. That lives would be saved, deaths averted, and illnesses cured, even prevented. More, that there would be *Shalom*, the good news of Jesus lived out in word and deed among communities.

And into that decades-long story stepped a young doctor, fresh from America, who had come to stand in the gap for two years, hopefully serving patients well, hopefully offering some encouragement and friendship to the medical team, perhaps leaving a mark for the better on some trainees in future practice. Seen or not. Known, even to me, or not. "Standing in the gap" seemed the best way to describe my role here.

"God does not call us to be successful, Becca," Willem said, as if discerning this fresh train of thought. "He calls us simply to be faithful. Obedience is all He asks."

I thought back to what he'd once said about missions as "all about going, not much about doing, and everything about being." It seemed the definition of faithful service was broader than I'd thought. Willem was gently nudging me to see each of our individual callings as small yet vital contributions — even if they're often indiscernible in the far bigger work of God. And this was a work so vast in scope that we could barely glimpse it from our vantage point, this side of heaven.

As a result, the work I was called to do demanded far greater faith in God than I'd realized, for it required that I trust Him with whatever calling He gave me, however small and inglorious it may seem. Jesus Himself seemed to view His ministry as best accomplished by discipling a handful of itinerant, sub-literate fisherman. He remained always at the periphery, carefully avoiding every circle of academic, religious, and political power. He eschewed the usual paths of influence, choosing instead the way of shameful death. Yet by doing, He made a mockery of those power structures, and dealt death's final blow three glorious days later.

In the same way, missionaries the world over — through their own quiet and humble outreaches in the unseen margins of the world — follow in Jesus's footsteps. There is no shame in being a small cog within God's big work. Over time, as that truth settled more deeply within me, I could better appreciate the gritty, hope-fueled faith in Jesus that sustained my mentors in their faithful service, living and loving in marginal spaces like Tansen.

CHAPTER THIRTY-SIX
Spent

"Take this pill once a day for the next five days," I explained in Nepali, "and come back in two weeks if your pain isn't better." I was finishing up with a middle-aged couple who had made the five-hour journey from their village by public bus. The wife came to our Emergency Department for indigestion following a bout with a stomach bug. I could find nothing concerning in her story or on exam, but a distance of five hours was pretty far to return if the antacid I'd given her didn't help. I figured that the day's allotted appointments must have already all been doled out. It was the only reason I could think as to why they'd have come to the ED for this relatively trivial complaint.

A benign-seeming problem, like indigestion in a woman in her late fifties, sometimes portends something far more sinister — a gastric ulcer, perhaps, or even a growing cancer. I always worried about missing something like that. For patients who lived "close enough" — usually defined as within a three-hour bus ride to the hospital — we would give an appointment slip to return in a week or two and think nothing of it. Yet some of our patients came from much farther, in some cases hailing from villages that took a week to reach by some combination of bus, car, and foot. By the time these patients grew sick enough to justify that kind of journey, their illness was usually far advanced, if they even managed to survive the journey. Regardless, many of the patients coming to Tansen's ED were very sick, often requiring admission for at least a night or two.

From time to time, though, a patient would travel far, yet seem to have a relatively mild malady. In such instances we sometimes asked them to stay for a few days in one of the local "inns," and be seen again a day or two later to make sure they didn't get more ill. These inns were single-story cinderblock homes lining the road to the hospital, and had several beds in an open, shared space. Though similar in concept to hostels dotted across Europe and South America, they were more stylistically reminiscent of a medieval stopover for wayfaring pilgrims. It always seemed, as I walked past these bustling inns on the way home from work, that they were full of the jolly warmth you might expect in an ancient tavern on a frigid night.

I was about to hand this couple a prescription and suggest that they consider staying nearby for a day or so, to make sure the pain wasn't a sign of something else, when Khirel came rushing over. I had learned early on that, as one of our many highly experienced medical assistants, his level of a worry could be trusted. Whenever he asked for help, you'd better drop what you were doing.

"Timi awa aaunu-parcha, Daktara." You must come now, Doctor. He had used the more informal, casual address *"Timi,"* which I found heartwarming. In the age-based hierarchy of Nepali language structures, an older man never used the deferential high form of "you," *Tapaain,* for a woman many years his junior. Yet because of my standing as a physician, all of the medical assistants did. It always felt strange, like the inversion of these linguistic norms was demeaning to my older, more experienced counterparts. After months of formality, his use of *"Timi"* felt full of warmth and familiarity, one small, cultural step closer to the inner circle of friendship.

Aaune, Daktara. Come. As he called me over, I detected a note of hesitation in his plea, and saw in his face a troubled, unsettled look. In a few strides, we had crossed the cavernous open-bay emergency ward lined with gurneys along three sides. Each bay was separated by faded polyester curtains in a beige, industrial pattern. They slid open and closed along metal wires suspended above our heads.

A commotion was brewing in the area outside one of these bays, in which three middle-aged Nepali men were gesticulating wildly, with great emotion, toward the curtained area. One, his face contorted with grief, had begun to weep. Another looked to be on the verge of outrage, while a third appeared to be trying to soothe them both. All three were dressed for farm work in the fields, their worn trousers cinched around lanky hips, and loose shirtsleeves rolled back to the elbows. I wondered if my own father's grandfathers, themselves farmers and coal miners in the valleys of Western Pennsylvania, dressed in similar fashion more than a century ago in their own, pre-industrial world.

Just then, the cluster of men parted as another medical assistant emerged from the curtained-off trauma bay and beckoned me inside. Khirel and I stepped past the older men, their eyes fixed on me, the *bideshi* physician on duty. We slipped behind the curtain, and I pulled it closed again around us, shimmying the curtain's rings along its rusty suspension wire. Softly, in the succinct language of an experienced professional, the medical assistant explained the situation.

Two young men had been brought in, apparently electrocuted by a live current pulsing through their rice field's irrigation ditch. The first man, he said, had dropped instantly when he walked to the edge of their field. The second ran over to see what had happened when he, too, fell to the earth. One of the elders present had witnessed the whole thing and called for the others to help bring them here in a taxi. Both young men, however, were dead on arrival, the flat lines of their EKGs confirming that nothing could now be done for either.

None of my personal records from that time — journals, emails, and many scratch-books of musings — mention this incident. It occurred over a year into my time at Tansen, far enough to have melded with all the other catastrophes filling each day. Such unthinkingly blind tragedy had by then, sadly, become routine.

Even so, the memory of this wantonly random waste of life stuck with me more forcefully than almost any other. The body remembers, even when thoughts and emotions have been pushed past exhaustion. Years later, grim images of two young men laid out like mannequins on their respective stretchers still remained starkly fresh in my mind.

Leveled in the prime of life, they looked to be in their mid-twenties, lithe and athletic and toned. It was likely that they were recently married, given their ages. If so, maybe they each left behind an infant in the arms of their young brides — women soon to learn that they were now marked with the stigma of widowhood in Nepal. When husbands die, widows are traditionally expected to observe mourning rituals — cultural practices meant to honor the dead — for the rest of their lives. These include austere proscriptions on clothing, food, and community engagement. A widow can never again wear red, the color of marriage and beauty. She must forever abstain from meat, and for a period of time, from salt. Until she herself dies, she must observe life-long chastity after the death of her husband. Financially, she is fettered by laws that require a male's signature on property deeds and other transactional documents. I sensed the tragic repercussions of these two lost lives rippling outward.

I stood there for a while beside those two bodies lying side by side on their backs, noting the muscular definition of their sinewy calves and thighs. The clothes they wore were more youthful than that of the elders with them, versions of the rip-off-brand athletic wear available in street corner shops across Nepal. With their eyes closed, the men looked more asleep than dead, except for their unnatural stillness, and a discarded bag-valve mask lying on one stretcher. They were not the shriveled, kyphotic frames of old age, nor even the mangled, bloodied corpses of motor vehicle accidents. These two young men, exemplary specimens of youthful health, were strangely pristine. Pristine, and utterly lifeless.

Perhaps it was this very aspect that shook me, my guard down, with none of the usual defenses that fly up in the face of more visceral, provocative deaths. In the world of medicine, death often comes only on the heels of attempted rescue, and is acknowledged only once the adrenaline of our actions is fully spent. I could do nothing but stand there, stunned into silence at the sudden, cruel senselessness of it all. Where was God to be found in all of this? Powerless, pressed upon by needs all around, I could feel nothing — not rage, nor bitterness, nor even grief. Nothing but inarticulate weariness.

Numbly, I realized I had to return to the day's remaining work. The woman with indigestion was still waiting on the other side of the room with her husband, and needed me to write a prescription for her to bring to the hospital pharmacy. A growing line of patients had begun to crowd the wooden benches lining the entrance hall. I could feel their eyes trained on this scene in the corner of the ED. I stood there a moment longer, my hand resting on the edge of one of the stretchers, unsure even of what to say to the aides standing there beside me. We looked at one another, my dismay and resignation mirrored in their faces. I didn't know how to make sense of this for myself, let alone for them.

Turning away from the bodies, I slipped out through the curtain and walked over to the three older men huddled nearby. I may have touched one of them on the elbow in a wordless gesture of comfort. There is no good term in Nepali for "I'm sorry." *Maaph garnos* is the closest phrase I know, though its translation implies culpability, an apology for the outcome. It didn't seem a fitting thing to say. I wanted to convey instead the grief and lament embedded in the English phrase, "I'm sorry." *I have sorrow.* The translation of the

Nepali phrase for "I'm sad" — literally, *"My heart is in pain"* — would have been a closer approximation. Still, words failed me in Nepali that day. Truthfully, they would have in my own language as well.

Instead, I looked at them with all the compassion I could muster, holding each gaze briefly, one by one. Then I gently shook my head, turned, and headed to the nursing station to sign two more death certificates.

CHAPTER THIRTY-SEVEN

Shaken

No one panicked that day, exactly. I'd say we held it together remarkably well.

Unnerved? As you would expect.

Shaken? By definition. Of course.

The sense of unraveling, heart-in-your-throat, diaphragm-contracting terror was not to be found in the naïve commotion of those early hours of the earthquake. That would take weeks to settle in. And then, like a houseguest unwelcome even at his arrival, it would stay, pervasive and unnerving, for months to come.

But not on that first day. That day was akin to Day One of medical school when, as a novitiate medical student, I marched to our cadaver lab for the first time and, garnering all my inner toughness, refused to show fear. The poker face that had served me well through years of medical training was helpful in disaster, too. Inner emotional distance, the capacity to compartmentalize, the discipline of disengagement, has its benefits — if also its more subtle dysfunctions.

It was nearly noon, 11:56 AM, to be precise, a Saturday in late April. Houses were empty, people already long at work in their gardens and terraced fields. Classrooms stood vacant on the one weekday of leisure observed in Nepal. I had joined most of the expatriates in our organization, including the entire executive leadership team, for an annual retreat in Lakeside Pokhara. Team members had traveled from communities across Nepal in which they were living and serving in order to attend this time of rest and spiritual refreshment. I'd been looking forward to this retreat for weeks.

The morning started innocuously enough with a time of communal prayer. Our group was seated in small circles on the carpeted floor of the hotel's large conference room. The walls were tastefully done in an eggshell-white stucco, framed by exposed wood beams. It was designed to evoke the charming, ancient *Newari* style of traditional rural homes — a fact that proved ironic, given the modern stability it would soon demonstrate. Far more stable, it turned out, than thousands of authentically traditional Nepali homes across the country.

It's strange to think of the moments before disaster strikes. News of a cancer diagnosis. The phone call that tells of a loved one's death. A stroke. A car accident. An earthquake. These events unsettle at the deepest possible level, shaking your sense of what's real, what can be trusted. An earthquake, of course, does so quite literally. And it continues to do so hundreds of times a day, for weeks to follow, in the psychologically wearing phenomenon known as "aftershocks."

When it began, our team was sitting on the floor in small groups of three or four people. Eyes closed, heads bowed, absorbed in prayer for one of our organization's village-outreach ministries. I heard the faint rattle of windowpanes high up on the walls above my head. It started lightly, like the vibrations that accompany a close-passing train or low-flying aircraft.

"*Is* that a train?" I wondered. "Why is an airplane buzzing our building?" It was mere milliseconds of fragmentary, pre-rational thought. The gentle rattle swiftly grew to a dull roar.

Before I'd gathered what was happening, someone screamed. *"EARTHQUAKE!"*

Everyone was instantly on their feet, everything in motion, a blur of bodies rushing around the room. One of our team members, a petite young woman from the West Coast, attempted to crouch beneath one of the conference chairs scattered around the room, a panicked look on her face. It seemed a desperate move, odd even at the time. Yet I didn't have any better ideas.

In the end, we all did what the experts say not to do. We filed out of the room as quickly as we could, making our way across the creaking wooden boards of our hotel's second floor balcony, and down the only egress in the building: a set of outdoor wooden stairs leading to the flagstone patio below. The lights in the building flickered out. I glanced down at the floor as we went and saw fine cracks in the floorboards, highlighted by sunlight. It crossed my mind that the entire balcony could break apart with us on it. Yet there was no choice but to go forward.

As we shuffled down the stairs, that initial rattling sound transitioned into a swaying sensation, and the stairs beneath us began to heave. Earthquakes generally follow a pattern, I remembered Maddy describing to me once. They start with "P-waves," the first, high-frequency phase of the quake. These waves squeeze and expand material in the same direction as the traveling tectonic plates, which creates that early feeling of vibration. "P-waves" soon give way to "S-waves," a second phase of swaying, undulating movements. It's these waves that do most of the damage, destructively rolling the ground upwards and forwards, back and forth.

The balcony did not come down that morning, nor did our hotel collapse — at least, not for us. The grout-loosening P waves and brick-toppling S-waves of a 7.8 magnitude earthquake brought low many thousands of buildings that day, just as Maddy had worried would happen all those months earlier. Yet our group was sheltered in the popular tourist district of Nepal's famed Pokhara, protected by the safety that wealth often confers. Nine thousand people died that morning, but none where I stood. Though it may have been close geographically, our mere accident of birth had put it a world away from us that day.

There was a decorative swimming pool built into the center of the hotel patio's garden, artfully inlaid with stone and shaped like a huge lima bean. As the ground beneath us swelled and rolled — as we all stood, frozen, waiting for it to end — I was astounded to see huge waves of water splashing over the edges of its stone wall. What kind of force *was* this that could send a semi-underground swimming pool sloshing around like coffee in a mug in my hand?

And then, after ninety preternatural seconds, it was all over. We gazed around, looking at one another with the realization that we had just survived a profound experience. My first thought was one of surprised relief. "This was *it*. The earthquake that had been so long overdue has *just happened!*" From my limited perspective, it had gone surprisingly well. All seemed in good order. "That could have been so much worse," I murmured aloud to no one in particular, as we milled about in disbelief.

The group tried to go on with life as usual, hoping to convince ourselves that everything was normal. That afternoon, a few of us walked down the road into town, past faces bearing a similar mixture of nerves and relief. One of the buildings we passed had an enormous crack threading up through one white plaster wall. I pointed to it, yet felt speaking at any length about the earthquake seemed *gauche*, out of place. The experience was still too close. Perhaps it's a protective mechanism, this tendency to fall back upon silence to cradle our own vulnerability. Shared trauma can be like that, simultaneously uniting and isolating people from one another in a pact of silence.

On the way back to the hotel that afternoon, I realized I hadn't even let my family know that I was alright, in case they happened to hear of the earthquake on the news. I wondered if such news even registered on American cable networks, since so few of the world's noteworthy events ever seemed to. Glancing at my watch, I looked at my watch, 3:30 PM, and made a quick calculation of the time — 5:45 AM, New York time. A little early, but best to reassure them when they first wake up. I quickly typed out a text, "Not sure if you heard, but Nepal just had an earthquake. Don't worry, no issues here, I'm totally fine. Talk soon!" and hit send, making sure I was connected to the hotel's WiFi network.

An hour later, my cellphone rang, something that rarely happened in Nepal. Glancing at the caller ID, I saw it was my mom. "She must have just woken up and seen my message," I thought.

Tapping the screen to answer, I heard her voice on the other end, nearly hysterical as she shouted, "Oh *thank God!* Becca! You're there! Jessica just called us — she said there was a huge earthquake in Nepal overnight — are you *alright?*"

I could hear my father saying something loudly in the background that I couldn't quite make out, but it was inflected with anxiety. "We hadn't heard *anything* from you," she was saying. "We thought you were. . . you were. . . Oh thank God, you're *alright!*"

"Oh yes, definitely!" I replied hastily, "I'm fine! Totally fine. Didn't you get my text?" She said it hadn't come through. I groaned inwardly, thinking of how frightened they must have been to hear about this on the news, with no word from me for hours.

I reassured them that we were all fine, surprisingly no damage to any of the buildings around us. "It was quite an experience, so surreal. But now it's over! Thankfully the worst is behind us."

"Are you sure, honey? It sounds so terrible on the news!" As if resigned that her daughter would do whatever she would do, she added, "Be careful, will you? *Please?*"

Part of the process of getting "back to normal" was resuming the rhythms of our annual retreat, which Callum and Midge had planned out with great thoughtfulness and attention. That evening, we reformed our retreat groups and tried to carry on as before. Sleep that night did not come easily, though. Tremors continued to rattle the buildings in which we slept, bringing with them unnerving visions of collapse.

The following afternoon, my colleague Dan motioned me over to a small group of Tansen staff gathered on the balcony. He, Anneke, and a few others were speaking on the same portico from which we'd evacuated the day prior. Our team's engineers had already assessed the property for any damage, and cleared it for use.

"Becca," Anneke began, "would you be willing to join a relief team that INF is putting together?" The International Nepal Fellowship, an organization similar to ours in many respects, was looking for physicians who could travel with them to Gorkha, the district of the earthquake's epicenter. "They'll leave tomorrow morning at five."

"What about Tansen? Won't you need us at the hospital when you all head back? Patients are supposed to be scheduled for their usual outpatient clinics tomorrow, aren't they?"

"That's alright, Becca. We'll manage." She spoke in a rich, familiar Dutch accent. Concise, clear, and courageously matter of fact.

I hesitated for a second, weighing this prospect of an emergency outreach that suddenly felt a little too real. But it sounded like a need I could meet, and after all, when would an experience like this ever come up again? "Okay then. . . I'll go. Yes."

I called my family back and casually mentioned that I'd be heading to the region of the epicenter the next morning. "But it's fine, really no big deal," I assured them. "We're going with a well-equipped group, and the leadership is solid. . . Don't worry, I'll be fine!" I wanted to project more confidence in my voice than the cracked foundations and tense faces around me seemed to warrant.

An hour later, after making a few stops at local stands, I had all that I imagined I might need — wool socks, hiking pants, a small backpack, my stethoscope, Bible, pen, paper, and a bag of granola. At the last minute, I thought to pick up a fresh NCell calling card to top off my iPhone's data supply, just in case.

CHAPTER THIRTY-EIGHT

Gorkha Bazaar

Early the next morning, Dan and I trudged through the hotel's pitch-dark courtyard to meet our INF team. A white, seventies-era Land Rover pulled up to our hotel's front entrance and we climbed in, introducing ourselves to the eight other team members. I took a seat between Dan and a young Australian who managed communications for INF. It turned out he was also a field correspondent for the BBC.

As we drove further from the outskirts of Pokhara and eventually began rattling along unpaved roads, this INF staffer narrated live updates of the unfolding crisis via his cellphone. His coverage had the cadence of those real "front-lines news anchors" I'd listened to for years on NPR. When I heard him describe Dan and me as "American physicians working in Nepal, en route to support local rescue efforts," I nearly choked at this surreal glimpse into realities previously confined to my radio. I recovered and tried to play it cool.

Those international news reports had intrigued me ever since I was young, listening with my father to hourly news on the classical music station he always had playing in the background. Those brief reports had the aura of a world in which everyone was an expert, eminently capable with their top-notch skills and preparation. They seemed unflappable, taking conflict and catastrophe in stride. Now, as if in a movie, I had fallen down the rabbit hole to find myself on the other side of the screen. True, I had the medical experience, and I now spoke the language reasonably well. Yet I didn't feel anything like the experts I assumed those disembodied radio-voices to be.

Is this how field correspondents on the radio ever feel? I wondered. Was it possible that they sometimes felt as uncertain as I did now, unsure how to navigate the political crisis or natural disaster they were reporting?

After driving for several hours, we arrived at Gorkha Bazaar, the district's capital. Official-looking U.N. and Red Cross vehicles were haphazardly parked all along the unpaved road as we pulled in. Our team leader went to connect with the local government team that was coordinating relief efforts, and returned forty-five minutes later with our assignments. We were to travel another few hours to Pokharidada and Mailung, two remote villages still technically accessible by land, though we discovered sections of the dirt road to be nearly impassable.

When we finally arrived in Pokharidada, we got to work setting up a makeshift medical clinic, choosing a location under the shade of an enormous tree. Our pharmacist sorted through a slew of medication boxes nearby, which I realized had been brought in the truck traveling with our SUV, along with other supplies like tarpaulins, shovels, and bottled water. The four physicians on our team found two picnic tables off to one side, and we began seeing patients. Dan and I settled onto opposite sides of one picnic table, as lines formed in front of either bench. Very quickly, those lines streamed so far back that I couldn't see the end of them. It felt like everyone in walking distance had come to talk with a doctor. With rare exception, each person who came during that long, hot, dusty afternoon had one, understandable affliction — Fear.

A woman in the line stepped forward, and I asked her how I could help. "*Ringata lagcha,*" she replied, "I'm spinning."

Her finger encircling her head in the universal symbol for dizziness. She went on to describe feelings of *"jhum-jhum,"* *"tsarik-tsarik,"* and *"ssrhing-sshring,"* a sort of symptom onomatopoeia that loosely translates to sensations of "tingling, shocks, and irritability." Along with headaches, dizziness, and poor sleep, her symptoms were all characteristic of stress. It was the same for virtually every patient.

What they needed — what we all needed — was a caring, listening ear, and reassurance that they would be okay. I could see that the patients before me were strong, resilient men and women, embedded in a community that was likewise strong and resilient. Yet they were also racked with the suffering of anxiety and uncertainty. It was clear in their eyes as they pressed around us, edging to be seen. I could hear it in their frantic *jhum-jhums* and *tsarik-tsariks*, as they struggled to give voice to feeling.

We stayed in Pokharidada for several hours, getting through the lines and seeing everyone who had come, then packed everything up and headed to the second village on our list, Mailung, where we did the same thing again. When dusk fell and it became too dark to continue working, we loaded the vehicles again and returned to Gorkha Bazaar. Ravenous, we consumed *dal bhaat* by flashlight on white plastic chairs in front of a local restaurant, and debriefed our day. I learned that while we were seeing patients, our team's leaders — a German engineer and a Nepali operations manager — had spent those hours surveying the damage in both villages. They estimated that upwards of ninety percent of all homes and buildings had been leveled, a staggering degree of destruction.

After dinner, it was time to sort out where we would spend the night. We drove to a nearby Army Camp with a large area designated as "marching grounds," and set up a makeshift tent by slinging a huge orange tarpaulin over ropes tied between two parked trucks. A crowd of aid workers and military personnel from across the district had converged on this field after that day's efforts, probably assisting in villages similar to the ones we'd seen. Exhausted, I crawled under a blanket and fell into a deep sleep.

Sounds of the camp stirring woke me early the next morning. I emerged from under our tarp to see that the whole area, several football fields in size, was covered with other tarp-tents like ours, many of them housing entire families. Overnight, an informal refugee settlement had sprung up to shelter those escaping nature's destructive hand. All across the country, in fact, people were sleeping outside, as they would for months to come. The palpable and well-founded fear was that their homes could collapse, since nearly every building still standing was rendered unstable by the earthquake and its near-constant aftershocks.

That morning got off to a slow start. After a breakfast of powdered orange juice from our stocks, we regrouped with the rest of our team and waited, the plan for the day still unclear. I heard stirrings of conversation about wanting to assemble a team to access villages deep in the mountains, some of the places that had been hardest hit.

After a few hours of waiting, we finally received word from the officials. Our team had been assigned to Keraunja, a village at 6000 feet elevation in the Gorkha district, whose people were now accessible only by helicopter.

CHAPTER THIRTY-NINE

Keraunja

I don't know why they chose me and Dan to go. In part, we were both family physicians, and used to thinking on our feet. We were the youngest members of the group, and maybe the leaders felt we were, at least theoretically, in the best shape to trek over mountains. Perhaps it was because our mastery of the Nepali language was sufficient to the task. Or perhaps it was simply because we knew one another well enough to cooperate well in stress and uncertainty. It was a relief to be serving with a friend I knew, one who had proved sensible and trustworthy in the long course of our hospital teamwork. Dan and Leah had arrived in Nepal just one day earlier than I had, after all, and we'd been through everything together over the past two years. As I'd heard Willem and Anneke once put it, we'd formed a "bomb-shelter friendship."

Our team leader outlined the proposed plan. We would be dropped off in Keraunja by helicopter to assess needs and provide basic medical care. Then we were to trek back out again on foot to the nearest town, where paved roads could afford vehicular access back to our team in Pokhara. He didn't go into much detail on that last part. It seemed more of a "figure it out as you go" sort of plan. Given how remote these villages were, I knew the "nearest town" could be at least a day or two on foot, maybe more. I imagined hiking over the rough terrain of mountain ridges and deep valleys between them, terrain that was by now a familiar backdrop. Since Dan and I had both done some trekking, and we were wearing decent shoes, it seemed possible.

"It should be two, maybe three days' trek to the nearest town. From there, you can hire a vehicle back to headquarters," he said. "Plan to sleep on the porches of houses you find along the way. Nepalis are usually fine with that when people are trekking through remote areas." It seemed a strange idea, but everyone else nodded, agreeing it was a fine plan, so I didn't question it.

Now that our "two-man" team had been assembled and briefed, we hastily threw our stuff into bags and squeezed back into the same seventies-era Jeep to head to the "helipad." It was just a level area of dirt cleared from an embankment that was set back a few feet from the mountain road. We hung around at the edge of the banked earth and watched as helicopters took off with aid workers or military personnel aboard, and returned with injured patients evacuated from villages high in the mountains. Some of them were moaning on stretchers, while others limped along, supported between soldiers wearing military fatigues. Everyone wore a weary, stricken look.

We waited for hours. Doubts began settling in about whether we'd get a chance to take off. Nothing appeared to be tightly coordinated. The only evidence of order was one harried looking man holding a tattered clipboard on which was pinned a grainy, black-and-white photocopy of a map. I could see various towns highlighted in blue, green, and yellow.

Waiting at least afforded a chance to people-watch. I studied the flurry of activity all around, trying to parse out what mysterious system might actually be at work here. After a while, a man with sandy blond hair wandered over, looking interested to start a conversation.

"I'm a reporter with the *Financial Times*, based out of

London," he said casually. "What's your role in all this?"

"I'm a family doctor. I've been working in Tansen, west of here, for eighteen months now."

"Interesting. What is your perspective on this whole situation so far?"

I began to share how our team had seen around four hundred people the day before, remarking that the stress people were feeling is real. "It's such an anxious time for everyone. And it's hard to know what we can really do to help, but we're trying to hold these makeshift clinics."

As I started to tell him about the utter devastation of buildings and village infrastructure in the places we'd been, two other men came over, one introducing himself as a reporter from *Le Monde,* and the other with the Associated Press. It was all so surreal, as if I'd fallen down yet another rabbit hole, or inadvertently wandered into someone else's life.

We were interrupted when I saw our team leader frantically waving me over. It was finally our turn, now shortly after 1:15 PM. I signaled to Dan, slung my pack over my shoulder, and jogged across the helipad to a five-seater commercial helicopter being loaded with government-issued supplies and the large box of medical items we were to bring along. Glancing up, I could see huge black thunderheads materializing on the horizon, growing darker and more threatening by the minute. The team leader thrust a satellite phone into my hand, saying this was a really expensive way to communicate, but it would work if we absolutely *had* to get a message through.

"But remember — satellite phones need to have a direct line of sight to the satellite in order to work. You can't use it inside a building, or any kind of enclosure. Get out into a wide-open space before you try to use it." I'd never even seen a satellite phone, and definitely didn't know that. As he finished giving his rapid-fire instructions, I overheard two uniformed men debating whether they could squeeze in one more takeoff before the storm.

The pilot sitting in the cockpit looked every bit the part of the intrepid aviator. His bearing was that of a *Gurkha* soldier, with his lean, square-cut jawline and a jauntily tied cravat. He was even wearing aviator sunglasses. His vote? Sure, we could do it, this storm was no big deal. Minutes later, Dan and I climbed into the helicopter, crouching on eighty-pound bags of rice and other supplies. As we tried to find our seatbelts and strap ourselves in, two Nepalis — a young woman named Urmila, and an older man wearing a blue vest that said "Press" in large, blocky white letters — jumped into the remaining two seats, and we lifted off. Through the helicopter's front windshield, it looked like we were heading straight into a wall of black cloud that had precipitously darkened in the few minutes since takeoff. I tried not to imagine that the tallest mountains on the face of the earth were also looming ahead, buried in those clouds somewhere.

This is how it happens, I thought. *This is how relief workers die.* Without wanting to, I pictured my family reading in their morning paper, "Humanitarian aid workers killed in helicopter crash. . ."

Ten minutes into our flight, the wind became too strong to continue, and our pilot made an emergency landing. He perched the helicopter on the edge of a narrow rock outcropping high in the mountains, as huge gusts buffeted and rattled the craft. It seemed entirely possible that the heavy winds could send us pitching and rolling right off the edge of the cliff, and I wasn't keen to be inside of this huge steel coffin if it did. Dan, Urmila, and I climbed down to wait out the storm under an abandoned cow shed tucked thirty yards in.

After an hour, the storm lifted and we were off again. Far below, we could see orange tarps dotting the landscape as we flashed by. They were replacing roofs and entire homes that had collapsed. Life in Nepal had already begun to change dramatically. It felt odd to be coasting smoothly along, several hundred feet above these hamlets where orange tarps represented traumatized families, destroyed capital, and lost lives.

Thirty minutes later, we approached the side of a steep mountain into which had been cut a series of rice terraces. The pilot landed on one of them, his helicopter runners sinking deeply into the rain-drenched mud. This was Keraunja, our target village at a moderate 6000-foot elevation. The whole village, it seemed, had come out to watch our arrival. Villagers were standing along the edge of the field, and many held burlap sacks over their heads to shield themselves from the driving rain.

Dan and I climbed out, and I walked over to one of the older men in the group to ask, in Nepali, where we could set up a medical clinic. He gestured with a wide sweep of his arm and asked in response, "Where? Nowhere. We have nothing left."

This was no exaggeration. There was not a single building in that village left standing. As Dan and I walked along the narrow dirt path snaking up the side of the mountain, we could see that their infrastructure damage was total. Everything in sight had been reduced to rubble. All roads and footpaths were out too, a fact that became clear later on, when we inquired about the best route out on foot. "*Yo garna sakindaina, didi.* Sister, it can't be done," said one of the elders. Another man added in Nepali, "The people of a nearby village tried to evacuate yesterday, and everyone was wiped out. They were trying to get to a town with supplies and food. A landslide took them." The image of hundreds of people being washed away and swallowed up into the earth was horrifying. As if to emphasize his point, a dotted line of people came into view along a dirt path far below us — displaced residents of a nearby village, their connections to vital goods also cut off by landslides.

Unsure of what to do, we offered to evaluate and, if possible, treat any injuries among the villagers. Urmila, the young woman who had joined us in the helicopter, was from this village, and she took charge of the situation. Speaking to the gathering cluster of villagers, she urged everyone to cooperate in sharing the food and shelter that had been brought in the helicopter, then announced that doctors were here to see anyone that had been hurt. She connected Dan and me with the village's health-post medic.

We headed over to the health post building, which we were told was the nearest one in a three-hour walk's radius, but saw it had caved in during the earthquake. There was no way to use it, or even to extract supplies from the rubble. People began forming a line. A few had minor injuries, scrapes and cuts mostly, from the falling debris. One teenage girl had a knee that was badly bruised, so tender and swollen that I worried the joint was filled with blood. Just as we had the previous day, we gave ear to the people's concerns, offered what comfort we could, and dressed what wounds were visible.

It wasn't entirely clear what else we could really do. Our medical training was our main qualification for being there, as if somehow it was comforting simply to have doctors around. I wondered how true that was, even though fettered by our lack of useful equipment, space, and supplies. There's no replacement for professional training, yet I could see that even our skills and knowledge were of limited value outside of the hospital or clinic setting, and the supports they offered in patient care. As we went along, we tried to at least make mental notes of patients that could be evacuated with us, if they wished, for treatment in a Pokhara hospital. Assuming, of course, that we could be evacuated. It didn't feel like much. In truth, those who were going to survive this ordeal already had.

It was still drizzling a cold, steady rain when we finished with the last patient's concerns and packed away our few supplies. Several orange tarps had been set up in the few flat patches of ground this steep mountainside afforded. I could see families huddling in loose groups beneath. An uncomfortable thought began to surface, as I considered how vulnerable these families were. Disconcerted, I realized that our very presence — two more people to feed and shelter — could pose a burden to the community we'd come to serve.

CHAPTER FORTY

Under the Tarp

The temperature began to drop as dusk approached, and we'd already noticed a few leech-bites oozing blood from our ankles. Peeking through a flap into one of the tents, I caught the eye of a woman inside, and asked if we could come underneath to get out of the rain. I asked her in the same way you'd ask for something you are certain will be granted, knowing how gracious the Nepali people are in their hospitality. I remember this because of the shock that came with her flat rejection, her shake of the head, her firm *"Hoina."* No. It was then that the full gravity of this crisis hit me. Her eyes had the look of one hardened in self-protective resolve. She was unhesitating, unequivocal, but still seemed disturbed that she could not meet the pressing need of a fellow human.

With a feeling of dread, I realized the vulnerability of our position, and how profoundly dependent we were on the people of this village to extend food, shelter, blankets, warmth, and welcome. A distressing thought came suddenly to mind, that perhaps we would have no choice but to sleep outside in the freezing, rainy mud. It was almost as disturbing as the rejection of her desperate, firm *"No."*

Dan and I exchanged a look that said all there was to say about the situation — uncertain, baffled, desperate. Then we noticed some sacks that had been tossed into the mud where the helicopter had landed. They were industrial sacks made from woven plastic fibers — yellow ones labeled *"Bhaat / Rice,"* and blue ones imprinted with the stamp of a government logo, *"U.S.A.I.D."* Never in my life had I imagined I could be so elated to see those letters. I was giddy with relief. In it were basic housing materials: rope, two tarps, a few utility blankets, and several ground-stakes. Urmila hurried over with her brothers and cousins, and we set to work.

After we finished putting up the tarp-tent, I had to urinate, and realized with panic that my period was also due that day. Not only had I failed to remember any feminine supplies, there wasn't even a private place to *pee* without exposing myself to the whole village. I couldn't see a single tree or low shrub in sight anywhere on that enormous, bare-faced mountainside of scrub-grass and scree. How was everyone else here taking care of business? Having no one I could ask without acute embarrassment, I tucked myself against a grassy patch of earth around the corner of a low concrete retaining wall and relieved myself, thankful that at least my period seemed to be late this month. Maddy had shared accounts of gender-based violence throughout remote villages in Nepal and elsewhere — stories of young women at risk, especially during menstruation. The nature of that vulnerability suddenly made more sense, taking shape in a reality I was unexpectedly, if only momentarily, living.

With our shelter erected and Urmila's large family gathered with us beneath, a few of her aunties began building a fire with the rain-soaked wood, thick smoke filling the tarp until the wood dried enough to catch into flame. I marveled at these women, clearly so used to performing such tasks in conditions only marginally better than these. How did they manage not to cough in the smoke, as we novices did? I teared and spluttered, my eyes burning, until finally retreating into the rain outside the tarp, trying to catch my breath and look as natural as I could. This was a normal part of village life, this wood-fire smoke. We'd seen enough patients with emphysema, including those stricken far too young, to know that.

Once they got a smoking fire going, Urmila and her family began preparing a simple meal of *dal-bhaat*, which we ate with our hands from tin plates. One of her older aunties, out of great courtesy, did what hosts often do when serving guests, and offered a demure comment about the simplicity of the meal. "This surely is not up to standards fitting for our city-dwelling *bideshi* guests, I'm afraid."

That was when we noticed that the Nepali man wearing the "Press" vest had also joined us under the tarp. He was a small-framed man with an irksome attitude, who often stood too close for comfort and had been giving me vaguely salacious glances earlier that evening. I now felt him again leering uncomfortably at my side. At our host's comment, he agreed heartily, chiming in, "Yes, well it *is* extremely bad fare, but even low-grade food will do when you're hungry," magnanimously adding — with a sly wink in my direction — that we would somehow bravely endure.

The exchange happened rapidly and in village-accented, colloquial Nepali, so I wasn't sure I had heard him right. In fact, I could not *possibly* have heard him right. Such a response was unimaginably insulting. I'd seen the hierarchies of power at work here, and coming from a city-dweller with some financial means, it was beyond the pale. I was appalled. Despite their impoverished circumstances, these women had shown incredible generosity to us, willing to host and feed three strangers in the wake of disaster.

I saw the woman's face tighten, a subtle scowl forming, and realized that I *had* understood his meaning, all too well.

Did he have no sensitivity? No insight, even, into the fact that we were guests in her "home"? That we were sitting at that most sacred of Nepali spaces, the kitchen hearth, no less? His brusque condescension was not only unconscionably rude, but unwise, and dangerously foolhardy. This family had provided for us out of their own great need at a time of national crisis. His insulting comment could imperil all of us, could send us right back out into the rain.

Jumping in, praying that I'd understood the situation correctly, I exclaimed in Nepali, "No, no! Food given with such generous care is a feast, indeed! This was a delicious meal by any standard." I hoped to draw a clear line that this other man was not "with us." Her expression softened, the injury to dignity somewhat assuaged.

If we were feeling vulnerable at that moment, I could only imagine how much more were they. While we helped clean up after dinner, I noticed a large plastic container of lentils with maybe four or five cups filling the bottom third of it, and a similar one with about the same amount of rice, propped up near a little bottle with some vegetable oil residue in the bottom. I asked one of the women about it. She held the lentils up to the light of the fire, and said, matter-of-factly, that this was it. All she had left for her family.

"How long will that last you?" I asked.

"Three days, maybe four."

This family — the entire village, in fact — was on the literal brink of starvation. Even the supplies of rice that came with our helicopter's food-drop would last probably no more than a week, two at the most. And how many of their crops had been damaged by our arrival, delicate rice plants crushed beneath the runners of our helicopter as it landed on their terrace? I thought back on the afternoon, and the myriad inadvertent harms that can flow from even well-intentioned efforts to help.

I also thought again, guiltily, of the fact that we were still three more adult mouths to feed. I remembered the bag of granola I'd bought in Pokhara, a place that now seemed a universe away. I'd intended to use it as an emergency food supply, and while Urmila's family was preparing *dal bhaat*, I'd reached into my bag, taking hold for a moment the plastic package hidden within. But then I thought to myself, *We can't pull out our own food stash and refuse to eat hers. That would be insanely rude. She'll think that village food isn't up to our standards.* I released my grasp on the granola in my backpack, and pulled the zipper closed again.

By that evening, both of our cellphone batteries were getting low, even though we'd put them on airplane mode to save power. There was no signal in the area. We had taken some photos of the area to document the degree of damage, reserving Dan's phone for that and saving mine for when we were back in network range. Once night fell, we laid down beneath the plastic tarp we'd erected a few hours earlier — Urmila and her family, Dan and I, and the reporter from Kathmandu, all lying shoulder to shoulder in a tight line on the ground. Restless, yet not wanting to disturb those around me, I stayed still and waited for sleep to come.

And so it was that I came to be lying under a tarp on the side of a mountain, wondering how I'd ended up there in the first place. I hadn't exactly volunteered for any of it, really. I suppose I'd neither volunteered nor declined. Wanting to be open to each step of this experience, hoping to be of some help, I felt as though we'd been carried forward on a current of decisions, drawn into a churning process with momentum of its own. When asked, Dan and I simply hadn't said "No."

I tried to reposition the backpack I was using for a lumpy pillow, and could feel the edge of my little pocket Bible sticking out. I had thrown it in while grabbing items from my retreat room a few days earlier. Filed between its thin pages was a small, familiar scrap of paper.

My mind flashed to a distant memory, of filing out of a yellow school bus as a high school freshman on a gorgeous day in late April. Our all-girls Catholic school had arrived on the grounds of a small convent in the town of Ossining for an annual Retreat Day. It was the sort of spring day you dream of on winter mornings in New York, hands numb and ankles soaked with snow-mush. It seemed to promise warm summer days were soon to come.

An elderly woman, hair cropped short and a long wooden rosary-bead necklace draped around her neck, emerged from a glass-paned atrium in the retreat center and strode over to us. She was a nun, clearly, and also our retreat host for the day. A few of the girls snickered loudly. I felt sorry for her, but still joined in with a cynical smirk, careful to avoid any sign of sympathy, anything that might somehow identify *me* with *her*. The last thing I wanted was to jeopardize whatever scant shreds of social capital I'd managed to cobble together that year.

She ignored our boorishness, welcoming our group of *tween* girls to the Mariandale Retreat Center, and laid out the day's plan. "There will be thirty minutes of silent retreat this afternoon," she announced, the only thing from that day that has stayed with me all these years later. That, and the tiny strip of paper she proceeded to hand out, a Bible verse printed on each, to guide our silent meditations.

That shred of paper, unbelievably, would remain tucked between the pages of successive Bibles for more than fifteen years, staying with me through moves across multiple state and national lines, surviving four different chapters in my academic journey, rotations on hospital wards, hiking and backpacking trips, and the periodic winnowing of paper shreds less valued. It would eventually endure even the relentless onslaught of Nepal's mildew and paper-eating earwigs, only to disappear one day in the most mundane of ways — slipping out one afternoon in a local New York park the year I returned home.

Yet by then the paper was, in truth, no longer needed. The words printed on it, a paraphrase of Luke 24:17, had grown so intimately familiar from countless reflections that they were firmly etched into my memory.

Jesus, Companion for the journey —
Help me to hear the echo of your question in my heart:
"What are you discussing as you go along your way?"

I reflect back on those thirty minutes of silent meditation, seeing it vaguely through the gauzy haze of time. I did not know it then, but that retreat would prove a watershed moment of my young life. For there, seated on a flagstone in the convent's garden, I first met Jesus as Companion, faithful

Friend. In the heady exuberance of youth, I found Him ever present in echoing questions of exploration and conversation, a God of *seeing* and of *being* seen. In loneliness, it was a space where I could be known to my depths, even regarded as someone whose company was welcome.

When the retreat campus began to stir again with distant voices calling out and feet crunching on the pebbled pathway, I rose from the large, flat slab of rock on which I'd been perched, transformed in a small but irrevocable way by the faithful Companion I met there.

I remembered those words now, praying them in the silent darkness of the night. *Jesus, Companion for the journey. . .* Yet where was God in all this now? It felt like a hopelessly dark situation. No real food, warmth, or shelter to speak of, no possible communication with the outside world, no one who even seemed to know where we were on this immense planet. Occasionally, scree and gravel could be heard sliding down the mountainside around our tarp-tent, threatening another landslide if the aftershocks were strong enough. We seemed to have no viable exit strategy.

Lying awake, it struck me that if anything, I'd gotten here by following God's call as best as I could discern it, responding to needs where I could. And I also realized, if God would have us survive this, then He — and He alone — could get us out.

I just wasn't at all sure He would.

CHAPTER FORTY-ONE
Runchet

At daybreak the next morning, over tin cups of warm salt water, we discussed the day's plan with Urmila and a few of her brothers. If we could hike up to the ridge above our encampment, there was a chance we could get cellphone reception there. Urmila's younger brother estimated that the walk there and back would take around forty minutes. Assuming we'd be back within the hour, I didn't even bring the pack containing my passport and other belongings. Two of her brothers offered to go with us, to make sure we followed the right footpath there. The walk was easy enough, although we had to navigate across rubble and boulders strewn all along the cliff's edge. At one point, we had to pick our way over two decaying cow carcasses, felled in the initial landslide while they were grazing on the mountain ridge above us.

Reaching the crest of the hill, I was thrilled to see we finally had a weak cell signal, and managed to get a call through to INF's Pokhara headquarters. The team had returned there the afternoon before, and our leader relayed that a briefing was scheduled for later that day.

I explained what we'd learned. "There are no passable roads out of here, so trekking out on our own isn't an option.

What's more, I'm worried that our presence here is a drain on their limited resources."

At the briefing, he said, he would look into ways to get us home. "I don't think there are any helicopters to spare, though," he added. "You know, with all the food drops and evacuations happening across the district." This wasn't great news. The last thing we wanted was to divert vital transportation resources away from relief efforts.

"Anyway, just text this number if you happen to hear that anyone's coming to this area," I said. "I think we have enough battery power to last a few more hours, maybe. But we can use the satellite phone too, I guess, if we have to." I was thankful that at least we had plenty of NCell data topped off. "We're still in Keraunja," I added, not sure if he even knew where that was.

"I'll do what I can. Let's regroup after today's meeting." We set a time to talk at two o'clock. It wasn't clear we had any kind of exit strategy. As far as I could tell, only a couple of people on earth even knew *where* on earth we were.

Urmila's two brothers walked over just then, urging us to continue on along the crest we'd just climbed. Instead of returning to Keraunja, they said, we should hike down the other side of the mountain to the neighboring village of Runchet. They gestured to the north, where I could just barely make out a cluster of homes nestled deep in the valley below.

"They need doctors there too," they said in Nepali. I looked reluctantly at Dan, who seemed to be considering the idea.

"But what if they send the helicopter back to Keraunja, Dan? No one will even know we're over there. I don't want them to think we've gone missing! Think of all the extra resources an unnecessary search party would take." I wanted to add that all our stuff was also back at the camp, feeling like a total fool for having left my passport and backpack behind.

We weighed the options. If we went to Runchet, we'd potentially be able to access additional villagers, triage them for injuries, and evacuate the more urgent cases with us. Assuming, of course, that we could secure a helicopter. It was also a chance to gather information that would help the government allocate resources like food and shelter. At the very least, by going along with them, we were more likely to stay in the good graces of our hosts, who seemed quite keen that we go. As in Keraunja, it seemed there was potent comfort simply in the promise of medical care — from time immemorial, the ritualistic reassurance brought by physicians and priests alike. Maybe it wasn't such a big deal after all. Dan and I looked at one another and shrugged our assent. It seemed clear that this other village might never get attention otherwise, and that's why we were here. So we started down the other side of the crest.

We spent the next two hours picking our way slowly down the steep mountain face, along a network of narrow rabbit-trails packed into the dirt and crisscrossing down to the valley. It turned out that this second village, Runchet, was larger than Keraunja, and appeared somewhat more resourced. Many of the buildings here were still standing, several of them apparently free of damage. Word of two *bideshi* doctors spread quickly, and we were hastily nudged into home after home as we made our way down the steep village paths. Several people were in need of care, including one man who could barely move his arms and legs because of extensive, painful crush injuries. I had no idea how we could get him down the steep mountainside footpath, even if a helicopter did arrive.

The writer in me had thought to stash a pen and paper in my pocket, so we could record any data gathered on situations we encountered. As in Keraunja, we moved through Runchet asking people anything we could think of that would be helpful to know. Because both Dan and I were family doctors, our community-based training had cultivated a good imagination for the sorts of things to explore, information we figured would help the local government direct resources appropriately. We got village leaders' estimates on how many people had been injured or killed. We asked about the ages of those who had died, how many of their homes and buildings had collapsed, whether they still had functioning water supplies, if the footpaths connecting them to main town centers were still open, how many of their community's livestock were lost, and estimates on their remaining stores of food. Loss of life was in the low double-digits, but around ninety percent of their cattle and sheep herds — their main capital reserves — had been decimated in landslides.

Some thirty minutes into our time there, as we wound our way down the zig-zagging mountain paths and past clusters of mud homes, we were astonished to hear the sound of a helicopter far above. Dan and I looked at each other, realizing that we hadn't seen or heard any since ours had left the afternoon before, and watched as an enormous military helicopter circled above us. It seemed to be making a gradual descent into the valley below. If this was a food drop, we only had a few minutes while it was on the ground, and the flat area where it could land was still several hundred meters below us. A huge wave of relief flooded through me. I couldn't believe it — we had arrived in a village *just* as a food drop was happening! Running down the mountain, I pleaded a silent prayer that we would reach the helicopter before it took off, and in the meantime not break an ankle, slip on loose gravel, or face-plant on sharp rocks jutting out from the path.

Dan arrived ahead of me, flying down the hill impressively despite a broken sandal strap, and he signaled to an Indian Army officer who was overseeing the food drop. I can only imagine how surprised that officer was to see two white *bideshis* emerge, sprinting with a slightly crazed look from the heart of this remote village. Somehow, over the deafening roar of helicopter blades whirring overhead and despite the officer speaking only Hindi, we were able to get our basic message across in Nepali: "Foreign doctors, injuries in village, people in other village, get to Pokhara. . ." It turned out they were picking up a group of five Nepali trekkers stranded in Runchet after the earthquake. Gesturing to a few young villagers, he gave the order that any injured patients should be brought right away if they wanted treatment in Pokhara.

They gathered the man with crush injuries and another woman in similar shape, and laid them both on the floor of the helicopter's enormous interior bay. It was far larger than the commercial five-seater that had taken us here. I couldn't get a cell signal where we were, and knew we had to alert our team that we'd managed to get a ride with the Indian Army, so they didn't keep working to sort that out. Turning on our satellite phone, I could find just one bar of service inside the helicopter bay. With minutes to go before takeoff, I leapt outside into the bright noonday sun, trying desperately to get a signal and send out a brief, typed message to headquarters. After an eternity of seconds, worrying that the helicopter might take off at any moment and leave me behind, the *Sent* confirmation popped up on the screen, and I scrambled back on board. Then the helicopter took off, as Dan and I tried to show the pilot with hand gestures roughly where we thought Keraunja was located.

We landed on top of another of Keraunja's rice terraces, the helicopter tucking into a small mountainside crevice that barely fit its huge, spinning blades. While military personnel loaded three more injured villagers from there, they pushed back against a crowd of others trying to jump aboard. We saw a few people squeeze in among the cargo on one side. It was difficult to imagine how desperate they were to get out. Meanwhile, I jumped to the ground again, asking them to wait another minute, and ran back up to the tarp where Urmila and her family were.

In a few words I tried to explain we were leaving, as I thrust the bag of granola and a couple of Snickers bars I brought with me into Urmila's hands. It seemed unlikely to help, given how dire the situation was, but I didn't know how else to convey the gratitude we felt for her kindness. I then grabbed my own small pack, ran back to the helicopter, and jumped back in.

It was finally over. Our INF team met us at the regional airstrip on the outskirts of Pokhara, where we landed half an hour later. After a quick debrief at their headquarters, they dropped us off at a familiar guesthouse to rest. Peeling off clothes bearing three days of sweat and grime, showering in gloriously clean water, it was impossible not to think of the frigid cold that Urmila and her family were enduring. Dan and I regrouped at a Lakeside restaurant in the heart of Pokhara's tourist district, where I ate a beet salad on an utterly different kind of terrace from the one where we'd stood just a few hours earlier, devastated by the dizzying whiplash between disparity and privilege.

Part 3 - Being

The other gods were strong, but Thou wast weak;
They rode, but Thou didst stumble to a throne;
But to our wounds only God's wounds can speak,
And not a god has wounds, but Thou alone.

- *Edward Shillito, "Jesus of the Scars"* -

But we know that when He appears we shall be like Him,
because we shall see Him as He is.

- *1 John 3:2b* -

CHAPTER FORTY-TWO
Seething

Less than a week after the earthquake, I was back rounding in the hospital. On the maternity ward that morning, our census was sky-high. The afternoon before, female OPD lines had stretched on forever. And we were short on doctors. Understandably, several of the residents had returned home to be with their families and communities, and to join the recovery efforts. Others were out on sick leave, or tending to ill family members. On my first morning back, Maya was the only resident assigned with me on maternity. The Nepali attending had inexplicably not shown up to handover that morning. The recent earthquake's devastation was explanation enough. Whatever the reason for his absence, I was on my own.

Sitting at the bedside of our first patient, my stomach sank as I read through her chart. She had delivered ten days earlier, by an emergency preterm Caesarean because of eclamptic seizures, a serious complication of pregnancy. Her preterm infant was still critically ill in the newborn nursery, and unlikely to survive. This patient herself had just been transferred back to our maternity ward from the critical care unit that morning, where she'd been touch and go for days with two other life-threatening complications of delivery:

disseminated intravascular coagulation and profound anemia.

She'd had a temperature overnight, with what looked like a brewing infection. She seemed unlikely, in her tenuous condition, to survive another complication. Primal fear fueled the anger swelling in my chest. A grim day loomed ahead, its tasks pressing down upon me with crushing weight. I blinked back tears and averted my gaze, focusing down on the chart in my hands. I felt in over my head. Here, yet another tragedy was unfolding.

And this was another day in a long string of hard days that seemed to stretch back a decade. I thought back to the sleepless nights and stresses of college, then med school, and finally residency. Every job I'd ever held required regular stretches of work lasting twenty-four to thirty-six hours without a break. I felt like I was being wrestled to the ground, face pressed down in the mud, unable to catch a gulp of air.

But it was even more than that. It was all the work beneath the work, the intense striving to prove myself as worthy and acceptable. Always seeking to be the best, the brightest, the most professional, the most punctual. I'd spent the entirety of my twenties and the better part of my thirties trying to become the ideal, perfect doctor. By and large, I thought I'd pulled it off.

And yet. . . here I was, fraught with stress and exhaustion, terrified to be found out as flawed. It took one careless mistake, one small misjudgment. With such complicated and sick patients, it felt inevitable. Not only that, but I was *angry* — furious at having to carry the entire burden of this service by myself, peeved at being punished with double the work just because I was the diligent sap who showed up every day. Sitting there at the bedside of this critically ill woman, I seethed silently with the pent-up frustration of years finally bubbling over. It all came to rest, as if in laser focus, on this one, absent colleague, and like a lightning rod, drew all that rage in full force.

I contemplated what to do with this patient. Lifting my

eyes to meet hers, I saw her face was pale and weary from what she'd endured. Yet in her exhaustion, she looked back at me hopefully, even eagerly, as if trusting that I, her stethoscope-draped doctor, held the promise of healing. It seared me like a hot knife to see her beautiful humanity. I fought back another surge of tears, seeing how my own self-absorption was clouding even my capacity to attend to her suffering. As I sat there, guilt washed through me, compounding my feelings of helplessness. I grieved the fact of her profound suffering at all.

Just then, Anneke darted in. "I'm just checking on each ward, Becca. Are you doing okay? Do you have everything you need?"

"Fine," I spat back, "Just *fine*. It's only me and Maya here. Where's the other attending? He didn't even bother to come in!"

Anneke looked at me for a long moment, registering my irritation. Then she said, "Right then. You don't need to worry about him, Becca. Please, just do your best."

I felt even more alone, and ashamed that I had gotten angry with her. I berated myself for speaking so unprofessionally to my friend and colleague. *Anneke must see me as so immature.*

The rest of the morning ground by painfully. Inching along, bed by bed, Maya and I got through all the mothers and babies on the ward. The whole time, barely able to focus, I couldn't shake the feeling that I'd acted terribly, and wanted to make it right. When rounds were finally done, I walked over to the administration building and climbed the steps to the medical superintendent's office.

I hesitated for a second outside the half-open door, then knocked and entered.

"Anneke, I'm sorry I got so annoyed when you came by. It's just that I'm really upset, and I felt so alone as the only senior doctor this morning!" My words started flooding out with an intensity that surprised even me.

"Why can't our staff just show up like they're supposed to?" I blurted out. It was as though a dam had burst. I'd never intended to let all this out, and certainly not to Anneke, whom I so deeply respected. But I couldn't stop, or even filter what was coming forth.

"I feel like I'm the *only one* working around here!" I all but shouted, in a hyperbolic finale of self-pity.

"Well, I'm sorry you feel that way," she pointedly replied. Her response stung, because I knew I was speaking like a fool. Plenty of others, Anneke included, had been working tirelessly, and for much longer than I'd even been a doctor. I sounded like a spoiled child.

"You know, that attending had to hold everything together while we were at the retreat, Becca," she continued, sounding weary all of a sudden.

In unloading my frustrations, I hadn't for a moment considered what the hospital must have been like in the immediate wake of the earthquake. I'd heard there was some unrest in those first days, while Dan and I were on the mission in Gorkha. The team here had to deal with all of that. Then I remembered that when the earthquake struck, all the ex-pat doctors were in Pokhara for the conference. This same colleague had volunteered to supervise the hospital while we were away, which meant he was the only senior physician there during that ill-fated weekend.

"He even had to calm crowds that were gathering outside the hospital, at the Upper Gate, trying to maintain a semblance of order after the earthquake. I doubt it was easy, Becca." When I imagined this, I realized how much his calm, competent demeanor would have helped quell anxious mobs thronging the front gate, threatening to riot.

I was suffocating beneath the burden of my own crushing standards, and sucking all the air out of the room by resenting and objectifying other human beings. I had no bandwidth to appreciate the challenges my colleagues faced, let alone the suffering of each day's stream of patients. I had no space left for compassion.

CHAPTER FORTY-THREE

The Emmaus Way

The interaction with Anneke continued to weigh heavily on me for the rest of the week. It was certainly on my mind one afternoon a few days later, when I sat down to prepare for a team Bible study I'd offered to lead.

The last time our study group met, several Nepali physicians had arranged a game of Scripture Trivia. *Oh cool, I thought, I know the Bible pretty well. This should be fun!*

We were divided up into two teams, and the leader pulled out a sheet of looseleaf paper. I could see that around twenty Bible verse references had been hand-printed on it in pencil. The game commenced, and the teams went back and forth, rotating through each player in turn, as the leader read aloud the references.

"Deuteronomy 28:9!"

The person whose turn it was had to recite whatever verse was referenced. From *memory*. Each team earned a point when their person recalled the verse correctly. Back and forth the volleys went, and to a *person*, every Nepali nurse, doctor and tech there knew the verses that were called out, reciting them with instantaneous precision. I'd never seen anything like it. (It's worth mentioning, too, that these were not your typical "blessing box" Scriptures — the kinds of verses popularized

229

by packs of mass-printed inspirational cards decorated in floral patterns. No, these all appeared to be relatively obscure verses, chosen seemingly at random.)

When it was my turn, the leader called out yet another reference — "Titus 3:8!"

I looked back at him blankly.

"Oh, you can say it in English if you want," he said magnanimously. "It's okay, you don't have to have it memorized in *Nepali*."

I grinned like a lunatic, then stammered something about how that wasn't *exactly* the issue, and deferred my turn to a teammate. The whole thing was so fantastically incredible that I simply had to laugh. It was truly impressive to witness how well my Nepali brothers and sisters knew and valued the Scriptures, and how they had committed so much of it to heart.

For our upcoming study, we would not be playing Scripture Trivia. Since it was nearing Eastertide, I'd chosen a story at the end of Luke's gospel, of Jesus encountering two disciples on the road to Emmaus after His resurrection, that I'd lately found particularly compelling.

I opened my Bible to Luke 24 and began to imagine the story playing out as I read along. It was late afternoon on a Sunday in Jerusalem's springtime. Two of Jesus's disciples were walking toward Emmaus, a town seven miles west of Jerusalem, speaking with one another about the tumultuous events of the past three days. Could it have been only three days since the execution of their leader, teacher, and friend Jesus, the man on whom they'd placed their deepest hopes?

He was the One, they'd thought more than once. *He was the One to redeem Israel.*

Jesus was supposed to be the long-awaited and longed-for Messiah. Yet a series of tragic events had unfolded faster than anyone could comprehend, and Jesus had died a gruesome death before their eyes. Even now, the events of His trial, beating, execution, and final cries replayed over and over in their memories, still raw on their hearts. It did not yet seem real.

They plodded along with defeated steps, making much of their journey in silence. After a while, another man approached, apparently headed in the same direction. He must have been going at quite a clip, for they hadn't noticed anyone else on this stretch of road all afternoon. He caught up to them, drawing alongside with a greeting.

"What are you discussing as you go along your way?" the man asked, with evident curiosity.

"Are you the only visitor to Jerusalem who doesn't know what's been happening around here?" one of them jabbed back, his voice laden with wonder and scorn.

They did not recognize this man as Jesus. Mysteriously, the text says, they were somehow "kept from recognizing Him." Yet here was the very One who had suffered all the horrors to which they alluded — the torture and suffering they themselves had witnessed, the death they still acutely grieved. As I envisioned the disciple's condescending, jeering question, I realized that even here, Jesus was being treated like an outsider to the very events He, alone, knew with a victim's intimacy.

Had it been me, hearing that question with the remembrance of those affairs still raw on my mind and body, I'd have become a bit. . . prickly. "Know? Oh I *know*. Look here, at these wounds. You can see for yourselves just how well I know it!"

But what did Jesus actually say at this juncture? He responded with a question that epitomized *listening* itself — listening not just to an account of events, but to the very depths of their hearts. He heard their grief, their confusion, and the cries of their wounded, bewildered hearts. And then He responded with a question astonishing in its simplicity.

"What things?"

It was as if He, who had more intimate knowledge of this experience than anyone else on earth, was saying, "Educate Me."

I can barely fathom such humility. It is frighteningly easy

to serve with a sense of having all the answers. Even if I am reluctant to acknowledge it, pat answers betray my proud heart's stance. I am too quick to speak, too slow to listen. It is humility that *truly* listens, patiently and thoughtfully. Humility listens generously, without generating a mental list of answers that impede the very act of listening itself. To hear with such openness, receiving the other purely for their own sake, requires first an assumption that they have something to share, something I do not already know. Impossible, of course, when I'm sure I know it all.

This stance of humility is a self-forgetful posture. I am tempted to fill the gap of silence with speech to ensure that I am heard, seen, and acknowledged — reassurance that *I count*. True listening is so deeply other-centered, so absorbed in the other, that it is not possible to be aware of, let alone concerned with, yourself. This self-forgetting humility is not the natural stance of the human heart. And in encountering those rare souls who do possess it, you realize that true humility is also hard wrought. It is a beauty forged in fire.

At his death, it was said of the missionary D. E. Hoste that "he lived to be forgotten, so that Christ could be remembered." Hoste served as the General Director of the China Inland Mission in the early twentieth century, though his name is far less known than that of his predecessor, James Hudson Taylor. Some might say that Hoste succeeded in his humble endeavor. Yet when I heard that, it reminded me of the missionaries Willem told me about — men and women who spent their whole lives waiting at Nepal's sealed border in the 1930s and '40s, simply praying to be allowed in. And it was Jesus who first demonstrated this way of humility. In becoming human, Jesus voluntarily gave up heaven itself. He emptied Himself of the eternally other-serving dance of love at the heart of the Trinity, trading its perfect harmony for the cruel brokenness of our world. It was a world He Himself had lovingly created, and a world that long ago spurned that Love.

I find it almost impossible to leave behind my sense of

agency, my power, all my privilege and entitlement. I cling to a resumé and credentials that provide ready access to power, and which feel like they give me an identity. If I'm honest, it's frightening to think of what leaving them aside would mean. Can I truly see myself as worthy, even without the things to which I look in moments of insecurity, when the fangs of self-doubt sink deep?

In contrast, Jesus's life and ministry was one of deep dependence and vulnerability, from the infancy of His incarnation onwards. His earliest childhood memories were as a refugee, his parents fleeing the genocide of a murderous dictatorship. As a teenager, He knew the ostracism of being presumed a bastard, his pedigree questioned in gossiping, middle-class whispers. As a young man, He withstood ridicule, coped with homelessness, endured singleness in a culture that brooked little tolerance for it, and died the ignominious death of public execution, unjustly condemned and lynched at the hands of an enraged mob. The Lord of Hosts relinquished the protection of His angel-armies; He who created all that exists withheld the power to yield bread from stones. In life, Jesus was constantly misunderstood by those closest to Him. In death, He was betrayed and deserted by even His dearest companions.

It is a wonder to me, then, how He could ask, "What things?" I am loathe to give up even an inch of my own self-reliance. Yet despite all His suffering, or perhaps because of it, Jesus was able to respond with tenacious, humbling humility.

"Learn to live inside this story," says theologian N. T. Wright of the Emmaus account, "and you will find it inexhaustible."

CHAPTER FORTY-FOUR

Mr. Kumar's Miracle

It was another busy day in the Emergency Department, each gurney occupied, every bench crowded with patients. All were waiting — some to be triaged, others for the results of labs drawn hours earlier, still others for their promised X-ray order slips. And all of them wanted to see the doctor.

That week in Emergency had brought with it a series of devastating patient stories. One twenty-seven-year-old woman had come to the ED with severe burns covering sixty percent of her body, following a suicide attempt in which she had set herself on fire. She died two days later. I heard of a nine-year-old girl brought in by her family with a broken neck, her arms and legs flaccidly limp because she was playing with her friends inside of an abandoned cement mixer that got suddenly flipped upside down. She would be paralyzed from the neck down for the rest of her life.

A skeletal thirteen-year-old boy had also come in that week, mere skin and bones, due to extreme malnutrition. He was suffering from severe PTSD following the earthquake, because when the shaking began, he'd managed to escape outdoors, only to stand and watch as his home collapsed with his younger siblings still inside, killing them all. Racked with guilt because his parents had put him in charge of looking over them that morning, he'd stopped eating.

Just the day before, a little baby girl with severe diarrhea and sepsis, only eleven days old, was carried to us in her mother's arms, already dead on arrival. And that was a fairly typical week in Tansen's ED. The suffering was unimaginable, and agonizing to witness.

Our morning's laconic start now seemed a distant memory. The crush of patients had been steady from just before lunch until around 8:30 PM, when our medical assistant Khirel touched my elbow to get my attention. I paused from filling out yet another packet of papers in the deluge of admissions and looked up, irritation momentarily flickering across my face.

"Manche heredinos. Gasping huncha." Please come see this man. He is gasping.

I hurried over to the gentleman lying on a gurney along the back wall, a nebulizer treatment steaming into the oxygen mask on his face. Through the clear plastic, his lips were an unnerving tinge of dusky blue, and I noticed the oxygen sensor on his finger was reading in the low 50s, half of normal. His eyes were closed, just a sliver of his up-rolled eyes showing. He had the look of desperation, the posture of a dying man. His expanded chest wall flickered with subtle movements, the only indication that he was still alive, if barely, and still trying to breathe. Nothing else moved.

When I listened to his chest, my stethoscope pressed over his ribs just beneath his collarbone, I heard nothing. A "silent chest" is one of the textbook features of a critical attack of asthma or chronic obstructive pulmonary disorder (COPD). It's an ominous finding, indicating that the airways are so tightly constricted that air can't pass through, not even enough to produce a wheezing or whistling sound.

I glanced quickly at his chart. Raj Kumar, aged sixty-five, male. History of COPD, longstanding. Discharged from Tansen that morning after treatment for a COPD exacerbation, only to return six hours later with a flare-up of exactly the same thing.

"We've already given him IV steroids, a series of nebs, antibiotics, even started a theophylline drip," Khirel said softly in Nepali, ticking off the mainstays of treatment. "No effect though." This combination is meant to relax the muscles around his tight airways, which were suffocating him from within like hundreds of tiny boa constrictors. Mr. Kumar was clearly about to go into cardiac arrest — "gasping" indeed. I tried to think of what else we could offer to buy him some time until the steroids kicked in, hopefully in a few hours. He was exhausted, and clearly didn't look like he'd last anywhere near that long.

The immediate response to this sort of problem is normally intubation and mechanical ventilation — putting the patient on a "breathing machine" — to give them a rest from the hard work of breathing, and a chance for their stressed lungs to recover. But our limited supply of ventilators — a total of two, both for adults — dictated strict criteria for their use. Functionally, they were reserved mainly for cases of neurotoxic snake bites, which caused a reversible kind of paralysis. Tansen guidelines were clear. They were not to be used in cases of chronic illness progression. And *chronic* is what "C" stands for in "COPD."

I racked my brain, thinking that there *must* be something else, and trying to suppress that old, familiar feeling that I was yet again failing the patient dying right in front of me. Then it hit me.

"Khirel, what do you think about IV Magnesium? We haven't tried that yet, right?"

Magnesium is an old treatment, used "off-label" for severe asthma attacks when nothing else in "conventional therapy" has worked. It was the one remaining option, at this point surely a last-ditch effort. Khirel drew up the two-gram dose in a syringe, which, as I read in the ED manual, had to be infused over twenty minutes. Sitting down on the edge of Mr. Kumar's gurney, I gave the slow IV push myself. Listening to his lungs again several minutes later, I was amazed to hear the faintest whistle emerging. *Progress*. I'd never been so relieved to hear a patient wheeze.

Ten minutes after that, back at the nursing station writing out orders for Mr. Kumar's admission, Khirel again hurried over and asked me to see a sick four-month-old baby in the gurney right next to his. Indeed, this infant was *sick*, chest heaving away at an exhausting 110 breaths per minute as he lay limp in his mother's arms. The baby's lips were blue tinged in spite of the oxygen, and his dry tongue, sunken fontanelle, and doughy skin were all ominous signs of severe shock. He looked like no infant ever should. Yet by now, it had become a look all too familiar. I sensed myself bracing. I just knew it. This was one of the infants who wouldn't make it.

One of the ED techs struggled to get venous access on the infant, but then miraculously threaded a catheter into one tiny, flat vein. We immediately started IV fluids and gave doses of IV ampicillin and gentamicin, the same combination long used for severe infections of virtually any kind in infancy, and somehow still effective. I squatted down in front of the gurney to discuss the care and prognosis with his young mother, who looked barely twenty. Yet I could see in her eyes that she already knew it too. A teenaged woman at her side, her younger sister perhaps, frantically protested at hearing the dismal prognosis.

"I hope he does alright," I said comfortingly. "We're giving him the very best medicines we have."

After all the admission orders were written, I looked back over to these patients. Both males, one old and one young, laying in adjacent beds, both in fulminant respiratory failure. Without the option of mechanical ventilation for either, there was nothing left to do other than wait for the medications to work. Or not. I watched as the two patients were wheeled to their respective critical care wards, following the infant to the pediatric unit. I sat there with his tiny body for over an hour, with nothing more than oxygen, antibiotics, and steroids to offer. Each breath, followed by a disturbingly long pause, seemed to be his last.

Finally, I met up with the on-call resident, who would help follow the patients through the night. He would be the one to get the call when they worsened further, as I was certain they would, and eventually to pronounce them when they died, so I wanted him to know everything about them.

In the darkness of the call room, now 10:30 PM, I stretched out on a bed and studied the ceiling. There was barely enough hope left in me even to pray. How many times over the last two years had I offered such prayers on behalf of patients? Prayers for healing, for deliverance, for life. Too often. And every time, it seemed, they went unheard, a cry into the silent, dark void.

These two were patients about whom I could entertain no delusions regarding my own ability to bring healing. I knew I could offer them nothing more than the treatments we'd given, and then place them in God's hands, asking for a miracle of healing. And I couldn't even do that. Instead, I asked for mercy, that they would at least have comfort and presence in their dying this night. There was no doubt that two empty beds would greet me when I returned to the wards. At some point or another, the only thing left would be the gurney's black plastic mattresses, freshly wiped down and glistening, ready for two more patients.

Yet somehow through the night, they both managed to continue breathing. By the next morning, as I made my checks through each ward, I was stunned to see the infant still there with his mother. They were both curled up in a pediatric crib, the infant laboring to breathe but still alive, and without the blue-tinged lips of eight hours earlier. Moving from there to the adult ward, I was even more astonished to find Mr. Kumar sitting up in bed, cross-legged and smiling, looking wonderfully alive with his bright eyes and the hint of an impish grin. He was an entirely different man.

It occurred to me then just how far I had acquiesced to the limitations of care here. Or perhaps more accurately, to my own limitations. Having offered all we could, with nothing left to do but wait and be present, I now no longer fretted anxiously at the bedside as I used to, wondering what more I should try. There was nothing else left. Our menu of options had been exhausted for them both. Only the grace of God could step in, doing what I could not.

In that understanding, I realized that my presence at the bedside was now free to be *only* that — presence. Waiting *with*. There was no diagnostic uncertainty here, only the uncertainty of whether these tired bodies before me would continue to fight, struggling along with whatever supports we could offer. I thought back to the man with kala-azar, the first patient I'd lost in Tansen, and realized that I'd been learning this lesson for a long time.

CHAPTER FORTY-FIVE
Debriefing

Four months after the earthquake, an email arrived in my inbox from two INF staff members, requesting a follow-up debriefing after the team's relief efforts. I happened to be passing through Kathmandu at the time, having just come back from a whirlwind two-week trip to America for my sister's wedding. I only had four months left in Nepal, which made returning a little easier this time.

Since I was leaving for Tansen the following morning, we arranged to meet one afternoon in a cafe near the Kathmandu guesthouse where I'd spent the night. After brief introductions, they asked how things were going since working with the INF team in Gorkha four months earlier.

"I'm not doing great," I confessed. "I still have earthquake nightmares from time to time, and every day, little surges of panic still come when anything nearby quivers, like when a nurse bumps the table where I'm writing notes, or someone runs by heavily. It's so weird, but even on the flight I just took, turbulence shook the plane a few times in exactly the same way that the earthquake had, and I thought it was another aftershock. It didn't make any sense, of course — we were at 30,000 feet! Each time it happens, I make a conscious effort to look relaxed, but all the while my heart is surging into my throat, adrenaline tingling in my fingertips, and I'm scanning the area for the nearest secure place."

They both murmured with understanding. I pressed on, keen to unload the real burden I was holding. "Whatever. I'm sure that will all improve with time. But I think what's bothering me even more is this vague, uncertain feeling about the *role* I played during those few days on our relief mission."

They looked at me quizzically, so I continued. "I mean, here I was, a random *bideshi* doctor literally dropping into these villages where all we were able to really do was ask a few questions and maybe hand out some Tylenol. I suppose we did identify a few injured people who could benefit from getting airlifted out. But did we really do any good at all?"

In truth, the more I'd thought about it over the last few months, it seemed possible we had unwittingly done harm, in fact. We'd arrived in Keraunja uninvited, eaten part of their precious food stores, and then left, plucked out as abruptly as we'd appeared. I thought back to the handful of patients we'd flown out of Keraunja and Runchet, some of whom had jumped aboard our helicopter at the last minute. They were airlifted to Pokhara, which was far enough from their town that it might as well have been a different country. Separated from family and community, with all overland routes wiped out, were they ever able to get back home? I also thought of the damage done to precious rice crops on the two occasions our helicopters landed on Keraunja's terraces. It seemed entirely possible that we'd done *only* harm.

These sorts of questions left me with a deep ambivalence about my participation in the relief effort. I voiced all of this freely, feeling my conscience lightening as I aired my confessions aloud. The INF counselors listened generously. Then they shared the reason why they were setting up meetings with all their earthquake team personnel — in part, it was to provide in-person updates to each of us about how some of those villages were doing.

"Well, apparently there was a huge landslide in Keraunja just two weeks after we were there," I said, telling them about a Nepali newspaper article Dan had forwarded to me soon after we got back. When he'd shared that, I immediately thought of the bag of granola I'd handed to Urmila, hoping at the time that it would help out her family, at least a little. But even that tiny offering had proved tragically irrelevant. The article reported that the landslide, unsettled by a second 7.3 magnitude earthquake in early May, had decimated the entire village, almost certainly killing Urmila and her family.

"Oh no, how terrible. Such tragic news," they both lamented. "Well, that could be the case. We weren't able to access any of the more mountainous villages by road — you can still only fly to those towns you visited that second day by helicopter."

The two staffers had, however, traveled back to Pokharidada and Mailung, towns our INF team reached by vehicle on our first day. As it turned out, both towns were doing surprisingly well — considerably better, anyway, than other villages located even closer to main roads.

"Pokharidada and Mailung had already repaired most of their buildings by the time we visited," one said encouragingly. "Their recovery seemed to have been faster and more comprehensive than a lot of other places we saw, despite being further removed from building supply shops and the like."

"You know," the other continued, "the only main difference was that your team was *there*. No teams made it to any other villages nearby. We think that simply having people come in from the outside — even just talking with them in makeshift medical clinics, like you guys did — showed them that they were seen."

It was a relief to hear this. Maybe our being there reassured them that they were, literally and figuratively, "on the map," and not invisible to the outside world. I appreciated the idea of that. Such hints are reminders that redemption is really happening in the broken places of our world. They hold the promise that, under God's coming reign, all will once again be made whole.

This way of doing missions — and life — is totally upside down from how we usually think of things. It demands that we let go of outward successes and clearly achieved outcomes, however noble those metrics might be. Such an approach is bound to make ministry promotion and fundraising more of a challenge. Yet the way of Jesus will always be different. "The kingdom of heaven," Jesus said, "is like leaven that a woman took and hid in three measures of flour, until it was all leavened." His is a way where small, unseen acts can yield massive, eternal consequences. It is a way that is often hidden, obscure, or forgotten. His call invites us on a journey of humility, which sometimes looks like humiliating failure. It can feel a lot like death. Until, in that great reversal that is *also* the way of Jesus, it unexpectedly bears life instead.

For this reason, I've found it best not to compare callings. Those who respond to Christ's invitation are called to follow Him in whatever vocation He entrusts to us, provided we recognize His own special preference for the poor, marginalized and vulnerable of our world. For the Christian physician, this may be a call to move halfway around the world, or a call to care for refugees right next door. Whatever our vocation, may we be able to rest in the truth articulated by the writer and minister Frederick Buechner, that "the place God calls you to is the place where your deep gladness and the world's deep hunger meet."

When I selected that quote as the title and theme of my very first blog in Nepal, its truth had not yet been tested in the ways it would over the next few years. Yet Jesus remains ever the perfect Companion for this journey of calling. He yearns for us to know Him in relationship as we make that journey, hearing the echo of His question still — *"What are you discussing as you go along your way?"*

CHAPTER FORTY-SIX

Demolition

"You know, Becca," he began, in his precise, impeccably erudite Queen's English, "I've been thinking about something."

Callum and Midge had come for a visit, and we were drinking tea out on the porch early one morning, catching up. These dear friends had been with me from my first night in Nepal, when they collected me at the airport in Kathmandu and brought me to my guest house. Their good humor and generous listening always cheered me during trips through Tansen every other month. Now, they had just patiently listened to another of my long rants about pent-up griefs — including the awkward outburst I'd had a week earlier. I always wondered at their astonishing reserve of compassion, tirelessly creating spaces that so many of us at Tansen needed in order to process our daily work.

Looking thoughtful, Callum continued, "I wonder if perhaps God has been doing something like a construction project in your soul?" I looked at him curiously as he went on. "What if these past two years have been Phase One of the project, the Demolition Phase?"

This was an unexpected angle. Could it be that this whole, challenging period was actually a path to growth? I hadn't considered it that way before. As Callum's words sunk in, I had a dawning, comforting sense that perhaps the discomfort of these months was not without purpose. In fact, it was perhaps the *only* means of achieving that purpose.

I looked out on the valley, lost in thought as I watched the mountains in the distance. Streams of white cloud flowed over their ridges, cascading like waterfalls into the valley below. It was lovely, although now I saw those mountains differently — as beautiful, but also as sources of intense hardship. I held the stories of my patients closely, knowing the hardships they faced eking out a living in that distant, unforgiving landscape. I thought of families growing what nutritive food they could on the rugged, terraced fields clinging to those mountainsides. I also held stories, by now all too familiar, of perilously sick men, women, and children traversing long distances and steep terrain to seek medical care at our hospital — sometimes arriving too late to be helped.

Ever since the earthquakes six weeks earlier, I also felt a deep ambivalence toward those mountains. It was hard to forget, now, that they had been formed from similar upheavals of the earth. With the ground beneath us no longer the stable bedrock it had always seemed, I still found myself jumping every time a loud truck or tractor rattled along rutted paths near our home. It was an instinctive bracing against tremors that could escalate into the "next big one." After all, we'd had hundreds of aftershocks and a second major earthquake in that first month alone. It turns out an earthquake is never just *one* earthquake.

Before that morning in late April, nature's capacity for violence was a theoretical matter. My sole understanding of its threat was based on news of distant lands and far-off people — tragic stories of typhoons and tornados, hurricanes, tsunamis and, of course, other earthquakes. Then I experienced a massive earthquake firsthand, and suddenly the earth was no longer just an inanimate rock beneath me. It now possessed living, potentially lethal force.

Spending two years in this land — learning its language, befriending its people, slowly grasping its nuanced culture, surviving its natural disasters — had been stretching in countless ways. It was an experience of learning to see differently, in large part through the eyes of beautiful new relationships I'd formed here.

I looked back at Callum and Midge, wishing there was some kind of shortcut to growth, without having to pass through this way of suffering. "You mean a demolition project in my soul? So God can build something good, something necessary?"

"Yes, Becca. Perhaps. And if so, it's because He's preparing a foundation, something solid, that can be built upon with grace, later on."

Suddenly, I thought back to the story of the rich young ruler, which I had re-discovered soon after arriving in Tansen. I thought about how Jesus asked the young man to give up his riches, in order to help him let go of whatever was getting in the way of His love. Maybe Jesus was doing the same thing in me, through all of this. If His aim was to help me to look more like Him — to love and serve and live as He did, bearing His Spirit in me with grace as I moved about in our hurting world — then maybe that's *exactly* what I needed. It was hard for that young man, of course. Why wouldn't I expect it to be hard, too?

I hesitated, a question forming in my mind. "But can I *trust* Him? I mean, with this whole complicated process? Because it's just that it hurts *so much. . .*" I trailed off, my voice beginning to crack.

Just then, Maddy and Anneke strolled by, and we waved them over to join us. They each pulled up a short Nepali stool, called a *mudda*, and Anneke asked how we were doing. Then, noting my stricken face, she gave me a smile of deep, empathic kindness. I appreciated the strength and compassion of these two women, and was thankful for these four dear friends here, friends willing to sit with pain and discomfort, and not run away in fear.

"We're just talking about the strange ways of God, Anneke, and the painful paths to growth in His love," Midge offered, as they exchanged a brief, knowing look.

"Oh my. Yes." Anneke said, pausing for a minute. "You know, it's funny, because last night I was just preparing the English service I'm leading this Saturday. I was reading about a particular tapestry, the *Bayeux Tapestry*, from the Middle Ages."

We all looked over at her, intrigued. I raised my eyebrows, wondering where she was going.

"No, really — hear me out!" she laughed, seeing the expressions on our faces. "The tapestry includes a scene portraying Britain's King Harold holding a spear in his hand. His troops are marching before him, as he goads them on with the point of that spear. Do you know what the tapestry says? 'Harold Comforteth His Troops.' That's strange comfort, no?"

I laughed with her, and we all nodded with admiration at this powerful image. Then Anneke continued, more softly, "I've found that sometimes, God's encouragement looks a lot like that — painful in the moment, but He gets us where we need to go, in the end."

"You know," she went on, "I was also just reflecting on the fact that God probably didn't have to send most of my friends halfway around the world. He didn't have to bring *them* to Nepal, in order to draw them to Himself. But I guess He knew *I* needed that. At any rate, I know this much. . . God brought me to Nepal to teach me what it means to be a Christian."

I considered my own experience over the past two years. Immersion in the brokenness all around me had brought to light deep fractures within myself as well — an unwillingness to identify with the need I saw in my patients, an inability to be vulnerable, a smoldering rage at my inability to be all things to all people. It unearthed a hardness of heart within me that only gentleness could shatter. It is God's kindness, as the apostle Paul encouraged the church, that draws us back to Him. I was grappling with this relentless tenderness of Jesus, suffering not just *for*, but also *with*. His ways had proved a severe mercy, showing me just how desperate my need of Him really was. I didn't have to come to Him perfect. That's the whole point of grace.

Jesus will always choose to align Himself with the homeless leper, the blind beggar, the grieving spouse, the shamed woman of ill-repute. He does so at infinite cost to Himself — relinquishing His position of ultimate glory, peace, and unity at the loving heart of the Trinity, in favor of suffering, grief, betrayal, and ultimately, death. Crossing an infinity of gaps, the incarnate God-Man died to draw an outcast world back inside that Triune inner circle.

I came to Nepal assuming that my call was to stand in this gap for a few years, maybe more. I had served as a physician, bridging gaps that medicine is meant to bridge. As a white, educated holder of an American passport, I did so from a position of immense power and privilege, certain that I had a lot to offer. I had also served as a Christian, all the while assuming that this same Christ-burden of incarnation, this task of chasm-crossing, lay squarely with me. Yet these years had taught me a valuable lesson — that sometimes, I had little more to offer than my own flawed, permeable presence to the pain of those I'd thought I could rescue.

Reflecting back on my growth trajectory, I began to appreciate the humble wisdom of Anneke's words. It certainly seemed possible that God's reason for leading me to Nepal was to show me how much *I* needed *Him*, and how little I could actually do on my own. In the days and weeks following the earthquake, a metaphor began to take shape for me — that I wasn't capable of effecting my own spiritual rescue, any more than I could have saved myself out of that mountainside village.

In short, I think Anneke was right. God brought me to Nepal to teach me what it really means to be His.

CHAPTER FORTY-SEVEN
Returning

Time is a funny thing. There is something especially strange about time at the margins. It's like the way a decorative mirror-pool appears motionless, until you see the speed with which a leaf in its stream cascades over the edge and down its black-mirror wall. Albert Einstein articulated a scientific basis for the relativity of time, yet even without knowing or understanding all the details, we have an innate sense of this. We never quite get used to the pace of time — sometimes racing breathlessly by, sometimes plodding along with interminable languor.

The literary scholar C. S. Lewis once observed, "We are so little reconciled to time that we are even astonished at it. 'How he's grown!' we exclaim, 'How time flies!' . . . It is as strange as if a fish were repeatedly surprised at the very wetness of water. And that would be strange indeed: unless of course, the fish were destined to become, one day, a land animal." He owned that the strangeness of time, and our being "so little reconciled" to it, was evidence that humans were made for eternity, created for a world that transcends time.

As with the mirror-pool, I've noticed that time seems to speed up at transitions both large and small. To cite a mundane example, consider the last twenty minutes before heading out your door each morning. For me, those twenty minutes are a veritable time warp, where I'm invariably rushing to finish twenty "last-minute" things. Similarly, time began to accelerate at a breathtaking pace as my departure from Nepal drew near. There were goodbye gatherings and final *dal bhaats* with friends, along with a ton of cleaning, sorting, and packing to be done. We began planning another goodbye party for the team — and this time, suddenly, it was for me.

Having dragged on for months, time now rushed along like water over the edge of a cliff, leaving far too much to do in far too little time. It seemed important to reserve a little space for deliberate reflection, sorting through all the memories and meanings I would carry with me as this chapter of life drew to a close. One day, I asked Willem for advice on the upcoming transition home, and he advised that I build a RAFT.

"Well, I like to think of it as a *GRAFT*," he confided. "That 'G' is crucial. It stands for Gratitude, which is an important part of transitions like this. It's something they left out of their acronym — whoever the *"they"* are who came up with this." I smiled at my Dutch friend's opinionated and direct manner.

The rest of the acronym, he went on to explain, stood for "Reconciliation" wherever needed; "Affirmation" of what went well; "Farewells" to particularly important places and people; and finally, if a bit obviously, "Transition."

I tried building my own (G)RAFT, but got only as far as the first letter. I was thankful for the beauty of Tansen's spectacular landscape, and took every chance I could to wander up Srinagar Hill, and through my beloved Tansen Forest. There, it seemed, I could do my best thinking, and my most honest praying. Work at the hospital, while certainly hard in so many ways, was at least straightforward when it came to note-writing. I knew I was about to re-enter an insanely complex healthcare system, trading short, handwritten paper notes for an electronic medical record that could inflict Death by a Thousand Clicks, just to satisfy the dizzying demands laid out in foot-thick insurance manuals.

Walking home from work one afternoon, as I passed a row of tin-roofed restaurants outside the hospital, I could smell onions frying in a *masala* of cumin and turmeric, wafting around me. As I breathed in, I realized how much I would miss that smell. Then there were the colorful *saris* and *kurta surawals* that many Nepali women wore. Their sartorial beauty swirled with rich hues of red, green, blue, and gold — not for any particular occasion, but just because it's what *everyone* wore, along with dangling earrings, elaborate nose rings, and glittering bangle bracelets.

During Team Dinner later that week, I looked around the Guest House dining room at everyone laughing and talking together, and felt a surge of gratitude for this community. I thought about the music, my favorite part of our worship services, which was often sung *a cappella* or with simple guitar accompaniment. Here I learned hauntingly beautiful hymns — well-known standards in Australia and Britain, I'm told, but different from those I learned growing up. It called to mind another unexpected joy of Tansen — the chance to hear Scriptures read, and prayers prayed, in many varieties of accented English, as missionaries converged from all over the globe to serve here.

We had been through so much together, forging bonds unique to our "bomb-shelter friendships." For two years, I'd been embedded in a community of single-minded devotion to patients' well-being, all of us pulling in the same direction. We were interconnected in virtually every aspect of work, life, and worship. While it could be cramped or insular at times, I sensed I would miss this tight cohesion back home. Everywhere I looked, it seemed, there was something for which to be grateful.

One evening, intending to do some packing as soon as I got home from dinner with Dan and Leah's family that night, I checked my phone and saw I'd missed an unexpected call from my mother. Panicked, I knew something must be wrong. My family never called my cell phone — I insisted on that, because of expensive long-distance fees. Instead, we'd established a regular pattern of checking in on Skype. I hit "play" on the voicemail, and heard my mother's voice in the recording. "Hi honey, I hope you're doing well. Things are okay here, everyone's fine. But your dad was admitted to the hospital with a small stroke. We wanted to let you know, but really, try not to worry. Just give us a call when you can."

I called my mother back immediately and got the details. "It started with some confusion when he woke up this morning," she began. I looked at the clock and realized it was around ten in the morning on the East Coast. "I noticed he was having difficulty speaking, like he couldn't think of the word he wanted to use. And he just seemed. . . *off*. Then, when he got up to go to the bathroom, he nearly fell over, so I called the ambulance right away. We're still in the emergency room, but the doctor said he didn't need any more medicine for now, just the aspirin they gave him when he got here. We're waiting for a neurologist to come by."

"Oh no, I'm so sorry to hear this, Mom! That must have been so scary for you both!" I heard her stifle a soft cry on the other end. "I should come home right away, I think. Don't you think so? I mean, I can call and move my flight around first thing tomorrow morning, it won't be a problem."

"No, no — you don't have to do that! You're coming home in two weeks anyway! He's fine, *really* he is. Just a little tired now. But his speech is already back to normal, almost. It was a very small stroke, they said, thank goodness!"

After we hung up the phone, I wondered what to do. It *did* sound like things were under control back home, and that amazingly, he was already recovering. Maybe he'd be back to normal in a couple of days. Still, it was awful being so far from home. If anything else happened — anything worse — there was no way to get home in time. Everything felt so uncertain. Talking it over with Leah that evening, I decided to take my mom's advice and keep my original booking.

Two weeks later, in early December — using only the second one-way ticket I'd ever purchased — I left Nepal.

Early on the morning of my departure, I said goodbye to the Tansen community. A dear group of friends had gathered to bid me farewell on the path behind our home — Dan and Leah, Anneke and Willem, Maddy, Didi, Maya, Tenzing, and even a couple of our visiting medical students. It had been a week of heartfelt, bittersweet goodbyes, a time in which to reflect on beautiful friendships formed, and look forward to the evolution of those friendships in a new chapter. But I was ready.

As the car pulled away, bumping down the road *en route* to the airport, I tried to parse through a tumultuous mixture of feelings. First among them was the sense of relief. This intense, two-year ordeal was over. Infiltrating that relief, however, was a worry that, in my eagerness to wish time away, I'd perhaps missed something vital. Had I failed to see and appreciate all that was right in front of me, the gifts of these years? It felt like a question I couldn't answer, at least not yet. Mostly, I just felt numb. I was tired of *feeling*, period. All I wanted was to curl up and hibernate for a long, long time.

A couple of hours later, my vehicle reached the Bhairawa airport. I easily caught my flight to Kathmandu that afternoon, then flagged a taxi to Callum and Midge's. They'd invited me to stay with them for a couple of days, to complete some final tasks in the city. Traffic in Kathmandu pressed in as usual, cars and motorcycles moving together as tightly and fluidly as people on a crowded sidewalk. They wove languidly back and forth, in and out, braiding a tapestry of casual chaos just outside my taxi window. I took in the stream of trucks, cars, and rickshaws one last time. How long would it be, I wondered, until I'd again see this world so close at hand?

Several days after leaving Tansen, I finally landed in the States, arriving through New York's JFK International Airport late one December night. The airport was empty at that hour, except for the planeload of weary travelers disembarking from our transatlantic flight, and a meager scattering of airport employees. The final leg of this years-long journey was over.

As I emerged from baggage claim, I immediately saw my parents waiting for me on the other side of JFK's vast "Arrivals" atrium. My father was sitting in a wheeled transport chair, but struggled to his feet when he saw me emerge. Standing next to them, I was surprised to see my dear friend Jane and her husband Bob, who had also come to welcome me home. We waved at each other across the large hall, while I hauled my overloaded luggage cart as quickly as I could. It moved me deeply to see those four, grinning faces gathered in a sea of strangers beyond the metal airport barricade. Reaching them, we all embraced for a long time, overcome with relief to be back together. My father cried, and I held him even more tightly.

I was finally home.

CHAPTER FORTY-EIGHT

The Weight of Poverty

I was glad to be home. Yet there were times in those first weeks back when it seemed I'd fall apart at any moment. Returning home around Christmastime, it was especially jarring to be surrounded by the holiday's glittering, abundant opulence everywhere I went. The local grocery store I went to one afternoon near my New York apartment had more varieties of cheese — as well as salad dressings, breakfast cereals, condiments, and preserves — than I could count. In Tansen, we were glad for the chance to buy a frozen block of bland Swiss whenever it happened to be available. Completely overwhelmed by the selection here, I left the store speechless, and a little bit sad.

Two weeks after returning home I was visiting my parents, and ran into some elderly neighbors who lived across the street. They invited me over for a chat. They'd just celebrated sixty-one years of marriage the weekend before, and I got the sense that, with their advancing years, faith had grown deep roots in their shared life. Settling onto couches in their cozy living room, the wife pulled out a slip of yellow legal paper from her Bible and said, "We were praying for you, Rebecca — the whole time you were in Nepal. We keep a list of everyone we know doing missions work, anywhere in the world." As she held up the dog-eared paper, I was humbled and surprised to hear that they'd even *thought* of me, let alone kept track of my time abroad.

For more than an hour, we talked about Nepal. They asked question after question, utterly absorbed in a world far removed from the rural cul-de-sac where we sat. At one point, something brought to mind the story of a twenty-two-year-old patient on our medical ward. She was admitted for kidney failure, and by the time she reached us, she was close to death. Her body was swollen with toxic fluids that her kidneys could no longer excrete. Confusion had slowly crept in over the past few days, finally causing her to slip into a coma. As so often happened in Tansen, it was unclear what disease was ravaging her kidneys, but we thought it was possibly an autoimmune condition known as lupus. A single, non-specific lab result was all we had to go on, as any other diagnostic options were limited. Knowing the disease's name wouldn't have changed the limited treatment options we could offer her, anyway. We didn't even have a dialysis machine to take over the job of her failing kidneys, let alone targeted immunotherapies or fancy drug infusions.

Sadly, this was a fairly typical story, similar to countless cases I'd already seen by that point. At the time, I remember leading the young woman's father out to a hallway corner, the ward's most secluded space, to discuss her prognosis. The man looked old — older, I suspect, than he actually was — and wore the threadbare clothes of a rural farmer. On his head perched a dusty *dhaka-topi*, the traditional hat worn by Nepali men. His wiry frame and thin, powerful shoulders were hunched forward, absorbing the impact of my words. He seemed to be trying to grasp news that no father should ever have to.

This had been a tough case. His daughter had very little time left to live — hours, a few days at most — and there was nothing more that we, or anyone, could do to reverse her disease. Although there's a role for palliative treatments in such situations, families instead would often choose to bring their loved ones home before death, both for pragmatic reasons as well as cultural and religious ones.

Yet it was what her father said next that I most vividly remember.

"I am such a poor man. Oh, if only I were not so poor! *Then* she could live," he lamented, his voice heavy with resignation. The memory of his words haunted me, betraying not only the wrenching pathos of grief, but also the vicious, exacting toll of poverty — physically, psychologically, and spiritually. I knew that anywhere in the world, his daughter's chances of survival, let alone recovery, would have been poor. I tried to explain this to him, wanting desperately to give him at least this one, meager gift I could, of alleviating his sense of regret. Yet he stood there and, in a voice choked with guilt, whispered, "*Yadi ma tyasto gariba manisa nabhayeko bhaneh.*" *If only I were not such a poor man.*

It seemed important that this man hear from me that his daughter's death was *not* his fault. She was not dying because of something he'd failed to provide. His daughter was indeed very ill, but I could confidently say that nowhere else in the world, not even with the most sophisticated level of care, would things likely have gone any differently for her at that point. Kidney failure from lupus, if indeed that's what it was, carries a dismal prognosis. I wanted him to hear it from a doctor, whose words carried authority — words that might not mean much in that moment, but might offer him a degree of solace when he recalled them weeks or months later. I wanted to ensure that, of all the grievous burdens he would carry home with him, the weight of guilt would not be among them.

As I shared all of this with my neighbors that afternoon, relating a story I hadn't yet processed with anyone else, sudden, unexpected waves of emotion surged forth. Of course, this kind of story was far from unusual at Tansen. Similar stories played out day after day in our hospital, across Nepal, and around the world. It hadn't even been a particularly emotional experience for me at the time. With the pressure of the day's tasks shuttling us all from one crisis to the next, there was rarely an inch even to pause and breathe. Now, caught completely off guard, I lost my composure right there in the middle of their living room, and began sobbing. Not until that wintry afternoon, seeing their story through the lens of my own affluent culture, did the tragedy of it fully land.

CHAPTER FORTY-NINE
Transplanting Flowers

By and large, my first weeks back were wonderfully restful. I lived with Jane and Bob in New York during my first few months home, while searching for apartments in the area. There were a few things to do, like sort out the requirements for medical license renewal and review apartment lease contracts. Yet the absence of many pressing responsibilities was lovely, if also strange. And it was a transitional space, full of reminders of just how long I'd been away.

One unseasonably warm afternoon during my first week home, I stepped outside for a minute in a tank top and, glimpsing myself in the tinted window of an SUV parked nearby, became sheepishly self-conscious. I felt so *exposed* — my bare shoulders hadn't seen the light of day in over two years! I used to wear sleeveless shirts and dresses all the time. Now, after living in a culture where that was strictly taboo, I felt like a tramp, and realized yet again how much of Nepal's cultural ethos I'd absorbed. Certainly more than I'd thought.

On another evening during my first month back, I was hanging out with friends at a restaurant, when someone brought up the topic of "predictive texting" features. "Can you believe that now it's suggesting emojis to replace certain words?" someone asked the group. "Isn't that *wild*?"

I wasn't sure what "predictive texting" meant, and definitely had no idea what an "emoji" was. When I surreptitiously looked up the word on my phone, I learned that it was "a small digital image or icon used to express an idea or emotion." The search engine also highlighted "emoji" as that year's Oxford English Dictionary Word of the Year. Specifically, OED was commemorating the "face with tears of joy" emoji.

Emojis? Is that what they're called? I wondered. *Sure, I've seen those pop up on my smartphone!*

Medical practice was also wildly different back home, generally far removed from the perils of tropical disease. After joining the faculty at a family medicine training program in the Hudson Valley, I was supervising the residents one afternoon in clinic during my first year back, when one of them presented the case of a woman with fevers and headache. Thinking back to our patient in Tansen with those same symptoms — the young man who received only Tylenol for a missed diagnosis of florid meningitis — I considered whether that could be the cause. My mind continued to scroll through other possibilities: *Dengue, typhoid, leptospirosis, malaria. . .*

Then the resident said confidently, "I think we should test for Lyme."

My mind was blown. *Lyme disease? That's an option?* I thought. *Of course! We're in New York's Hudson Valley — the Lyme capital of the world!*

I recalled how my own medical school had pioneered decades of groundbreaking research at the front lines of Lyme Disease. And Lyme, Connecticut — the town after which, in 1975, the disease was named — was less than two hours from where we sat. Still, I hadn't considered that diagnosis in years. As the resident finished his presentation, he turned to me and asked, "What do you think, should we treat her while waiting for those results?" I nodded, thankful that the resident had done his homework that day. Just as Tenzing had, my residents often taught *me*, in an academic, bidirectional learning environment that kept everyone on the cutting edge of medicine's best evidence.

Six weeks after landing at JFK Airport and gradually adjusting to life back home, it was again time to board a plane — this time to Denver, Colorado. I'd researched options for various "re-entry programs," and finally settled on one that seemed to fit well. These sorts of programs were developed to meet a recognized need, as returning missionaries sometimes struggled to integrate challenging or complex cross-cultural experiences in their lives, moving forward. By holding space for personal reflection, group discussion, and individual counseling, these programs help missionaries in transition process their experiences. In doing so, they are better able to discern where God was present in their story — even in times of suffering or trauma, when He can feel absent.

I was eager for this week-long retreat, where I would connect with others transitioning back from global ministry service lasting at least one year — though many were on mission for much longer than that. My memories of Nepal still felt distressing and confusing, far too jumbled up to reveal any clear narrative thread woven through those two years. The week proved to be a profoundly important one, helping me contextualize the suffering I'd witnessed in Nepal, and giving insight into experiences that had seemed devoid of meaning or purpose.

Our group of ten was assigned two guides to lead us in reflecting on our own experiences. We processed aloud with our group, then meditated on Scripture in solitude to inform those reflections and further shape our perspectives. They also introduced several operative metaphors to help us navigate the uncharted, murky, and often disorienting waters of re-entry. I found one metaphor in particular very helpful — though, as with so many of the illustrations they shared, it seemed deceptively simple.

One of our guides was an amateur gardener, and began walking us through the details of how to transplant a flower. She described buying a plant at her local garden center, bringing it home to her greenhouse, and then getting to work on it. First, she'd flip the flowerpot completely upside down, squeezing and crunching the plastic bottom until the plant inside came loose, much of its dirt falling out in the upending chaos. Then, grasping the revealed root-ball, she described slicing into the matted, entwined roots with a knife to rough them up.

She paused, looking at each of us tenderly, and said, "This was what you have each been through to some extent, in returning to America." Then she turned to an easel pad propped in the front and sketched out a few colorful cartoons to illustrate these steps.

"Your worlds have been upended, and such rough handling can seem inevitable with a huge, cross-cultural transition. You may feel that the word 'home' is a lot more complicated than it used to be. Maybe it's not just the country stamped on the front of your passport, anymore. You've experienced being planted for a long time in another culture, perhaps even *multiple* cultures. You may even feel like a big part of you is still back in that other place. And I imagine friends and family don't always get that. Maybe they think, 'Now you're back home,' right?"

A few people nodded. Everyone looked pensive.

Drawing a cartoon of a new flowerpot, with the transplanted flower sitting in it, she continued. "Now you're repotted into this nice, shiny ceramic pot, surrounded by fresh new potting soil. *Voila*, process complete, right? New pot, new home, new life. *Done*." She drew another cartoon of the newly re-potted plant as if seen with X-ray vision, a dotted semi-circle within the pot.

"But that's only how it looks on the outside, right? You all know that. See how the old root-ball is still there in the new pot, even though it's invisible from the outside?"

We could all see how the old root-ball remained, holding its old dirt closely, even in its new pot.

She looked back at us and said, "That root-ball might even stay a little bit separate from the rest of the soil forever. Even as you transition 'home' — and I know how 'home' can be a complex word for some of you — some of *your* root-balls may never fully integrate into this new soil you're in. And if so, that's okay."

This analogy's platitude could have fallen flat, had we not all felt so vulnerable. Yet she brought her cartoon drawings alive with metaphoric detail that resonated powerfully with my own experience. For most of the people in that room, their "uprooting" trauma was the move from "host" to "passport" country. For me, however, the uprooting actually felt broader. It was the entire experience of missions, those upending two years in Nepal that were a thorough disruption of *self*. Either way, it was poignant to think of that little flower being flipped upside down and roughed up so terribly. I felt sorry for it, even as I could see how necessary those steps were for it take hold in its new soil.

The validating metaphor offered permission to let this process unfold over time. Perhaps a shadow of my root-ball would always remain. Nepal had shifted something in my heart and soul, in some ways changing me forever. How could these last two years *not* have done that? I saw now that the work of processing my experiences would continue even in this shiny, new pot. For the first time that felt okay, too. Permission for whatever was, and whatever would be.

It also seemed fine that only a few people closest to me knew my old "root-ball" was still there — those precious few who'd held that space so tenderly since I'd returned home. I thought of the many hours that Jane, my sister, and other close friends had held my stories as I processed through Nepal's experiences and emotions. It was enough. With a small, core group of support holding me close, it didn't seem necessary that *everyone* know about my inner "root-ball."

Later that week, another one of our guides opened his session by reading a passage in Mark's gospel, where Jesus had just celebrated Passover with His disciples. It opens when they've just finished, and Jesus knows He is about to be arrested, on the cusp of events that will soon lead to His torture, crucifixion, and death.

The study leader began to read, "And they went to a place called Gethsemane. . ." Then he stopped and looked up at us expectantly, as if he had just said something crucial to the narrative.

What could he possibly say about that? I wondered to myself. *He's not even ten words in!*

Emphasizing every word, he explained that "Gethsemane" means "Place of the olive press."

"An olive press is a place where an ordinary, ugly little piece of fruit is squeezed and crushed to pieces." He looked at each of us meaningfully before going on. "But under that incredible pressure, it exudes a tiny yield of precious oil. As it turns out, there's really no way to extract that oil without the olive suffering some damage."

The meaning embedded in his metaphor was clear. Pain was an invitation to notice God's particular, intimate presence with those who suffer. And what was true of Christ's suffering in Gethsemane would soon prove true of His disciples as well. For like Him, they would also endure crushing loss, pain, grief, and death. Yet none of that suffering was worthless or lacking in purpose, when held with God. In fact, their suffering was, metaphorically speaking, a source of "oil" in the world. It is the source of new life through the enduring love of Christ's presence, embodied in His church, across time and space.

By enduring such suffering first, Jesus suffused it with meaning, because He did so sacrificially. He withstood the suffering and shame of Calvary for the redemption of our world. In a similar way — in kind, if certainly not in degree — our own suffering has redemptive potential, if borne with the aid of His Spirit. I believe this to be especially true of pain endured with and for others. Through the courageous witness of presence, compassion's grief stretches your heart, expanding it wider and wider in love. Because someday, in that final day when all wrongs are put right, and all brokenness healed, your overstretched heart will be filled with joy at God's healing of the world. And that joy will be proportionately greater, for having been stretched wide open by grief.

Just as Jesus willingly endured unimaginable suffering out of love, I realized I could trust His hand to extract precious oil through suffering from me, too. *Jesus, Companion for the journey.*

CHAPTER FIFTY
Empathy's Imagination

One morning during my first year back in the States, I was seeing patients at our local community health center. I knocked on an exam room door where the next patient on my schedule was waiting. After introducing myself to the young woman, I went over to the wall-mounted phone and dialed our Spanish interpreter services. My Spanish language skills, which were never that strong, had grown rusty over the past two years. I perched myself on the rolling exam chair, swiveled the wall-mounted computer to one side, and scrolled briefly through her record, noting that she was thirty-four years old and had recently emigrated from El Salvador.

"What brings you in today?" I asked in Spanish, practicing my language skills with the official interpreter's safety net securely in place. She explained that she wanted to see a doctor for chronic headaches, and began to share through the interpreter that they were worse when she was feeling anxious, or at the end of a long workday. *"Tengo dolor aquí,"* she said, tenting her thumb and fingers against the sides of her forehead to show me where the pain was. It formed a squeezing band of pressure from her temples across her forehead and around to the back of her neck — a classic tension headache, without any red-flag features. I began to explore stressors she was having in life. From conversations I'd had with other patients, I suspected there would be some. She told me that her father had died ten days earlier. She received word from her family that he was very sick, but because of her own undocumented status, and the threat of violence against young women in the town where her family lived, she couldn't travel back to El Salvador to be with him, or to say goodbye. She was unable to attend his funeral service, or stand at his graveside to mark the place where he was buried. She couldn't even hug her mother, or receive comfort from her siblings, family, and community.

Sharing all this with me, she began to weep freely, grieving anew pain that was still so raw. As I handed her tissues and offered space to feel this tremendous loss, I thought back to my last few months in Nepal, recalling the night I came home from Dan and Leah's house to news that my own father was sick. I remembered how terrified I was for him that day, and how difficult it was to be so far away from family.

At the time, I needed to decide whether to travel home earlier than planned. Yet it never occurred to me to ask *whether* I could go home. Of *course* I could — I had every financial and political freedom to do so. My U.S. passport, coupled with the purchasing power of my bank account's U.S. dollars, afforded incredible clout. So much so, in fact, that I hardly noticed it at all. A door is most visible when it's closed. And doors open to me remained impassable to many of my patients, including this woman before me. She was my exact age and, like countless generations before her, came seeking a better future for herself in America.

There was little to say, though we sat for a while in the exam room as she wept, then eventually composed herself.

"*Lo siento,*" she said, again and again.

"No, really," I soothed. "Please don't apologize. Your tears are real. Your grief is real. *I'm* the one who's sorry, for all you've endured."

When she left, a treatment plan in place for her headaches, I began thinking about how much my views and attitudes had been shaped by the experience of living abroad. Especially in a context radically different from your own, such immersion is powerfully able to expand the imagination. It did for me. Once back in the States, conversations with my patients helped me to see life through their eyes. It became clear how much of their health and flourishing depended on factors beyond their control — factors strikingly similar to those I encountered in Nepal.

The location of grocery stores mattered, it turned out, and also whether those stores had a good selection of vegetables and other fresh foods. Most of my patients did not own a car, and thus relied on public transit to get to their appointments. It's time-consuming to navigate two or three bus transfers with, for instance, a toddler and unwieldy stroller in tow. One such patient, arriving twenty-five minutes late for her appointment, explained to me in a mix of Spanish and English that her last doctor's practice charged her thirty dollars each time she was late, and then fired her after her third missed appointment. Her pre-paid phone had run out of minutes, and she was waiting for her next paycheck to buy another, but they'd released her from the practice in the meantime. I wondered if some snippy message from their office manager was waiting for her when she finally reactivated her service. From that posture of more empathic listening came a depth of connection, and was on my mind with another patient I saw that year.

An Indian man in his late fifties came in one morning, accompanied by his young adult daughter, for a sore throat and viral symptoms. His daughter made the familiar head bobble in response to something I said, and I was overcome with a wave of homesickness for a place that was never even truly my home. It had been a tiring day, and all I wanted was to sit with the two of them in that cramped exam room and listen to them speak, wishing we could do so over a cup of *chiya*. I lingered a bit longer than usual, affirming his daughter's adamant assertion that he'd caught this cold because just yesterday, he'd eaten some food straight out of the fridge, and followed that indiscretion with a glass of cold water immediately afterward.

"Of course he got a *cold*, after all that!" she exclaimed. At this, I offered a vague head bobble of my own, then nodded vigorously when she asked if an Ayurvedic mixture of honey, lemon, turmeric and ginger, steeped in *hot* water, would be good for him. That was, after all, pretty close to what I'd instructed the fifteen patients before them to do, during a season when it seemed everyone was combating these lingering head colds. She looked startled at how quick I was to support this remedy. I wondered how other physicians might have responded to her suggestion in the past.

I hoped this man and his daughter sensed an unusual openness in their physician, especially at the mention of Ayurvedic therapies. I didn't share with them that I'd just returned from living in South Asia. I didn't want them to think the only thing I saw about them was their Indianness. I viscerally recalled how frustrating that was for me in Nepal — when the first or only thing people saw about me, a *bideshi*, was my foreignness. It was isolating in a way I could never have imagined otherwise, without living it for those two years. Perhaps they assumed I was just another white doctor, one with little knowledge of the world beyond my own borders. If so, then that was okay, too.

CHAPTER FIFTY-ONE
Tragedy Reprised

After returning home, I joined the faculty of a family medicine residency program in New York's Hudson Valley region, and had a chance to help develop Global Health training opportunities for the residents. We designed and led an annual, medical-cultural immersion trip in partnership with a Caribbean-based residency team. Hoping to facilitate a medical, linguistic, and cultural exchange between our two programs, we chose not to focus on providing high-volume medical care, like to many other "short-term missions" models, but instead designed it with a more observational approach aimed at cultural humility. Mid-morning on our first day visiting their hospital, I was accompanying three of our interns to observe a shift in the Emergency Department.

Introducing ourselves to a patient behind one of the curtained cubicles, we began to gather his story. He was sixty-seven years old and had arrived at the hospital the evening before, but was still awaiting care. He'd come in for severe pain in his groin, along with massive swelling of his left testicle. It all began after he was kicked there by his wife during a domestic altercation the week before. Since then, his scrotum had become unbearably painful and distended to a large, purplish mass nearly the size of a basketball. He'd come in because he could no longer walk, and he was vomiting anything he ate or drank. He also hadn't moved his bowels in three days, and couldn't recall the last time he'd passed any gas. As we explored his symptoms, he noted that some mild swelling in his left groin had actually been there for a long time.

"Eight years at least!" he exclaimed, in awe that something so long quiescent could turn bad so quickly.

This sounded serious. I was troubled that he'd already been lying here in this condition for over twelve hours. I was also troubled that he, as an immigrant laborer, was known to be part of a discriminated ethnic group in the region. His mouth was dry, and he was clearly dehydrated. His belly was swollen — not with the fat of the well-fed, but with air, an ominous finding consistent with bowel obstruction. This would easily explain his inability to pass gas or bowel movements, his nausea and vomiting, the silence of his belly when I gently pressed stethoscope to skin, and the exquisite tenderness he experienced when I did so.

He had received no treatment since arriving in the emergency room, other than some hydration dripping into one vein. Or, as it turned out, not even that. When we looked more closely at the IV tubing, we discovered that it was kinked near the insertion site, and virtually none of the saline in the bag hanging above his bed had gone in. I wiggled the catheter a bit and got the fluids flowing.

Speaking with our three interns, we talked over potential causes for his presentation. Testicular rupture was a concerning possibility, but I was also worried about an incarcerated, strangulated inguinal hernia. That's when a weak spot in the muscles of the abdominal wall bulges into the groin, and the intestines filling that protrusion get trapped. Sometimes when that happens, the pressure on the bowel cuts off its own blood supply, so that part of the bowel begins to die. Another option, equally bad, was testicular torsion, where the traumatized testicle flips around on itself, similarly cutting off its own blood supply. Any of the possibilities we considered were surgical emergencies, and required quick action. All of them were potentially fatal.

Emerging from the curtained cubicle, we looked around for the young clinician on duty, curious to hear her thoughts as the covering physician that morning. We found her standing by the nurses' station, looking bored.

"Oh, him?" she said, in Spanish. "That's a case of constipation." She walked over to the lightbox, where X-ray films were viewed the old-school way, which brought me right back to Nepal.

Just the way we did it in Tansen, I thought. The doctor placed her film up on the lightbox, confidently shoving it under two metal clips. It was an upright X-ray of the patient's abdomen. Multiple loops of air-filled small bowel crowded the space. Several air-fluid levels were visible — I counted five, at least — further evidence of a serious bowel obstruction. Bending forward to scrutinize the right side of his diaphragm, I made out a thin, dark black line tracing the top edge of his liver. *Free air.* Somewhere along those pressurized coils of bowel, a small hole had already formed. This was a surgical emergency.

How could he have been sitting here for nearly fourteen hours? I narrated the findings to our residents in English, speaking quietly and quickly under my breath. The attending eyed me a bit uneasily. I knew she probably already felt judged by our presence. A physician there had shared earlier that when American doctors visit, the staff often assume it's only in order to catch errors and document poor care. It had surprised me to hear that, so I'd resolved to avoid anything that could appear judgmental of them, or their system.

As deferentially as I could, I asked my colleague in Spanish if this could possibly be something else, something *other* than constipation. Had she considered the possibility of an incarcerated hernia? Or perhaps a traumatic rupture of the testicle, or testicular torsion? But she waved her hand dismissively, not giving it a second thought.

"Of course not. He hasn't stooled in three days. This is obviously a case of constipation. I've already given him a laxative." And with that, she turned away, our conversation clearly over. She seemed irritated that we had already taken so much of her time. I struggled to conceal my disbelief and anger.

"We're visitors here," I quietly reminded the residents and myself. I knew we were guests, only there at the invitation of this hospital's leadership. "And this is just our first day. We should be careful in what we say." I'd already questioned her in front of my own residents, perhaps putting her on the spot, and she'd seemed ruffled. I didn't know how else to push her to address a diagnosis that she had apparently failed to consider, however unimaginably. This was a problem too impossible — and too crucial — to miss.

As I stood in that Emergency Department, two inner voices competed for attention. *On the one hand,* I reasoned, *these kinds of decisions have been going on for years, long before our arrival. And this care will continue long after we go back home. Besides,* I chided myself, *you barely made any difference in two years of work in Nepal. What makes you think two* hours *will change anything here?*

But this is a life *before us* — another voice within me chimed in. *This man's life is in jeopardy. What duty do I owe him as a physician? As a fellow human? Isn't that worth the risk of making myself a little odious to the senior doctor here?* the voice pleaded. *Is that even on the same scale as his life?* I was as conflicted as I'd ever been. In the end, I negotiated with the physician to at least request a surgical consult, hoping that another set of eyes might make the difference. Then, disappearing again into the patient's curtained cubicle, we stood with him and learned more of his story.

He had emigrated from Haiti at the age of ten, he said, and had worked in the *bateys*, or sugarcane fields, ever since. His journey fit a larger pattern I had recently learned about, one of human trafficking across the border. Families facing poverty are promised a better life, others simply abducted from their homes, only to be dropped off in fields, forced to plant and harvest sugarcane. With all their documents confiscated by traffickers, these victims are rendered stateless, condemned to lives of bonded labor in the *bateys* without any official recourse.

I'd also learned that ridiculously inflated rates were charged for basic food and goods at the "company store," where everything was bought on credit, a tragically common means of enslaving people in generations of bonded labor around the world. On a prior trip, I had also witnessed first-hand the conditions of plantations deeper inland, further removed from main routes, and had never forgotten the miserable conditions I saw there. Such was the situation, human rights advocates claim, for workers across a network of Caribbean *bateys* — on land that is frequently owned or funded by American conglomerates, to supply an insatiable American sweet tooth.

I also wondered how much of this man's care reflected a long history of systemic racism perpetuated against darker-skinned patients, people who often happened to also be poor, and usually non-fluent in Spanish. It seemed that this patient's membership in a discriminated group could certainly play a role in the neglectful care we were witnessing. I had a hard time imagining a light-skinned, Spanish-speaking, well-dressed patient from the city being treated for "constipation" in the same scenario.

We lingered by the man's bedside for another hour, learning more of his story, at times standing with him in quiet solidarity as he endured excruciating spasms of pain that tore through his gut. It felt like a mixed blessing to be standing there — exempt from the pressing obligations of patient care, we were frustratingly unable to provide what he urgently needed, but at the same time, we were free to simply be present and bear witness.

Eventually, the time drew near to meet the rest of our group. As we said goodbye and turned to leave, he reached out and grasped my hand powerfully, with a strength that surprised me. He held on firmly, and began to speak rapidly, in fragmented Spanish mixed with Haitian Creole. I could make out words like *El Señor* and *Jesucristo* peppered throughout, but caught little else. His face was radiant as he pointed to a small cross hanging on a thin silver chain around the neck of a resident standing beside me. He seemed to be trying to thank us, indicating that God had sent us to him, grateful that He was at work, grateful that we had come. I cringed inwardly at the thought of being given any credit, when I knew how unjustly he had been treated by the medical system we represented. I also knew how little we had really been able to do to save his life.

With one final squeeze of his hand, we slipped back through the curtain and left the Emergency Department to meet our team rounding in the rest of the hospital. I remained pensive that afternoon, praying that by some miracle he would receive the medical attention he so desperately needed. The next morning, returning to the same ED, we were unable to get any word on how he'd done. Nurses at the front desk had no records of any patients from the day prior, or at least couldn't find any for him, when we provided his name. The doctor on duty for the day was new, and hadn't heard anything about the patient or his case. I wondered whether the few hours we'd spent with him were his last, whether he had died soon after we left. It was unsettling not to know, and to have no way of knowing.

CHAPTER FIFTY-TWO
Contextillence

There's a perception in the West that medical care in the developing world is hampered by insufficient resources. "If only those countries had access to a CT scanner," I've heard people say, "or an ABG machine, or a shiny new ICU with the best ventilators, *then* they'd be able to deliver good care. Then they could really save lives."

Yet the reality is more complex than that. In fact, the solution is as challenging as it is mundane. In the ED with my residents, we were standing in our own hemisphere, a world much closer than Nepal. Yet the same opportunity for attentive care was presented to the ED physician, just as it had to Dev, back in Tansen. In a bizarrely coincidental turn, it was even the same case: free air under the diaphragm. Generally not a difficult diagnosis to make — provided the doctor is paying attention.

I began to notice a systems-level difference between healthcare in "wealthier nations" as compared to that in the developing world. Across America, for instance, hospital administrators shudder when a surprise *JCAHO* visit is announced. The "Joint Commission on Accreditation of Healthcare Organizations," known widely by its oft-feared acronym *JCAHO*, is a regulatory body designed to ensure that minimum basic standards are met by hospitals and other medical institutions in which the public places its trust. Similarly, the *ACGME*, or "Accreditation Council for Graduate Medical Education," inflicts deep agita on residency program directors nationwide, with its periodic site visits to assess the quality of their medical training.

I used to roll my eyes at this alphabet soup and their Stuffed Suit Representatives, marching in with clipboards and nit-picking checklists in hand. They would move down the hallways, eyeing everything with critical suspicion as they searched for subtle deviations from protocol. It all seemed unnecessary, just another example of Big Brother interfering in the jobs of good people doing good work.

When I returned home, however, I stopped rolling my eyes. I've come to realize the value of such meticulous oversight, such careful attention to detail. In my global health experiences, it seemed to me that a lack of consistently rigorous care at the systems level, and the resulting glut of unnecessary deaths, came from a failure to consistently expect and demand these high standards for all hospitals. This starts at the ground level with expectations we maintain for medical students and residents, from standards of medical knowledge and procedural technique to professionalism and integrity.

The only way to maintain these standards is by deputizing organizations to ensure quality, including in all those irksome, nitty-gritty details. Such expectations, from the top down and the bottom up, are the only safeguard against slipping standards. Human beings usually mean well, no doubt. But we are a lazy bunch at heart. We will eventually cut corners if we think no one is looking. We need accountability to ensure that medical students, residents, and attending doctors do their jobs well. If the care we give is at a standard that you, or someone you love, would want, then there aren't any other options. Because sooner or later it *will* be you or your loved one in that bed.

When I pondered the big questions of health system improvement — especially where it all starts, in medical education — I recalled what my friend Anneke had shared about a government teaching hospital just twenty minutes from Tansen. The standards, she said, were sadly quite different there.

"You'd be shocked, Becca, if you think Tansen is bad. Try visiting other hospitals in Nepal." She reminded me how, over the years, slow but steady growth had transformed Tansen into one of the best hospitals in the region. "Tansen built a reputation for high-quality care, and Nepalis know our doctors can be trusted. That's not the case everywhere."

It was certainly true that Tansen had a reputation for reliable care. Patients did seem to trust me immensely, often lending more credence than I felt was due, in light of the limitations I knew I was working with. I voiced this reflection with Anneke one day.

"You know, Becca, I've recently been thinking of how some people say that we need to aim for excellence in our work in Tansen. That strikes me as a big idea, full of questions that come with it — *Whose definition of excellence? What values underpin that definition? And at what cost?*" Her words surprised and intrigued me. I hadn't thought that excellence could be anything *but* the sole, worthy goal. Still, I'd also seen the costs of striving for perfection, and, frankly, the limited resources we were invariably working with as we did so.

As if echoing my thoughts, Anneke went on. "I mean, surely there are some people who miss out if we aim for excellence for everyone, simply because there are not enough resources to go around. All people, in every setting the world over, are not yet getting excellent care. Just look at the unhoused, marginalized, and unemployed population in your own country, America. Even our *models* of excellence differ, from Australia to the Netherlands to Nepal."

She paused for a moment. "In thinking about all of this, Becca, I've come up with a new way I've found helpful in my approach — *'contextillence.'* It's the idea of striving for excellence, but within the context of the workplace. It helps us acknowledge and honor our limits, like the inevitable restraints around financial and human resources, cultural expectations, national and local politics, even the limits of medicine at its best. All the things you yourself witnessed and experienced as challenges to delivering excellent care."

I appreciated this shift in perspective, and the framing she'd placed around it. Anneke had always seemed at peace working within Tansen's system. I wondered if this was part of how she and Willem had maintained longevity there for as long as they had. It didn't mean we shouldn't aim for the best care we could give, but it helped me think about what a better balance would look like between the idealism of what ought to be, and the realism of what *is*.

Anneke agreed it was a slow process. Yet we'd both seen how diligent work had, over the decades, set Tansen apart — one faithful cog at a time.

CHAPTER FIFTY-THREE
When We See Him

It was mid-May, exactly five months since I'd landed back home in New York. Church had just ended, and I was thrilled to be back among the congregation that had been my heart's home for a decade, through all my travels. The sermon that day was about "putting on the new person" in Christ, and "putting off the old," a life-long discipline of rejecting all the usual things that define us — what we do, who we know, how we look, what we have — and receiving instead the freedom of Jesus's identity.

Sitting there, I realized yet again how thankful I was to be back home, how nice it was to feel happy, healthy, and well-rested again. I was surrounded by people who had known me for years, and who had loved me through many of life's ups and downs. These were friends who could affirm and reflect back to me who I really was. All the old wounds — the gritty challenges of life in Nepal; the foreignness of language, medicine, people, land, food, and culture; the constant sickness, poverty, suffering, and death; and the deep anguish that I could, in the end, do so little — all of it was in the past. A vital chapter in my story had finally drawn to a close. And despite new challenges arising in my new job, where work hours could be even longer and more exhausting than before,

I felt my reserves bolstered. Constant, brittle frustration had gradually been supplanted by resilient flexibility to meet those challenges.

Yet sitting there, I also knew the real truth about myself. Put me back in Tansen Hospital or somewhere similar, with all those same pressures and challenges, and I knew I'd revert right back to the same angry, frustrated person I so often was. What to do with all this talk of putting off the old self, exchanging that for Christ's, as if it simply involved a change of clothes? My identity was always going to be dependent to at least *some* degree on my circumstances. And when my best efforts — my ardently focused, intense pursuit of goodness — served only to fuel the touchy pride of that same old self? What then?

After service ended, Jane came over to say hello. Registering the discouragement on my face, she asked how I was doing.

"How are we supposed to 'put on Christ?'" I asked irritably. "What's that even supposed to mean, Jane? It's just an opaque metaphor, an analogy. . ." Then, to my own surprise, I began to cry. "I feel so trapped, Jane. The same old patterns are still there, the same vicious cycle of pride. I know it's all still there inside me. What if I never change? What if I never really break free from this cycle?" Despair seemed to billow up around me, choking out my breath. I felt a vise-like headache coming on.

Yet I couldn't let it go. This felt like a critical fork in the road, a reckoning. I sensed that to push this question away, unwilling to *face* myself and whatever brokenness and shame I found, would cause something within me to wither and die. This was a time to either confront whatever it was head-on, like the pain of a necessary surgery, or harden myself against it — at my own peril.

Jane stood facing me, taking it all in. Dear, sweet Jane — my friend, mentor, and model for life over the years. When I finished speaking, she took hold of both my wrists in her firm, gentle grasp. She looked up at me with tender, searching compassion. In that look, she saw my distress — not only the pain of that moment, but the pain layered throughout the past two years. She saw in my eyes a yearning to do right — restless and anxious to be sure, forever casting about in search of peace, but a struggle of honest intentions. She knew the longing I felt to root my identity in the God I so deeply loved, the One I was sure I had deeply disappointed by my failures.

"Oh, Becca, Becca," she began, tenderly. It seemed she was searching for the right words. "Remember First John?"

That wasn't exactly what I'd expected her to say. Still, I grasped her meaning. Years earlier, Jane and I committed to memorizing Scripture together, and had chosen the first letter of John. It was a passage well-worn over the years, dearly familiar to us both.

"Remember what he wrote? *'When we see Him, we shall be like Him.'* Don't you see how beautiful that is? Simply *beholding* Jesus will make us more like Him. But it's only *when* we see Him, Becca — and not until then. Be patient. . . there's time."

With those words, Jane was pointing to the hope of God's coming restoration. She had reoriented me to the promise that, when our noble King finally returns, He will put right all that's gone so terribly wrong in the world — healing for broken bodies and restoration of grieving families, the end of tragic news cycles and horrific natural disasters, the undoing of all intimately personal losses. Christ's bodily resurrection is the Christian's sure hope that, to paraphrase J. R. R. Tolkien, everything sad will come untrue.

For the first time, however, Jane's words had led me to receive this hope of restoration not only for what's wrong *out there* in the world, but for what's wrong *within me* as well. In the face of despair — certain that despite my best efforts, I couldn't root out my pride, impatience, self-centeredness, or shame-filled anger — it was deeply consoling to entrust it all to God, knowing that He could, and would, bring to completion the good work He'd graciously begun within me.

I walked back to my apartment, still with a headache and a

pensive heart, but sensing a glimmer of hope dawning in that dark and heavy place. Jane had uplifted me with her benediction, the "good word" of God's *already-but-not-yet* reality. It was a relief to realize I could give Him even my own, broken self, and trust His healing touch — in His time.

Epilogue

Time, the twentieth century revealed to us, is relative. It expands and contracts. My time in Nepal proved that truth to me as nothing else could. It seems unfathomable to me that, on paper at least, those two years comprised one of the briefest chapters of my professional and personal story. Yet it felt as if I were in a time warp, or Narnia — where two years there is a decade elsewhere. Truly, no other experience in my life looms larger.

When I finally came back to visit Tansen, seven years to the day after I left, I thought it was in order to place a period at the end of this incredible chapter. Yet, if anything, an ellipsis opened up in my story instead, and with it, new willingness to hold the future loosely. After seven years, it was as fitting a sabbatical journey as I could imagine.

In revisiting Tansen, I saw how tricky a thing it can be. Some events from those years were seared into my memory such that, after writing about them and going back to fact-check in my journals from that time, I found those memories had been preserved almost word-perfectly. In other things, however, I discovered my memory to be flawed. I have a distinct recollection from years ago, for instance, of seeing the snow-capped Himalayas one clear morning in Pokhara, enjoying a view of the famous, double-peaked "fishtail" that gives the sacred *Machapuchare* its name. Only, such a view is actually impossible from Pokhara. Those double peaks are only visible from the east or west, not from their southern view in Pokhara, when they line up behind one another *en face*. Either the mountains had moved, or my memory is, from time to time, errant. It's most likely the latter.

Everywhere I went during that sabbatical visit, the same question came — "Are you here to work, or just to visit?" The answer was easy at first — a quick, "Oh, just here to visit." That answer got more difficult and nuanced with time. "Well, for *now* just a visit. But in the future…who knows?" Nepal is a magnetic place, and Tansen is, for me at least, the center of its gravitational pull. Anyone who has been there will tell you as much.

After returning home seven years ago, I discovered deep affirmation in the chance to share and process my story with others who had "been there." Friends who had been with me in Nepal, or lived elsewhere in the world, could understand the relentless discomfort of being different, the vague uncertainty of political unrest and its repercussions, the ground-note of fear following a natural disaster. They could relate to the myriad pressures of cross-cultural living because they had lived it firsthand. They knew the sensation of anger tightening in the chest in response to witnessed injustice. They had wept over the effects of poverty, disease, and death that ravaged our patients, neighbors, and friends.

They could also laugh harder than anyone over the adventures of "daily life" elsewhere in the world — deafening truck horns, language foibles, bathroom creepy-crawlies. An unscheduled electricity black-out when dinner was only halfway cooked. The discovery of furry green mold — this really happened — transforming a pair of shoes into creatures that could conceivably walk out the front door on their own. I was fortunate to be surrounded by a tight-knit community of people just a Skype call away who understood that.

As I reflect on these memories, I'm conflicted. I now enjoy the gifts of reliable electricity and hot running water at the turn of any tap in our house. My clothes always smell freshly laundered and free of mildew. I am effortlessly understood by any customer service rep at the other end of an 800-number. I've reconnected with my community of family and friends, and reintegrated into meaningful life and work here.

Yet at the same time — at precisely the same time — there remains forever within me the pull of life in Nepal. I miss the pure craft of patient encounters, free of current bureaucratic burdens — but not the overwhelming volume or intensity. I miss the joys of living alongside amazing people that you looked up to as mentors, and loved as friends — but not the burden of always being a stranger and outsider to the broader culture. Mostly, I miss the singleness of vision that exists when you live, work, serve, and worship within a community whose sights are set on the beauty of a world Christ is presently healing — but not the frustrations and heartache that can so easily cloud that vision.

Within weeks of my initial arrival in Nepal, I began to taste a small part of what it means to be a foreigner, an outsider, far from that which is familiar and comforting, far from home. In short order, however, I came up against great brokenness in full force — that of bodies, and families, and societal infrastructure. It was a front-row view of the basic, grievous fact that resources are distributed unjustly in our world, allotted to those of us with much, and withheld from those — by mere accident of birth — with nothing.

When I returned to New York on that December night two years later, my own image of myself was that of seaweed strewn upon the beach. It had been a hard run; I was exhausted, drained, spent. It has been two long years of contending with God, having my head slammed again and again to the wrestling mat, in this journey of being brought to the end of myself. I was sure I had nothing left to give, and might never again. This image of limp and lifeless seaweed recurred often during my first months home, a sad but telling insight into where I'd found myself.

I was also coming to see the beauty of the profoundly other-centered ethos at the heart of Christian faith. Everything is not always about me. In fact, it's exhausting to live that way. Two years in Nepal had taught me that. Arguably, my biggest barrier to flourishing was my inability to get beyond myself — owing, perhaps, to the profound pain suffusing that space. Pain tends to contract the universe down to a minuscule, self-focused aperture. Madeleine L'Engle put it well when she wrote, "To grow up / Is to find / The small part you are playing In this extraordinary drama / Written by somebody else." I was eager to be taken up into this beautiful, cosmic story God was weaving in the world, so much bigger than any one individual story.

On the first day of January, two years after I'd landed back at JFK Airport, I chose to ring in the New Year with a fresh start at a local yoga studio where I'd been attending classes. Yoga was one of the most unexpected discoveries of my time in Nepal, and I'd grown to love it. In every other sphere of life — personal, professional, physical — the implicit (and often explicit) expectation is to find your limit, and then blow past it. I was part of a cultural ideal that sought always to push limits, expand your own margins. "Defy expectations!" is the popular cry. "No pain, no gain!" proclaim the tee shirts. "The sky's the limit!" promise banners decking the walls of elementary school classrooms.

But in yoga, the whole point is to identify your limit, "find the edge," then back off it a little. Embrace what *is*, not what could be, nor what *ought* to be. It's a call to recognize myself as a human being when the world is willing to acknowledge me only as a human *doing*. Our yoga teacher often guided us into the practice's closing space of rest, *shavasana*, with this invitation: "Notice who you are right now, in this moment. Notice who you are when all the *doing* has ceased."

On that particular New Year's Day class, we rose to a standing pose at the front of our mats, arms reaching gently above our heads in the shape of a "Y." I sensed myself growing ever so tall, feeling sunny and hopeful, open to receiving whatever the coming year had in store. I extended my palms upward in a gesture of trust, open to God. He had brought me into this new year, and I knew He would sustain me through it, come what may. I needed only yield, body and soul, to Him.

Then I heard the teacher say, "Now, my friends... Drape your arms to the side. Yes, flow over to the left — that's it! And now to the other side — very nice. Fluid, buoyant. You are like seaweed in the ocean..."

I had marked two years since returning from Nepal. Two years of healing, two years of restoration in loving community, two years of reflection and space for deep soul care. I had been home for as long as I'd been away. And I knew I'd finally come full circle.

Acknowledgements

I hope that *Though the Darkness* offers a measure of hope and encouragement to those on mission — in whatever form that takes, and whatever chapter of the journey. If so, then I am indebted to a number of people for it:

First, warmest gratitude to my incredible editor Jana Riess of Riess Editorial Consulting, who provided invaluable feedback and encouragement over the course of multiple manuscript revisions — thank you for your diligent and visionary help in getting this book where it needed to go. Huge thanks to my friend Carolyn Lee, who designed this book cover and realized its vision perfectly. Appreciation to the editorial staff of *Narrateur: Reflections on Caring*, a publication of the Donald & Barbara Zucker School of Medicine at Hofstra-Northwell, for featuring earlier drafts of content included here. A special thank you to the followers of various blogs I've kept over the years — I had the honor of sharing these stories publicly with you first, and you responded with kindness.

Thanks to Grace Mark for her early guidance in draft development; to Heidi Haverkamp, Kaya Oakes, and my writing group at the 2019 Glen Workshop for reviewing early material; to Elliot & Lindsay Drake, Dora & Jonathan Poarch, and the whole MTI team for holding space through your invaluable *"Debriefing and Renewal"* program; to Dana Walfish for her assistance in reviewing and proofing the final draft;

and to my fabulous memoir group members — Caroline, Mars, Mara, Ellen, and Jordan — for generously helping me process, write, edit, and hone this story over several years. A huge thank you especially to Caroline Wellbery, my dear friend and first mentor: you are a brilliant writer, phenomenal editor, and beautiful human being — in short, an inspiration.

A debt of gratitude is owed to my friends in Nepal — Becky P, Manju, Theo & Beth, Malcolm & Cati, Josh & Sarah, David & Hannah, Arko Josh, Rachel, Les & Debbie, Ansie, Ana & Steve, Ganesh, Marianne, Becky E, Tul & Christina, Tim & Leona, Kimberly, Namo, Sima, Laxmi, Pratima, Seesam, Subesh, Janene, Joy, Carrie, Tim & Val, Jackie, Joy, Becky T, Paul & Jessica, Luke & Cris, Peter & Valerie, Khila, Sandeep, Basanta, Rajiv, Dhiraj, Jim & Carol, and the whole Tansen community, past and present — you have touched countless lives, and continue to inspire the world with your witness. This book is for you.

To my "root-ball" friends — John, Robert & Jeehyun, Jill, Martha, Danielle, Molly, Erin, Marian, and my whole faith community at New Hope Fellowship — in love, you held these stories; through your listening, you helped me remember. You are amazing, and have my eternal gratitude, which goes beyond words.

To my family — Jessica, Matt, dear 'Nuther Mother, and Katherine — you've inspired this book in more ways than you could ever know. I am especially grateful to my father, whose encouragement predicted the dawning of this project, and to my mother, whose lifework bore witness to the beauty of medicine as ministry. Although they did not live to see it come to fruition, this story exists because of them.

To my husband, confidant and best friend, Ryan, who edited this book and has been an invaluable support, insightful sounding board, tireless encourager, and incredible friend through these years of writing — 143, my darling.

Most of all, to my God in Christ, who makes Himself known in brokenness, and whose Spirit is graciously restoring all things — even me.

About The Author

Dr. Rebecca McAteer Martin, M.D. is a Palliative Medicine consultant and Clinical Associate Professor, board certified in Family Medicine. Her published works of narrative non-fiction and poetry have appeared in journals including *Academic Medicine, Narrateur, The Intima,* and an anthology of poetry. From 2013-2015, she served as a volunteer physician at Tansen Mission Hospital in the Annapurna Himalayan foothills of central Nepal. She and her husband Ryan live in New York's lower Hudson Valley with their cat, Turtle. This is her first book.

www.ingramcontent.com/pod-product-compliance
Lightning Source LLC
LaVergne TN
LVHW041211080426
835508LV00011B/904